FORD MADOX BROWN
THE UNOFFICIAL PRE-RAPHAELITE

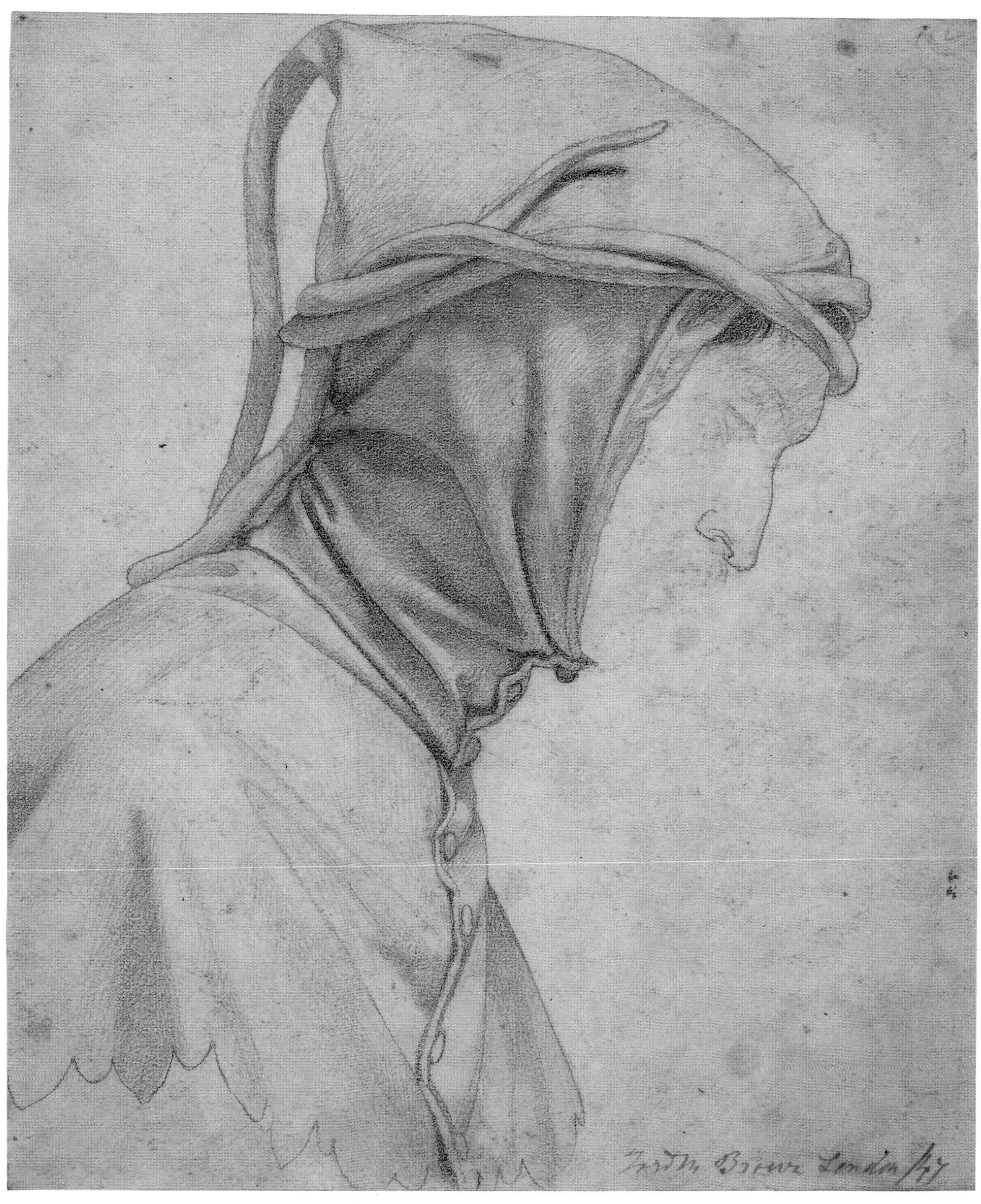
Forth Brown London /77

FORD MADOX BROWN
THE UNOFFICIAL PRE-RAPHAELITE

Works on paper by Ford Madox Brown
from Birmingham Museums and Art Gallery

with essays by TIM BARRINGER, ANGELA THIRLWELL
and LAURA MacCULLOCH

edited by TESSA SIDEY

includes a catalogue of Ford Madox Brown: Drawings, Prints,
Designs, Watercolours and Archive Material at Birmingham
Museums and Art Gallery

D Giles Ltd
in association with Birmingham Museums and Art Gallery

For Patrick, Sheena and Alex MacCulloch

First published in 2008 by GILES
An imprint of D Giles Limited
2nd Floor
162–164 Upper Richmond Road
London
SW15 2SL
www.gilesltd.com

ISBN: 978-1-904832-56-0

Edited by Tessa Sidey

For Birmingham Museums and Art Gallery:
Tessa Sidey, Curator of Prints and Drawings, Birmingham Museums and Art Gallery
Laura MacCulloch, Researcher, Prints and Drawings, Birmingham Museums and Art Gallery

For D Giles Limited:
Helen Swansbourne, designer
Sarah Kane, copy-editor and proof-reader
Ursula Caffrey, indexer
Produced by D Giles Limited, London
Printed and bound in China

All measurements are in millimetres

Unless stated otherwise, all illustrations are drawn from Birmingham Museum and Art Gallery
Photography by David Rowan

Front cover: *The Last of England: Portrait of Emma Hill*, 1852 (cat. 29)
Back cover: *Stages of Cruelty: Study for the Child (Catherine Madox Brown)*, 1857 (cat. 37)
Frontispiece: *Chaucer at the Court of Edward III: Study of a Man in medieval Hood*, 1847 (cat. 12)

Throughout this publication, Brown's idiosyncratic spelling and grammar has not been corrected.
However, when names have been misspelt 'sic' has been inserted.

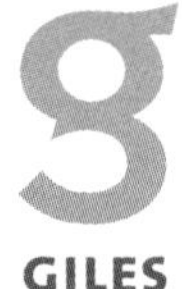 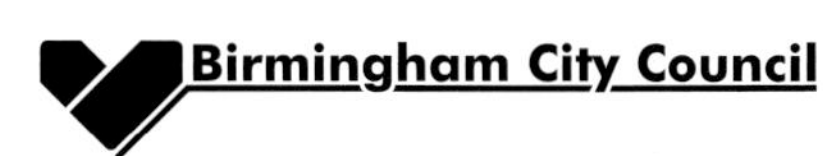 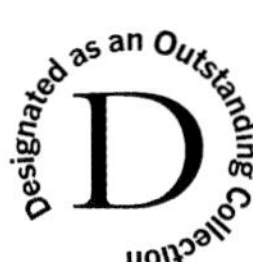

GILES

This publication accompanies the following exhibition:

Ford Madox Brown: The Unofficial Pre-Raphaelite
Works on Paper by Ford Madox Brown from Birmingham Museums and Art Gallery
Birmingham Museum and Art Gallery
Chamberlain Square
Birmingham B3 3DH
24 August – 14 December 2008

Contents

Foreword and Acknowledgements

Born in Calais in 1821, and some six to eight years older than his contemporaries William Holman Hunt, Dante Gabriel Rossetti and John Everett Millais, Ford Madox Brown was never officially a member of the Pre-Raphaelite Brotherhood. He nevertheless remains a central figure associated with the original 1848 ideals of this major nineteenth-century art movement. Contemporary critics recognised this relationship, as Brown himself described in 1851: '[They] begin to know that if not an actual Pre-Raphaelite Brother, I am an aider and abettor of Pre-Raphaelitism.'

Today the Pre-Raphaelite label remains the most familiar point of discussion for this considerable artist, whether as forerunner and follower or as teacher to Rossetti. Recent research, however, has also revealed the breadth of Madox Brown's achievements as a realist and modernist in a career spanning nearly sixty years until his death in 1893. Mary Bennett's catalogue is expected in the near future, as well as a major survey exhibition. The present project aims to be part of this reassessment process.

The Madox Brown collection at Birmingham Museums and Art Gallery (BMAG) ranges in date from the early 1840s to the 1890s. It includes sketch and study drawings, watercolours, stained glass designs, wood engravings as well as paintings and archive material. The unique breadth of this collection was largely acquired through public subscription from the collection of Charles Fairfax Murray in 1906, and is currently the subject of a series of research projects profiling the scope of Birmingham's Pre-Raphaelite collections. The last few years have seen exhibitions and publications on *John Everett Millais: Illustrator and Narrator* (2004) and *Hidden Burne-Jones* (2007–8).

Ford Madox Brown: The Unofficial Pre-Raphaelite has been realised as a collaborative PhD project, one of the first in the country, funded by the Arts and Humanities Research Council with the University of Birmingham. Over three years the postgraduate student Laura MacCulloch has catalogued the Museums' 174 works on paper by Madox Brown as part of her doctoral thesis. She has, in turn, worked with Tessa Sidey, Curator of Prints and Drawings, to select and organise this exhibition. Laura's findings will also be incorporated into a new online Pre-Raphaelite Resource Site for the Birmingham collection to be launched in 2009.

Over the last three years various people have contributed in all manner of ways to the Madox Brown project. We would like specially to thank the contributory writers to this publication, Angela Thirlwell and Tim Barringer; at the University of Birmingham: Paul Spencer-Longhurst, Richard Clay and Shearer West; at Birmingham Museums and Art Gallery: Gill Casson, Lee Handley, Carl Turner, David Rowan, Lucy Blakeman, Rachel Cockett and Kath Leahy; Mary Bennett for generously providing access to the numbering system in her forthcoming catalogue and for her comments on individual works and encouragement with Edward Morris for this project; Oliver Soskice, Paul Goldman, Briony Llewelyn, Kathryn Ferry, Charles Nugent, Melva Croal; Yale Centre for British Art; the staff of the Art Gallery of New South Wales, Sydney; and not least Dan Giles, Helen Swansbourne and Sarah McLaughlin for their respective skills and support for what will be their second publication of Birmingham's unique collection of nineteenth-century drawings.

RITA MCLEAN
Head of Museums and Heritage Services
Birmingham Museums and Art Gallery

Vieux Fordy: Death of a Modern Man

ANGELA THIRLWELL

On Sunday 1 October 1893 Ford Madox Brown worked for an hour or two on his replica of *Wycliffe on Trial*.[1] Stiff with gout, he climbed down the ladder from the screw-chair in which he painted. He felt inexplicably tired. As Cathy Hueffer, his widowed, younger daughter, helped him upstairs to bed, he said to her, 'Well, my dear, my work's done now.' On Monday he stayed in bed, at his home hung with Aesthetic golden wallpaper at 1 St Edmund's Terrace, adjacent to the green space of Primrose Hill, in north London. Later, Lucy Rossetti, his eldest daughter, visited for a painful farewell. Ravaged by tuberculosis, she was leaving the next day to winter in Italy. On Tuesday Madox Brown suffered an attack of apoplexy (stroke or cerebral event)[2] and remained in a comatose condition for three days. Cathy called in Dr Gill of Russell Square and Dr Roberts of Harley Street. On Friday morning, 6 October, the seventy-two-year-old artist regained consciousness briefly, had breakfast, then relapsed into a coma and died at 4.30 pm.

His thirteen-year-old granddaughter Juliet was living with her mother Cathy at Madox Brown's home:

> Something so terrible happened that I think I shall never forget it as long as I live. My dear grandfather died. He had only been ill a few days, and his illness began on the very night he finished the big picture…
>
> I was afraid of waking him, but all of a sudden he turned his head towards me and opened his eyes and looked at me…
>
> I felt I was going to cry, but I didn't, and he turned round and smiled just a little and said, 'Ah, little pigeon.'

But his thoughts were not in the present, with Juliet. Instead he was reliving Guy Fawkes' Night 1874, nearly twenty years earlier, when his brilliant son Oliver had died.

Juliet heard him saying in a low voice:

> 'Please to remember
> The fifth of November…

And then he went to sleep and didn't move again. She crept out of the room and cried because she felt he had not really been glad to see her.[3]

In the lost three days between his first stroke and his final attack, we know Madox Brown regained consciousness at least twice. On one of these occasions his thoughts went back to his son, Oliver Madox Brown. The boy had promised to become – like William Blake or Dante Gabriel Rossetti – that rare phenomenon, a poet-painter, before dying tragically, aged nineteen. Who knows where human thoughts drift when in a state of unconsciousness? Perhaps thinking about his lost son cast Madox Brown back to his own childhood and youth in France.

It had all begun in 1825 with a horse's hoof. When he was only four, young Ford had corrected an equine sketch his father was making. His parents, Ford senior and Caroline (née Madox) Brown, immediately recognised their son's artistic flair. 'In order to encourage his efforts', Caroline herself joined a local drawing class with young Fordy (his family pet-name).[4] Later the parents 'engaged the best drawing masters' in the Pas-de-Calais for their precocious young son and his elder sister, Eliza, always called Lyly.[5]

Reduced finances – Ford Brown was a retired officer on half-pay from the navy – forced the Browns to become economic migrants to France where the impoverished middle classes could live altogether more cheaply than in England. As his parents moved restively from Calais, where Ford Madox Brown was born, 16 April 1821, to Dunkirk, Bruges, Ghent and Antwerp, the picturesque towns and forests of northern France and Belgium left an indelible impression on the young artist.

Two key elements of his future life as an artist were already apparent in the child. The first instinct was an almost painful sense of what is beautiful and what is ugly. One day when his spelling book got ripped in a quarrel, his mother ingeniously repaired it with needle and thread. 'Because my mother had sewn it I thought it all right, but it was nevertheless an eye-sore to me.'

The second artistic trait rooted in childhood was an acute sense of the expressiveness, even the grotesquerie of the human face. At a family picnic in the forest of Guînes, outside Calais, he meandered off and 'lost himself'. Conjuring up bears or wolves behind every tree, he 'began to howl but no one heard me'. At last he was rescued by 'a sand-boy and a sand-girl with a donkey' who laughed as he howled, 'je veux Maman'. They propped him on their donkey and took him back to his parents. But their menacing faces seared his imagination. 'Not Gargantua and his sister could have seemed more terrible to my frightened senses than this ferocious looking couple.'[6] Contorted or grimacing human faces would feature throughout Madox Brown's work. His commitment to expressiveness made it hard for an audience accustomed to Victorian art to accept his principles of dramatic truth-telling rather than anodyne beauty. In 1871 Dante Gabriel Rossetti acclaimed Madox Brown as 'one of the greatest painters living anywhere, though the intensity of expression in his works places them beyond the appreciation of commonplace people'.[7]

Once the Browns had decided their son was to be a great artist, their removals were driven by finding the best academies of art in their corner of Europe. In a curious irony, a training that was first French, then more widely European, underlay Madox Brown's eventual reputation as a quintessentially British artist. His picture, *The Last of England*, would be voted one of Britain's ten favourite pictures in a BBC Radio 4 poll in 2005. But when he died, French newspaper reports naturally stressed his French roots.

He moved across the French border in November 1835, aged fourteen, when he became a private pupil of Albert Gregorius, director of the Bruges Academy of Painting. Gregorius was back in Belgium after many years in the atelier of the French neoclassical painter, Jacques-Louis David. A year later, another of David's pupils, Pieter van Hanselaer, taught Madox Brown at the Ghent Academy – though he was debarred from life-classes as he was still

only fifteen. He graduated to the Antwerp Academy in 1838, taking tuition from arguably his most distinguished teacher, Gustave, later Baron Wappers, noted for crowd scenes of heroic revolutions in Europe. This influence would resonate throughout Madox Brown's career and point to another contradiction in his art. Although a modern artist who chose subjects with contemporary significance – such as economic emigration to Australia in *The Last of England*, or the impact of the Crimean War in *Waiting: An English Fireside in the Winter of 1854–55* – Madox Brown was equally committed to finding modern significance in key scenes from British history. His heroes were either democrats who changed political history, such as *Cromwell on his Farm*,[8] or working people who rebelled against tyranny, as shown in *The Expulsion of the Danes from Manchester*.[9]

In Antwerp in 1838, Madox Brown lodged at Le Pot d'Etain with his friend, the 'slightly hot-headed' Irish artist, Daniel Casey. Both young men were enchanted by a blonde girl next door with 'very pretty small feet' whom they wooed, unsuccessfully, with bunches of violets.[10] Their mutual sympathy is apparent in the sensitive, clear-eyed portrait Madox Brown drew of Casey in 1848 (cat. 21). Casey called him 'mon vieux Fordy' and the two artists remained lifelong friends. Casey later lived in Paris, while Madox Brown settled permanently in England from 1846. Madox Brown always admired his friend's paintings and, almost forty years on, tried to intercede with the French government to rescue him from neglect and penury.[11] It was one of many occasions when Madox Brown initiated subscription funds to help fellow artists and their families in distress.[12]

He associated Casey in his mind with Paris and with happy memories of living there with his first wife, Elisabeth Bromley. Madox Brown valued his male friends, masculinity, and from 1855, his son Oliver above all else. The artist came from a line of proactive men. His grandfather, John Brown, was a pioneering Scottish doctor, famous for proposing a revolutionary theory known as the Brunonian system of medicine. His mother was a Madox who could trace her ancestry back to the English Crusaders. His father had been an officer on board the *Arethusa* in the British navy during the Napoleonic wars.[13]

Yet women shaped his life from an early age. Caroline, his mother, had been perceptive and loving. After her premature death, in Calais in September 1839, a Madox annuity gifted him a small measure of financial independence. A few months later, in June 1840, his companion and sister Lyly died, like their mother, of consumption. Madox Brown had literally lost half his family before he was twenty.

So when his first cousin, Elisabeth Bromley, broke her journey in Antwerp on her way back from finishing school in Germany, she seemed almost angelic. Natural serenity heightened Elisabeth's attraction. She modelled in a demanding head-thrown-backwards pose for the fainting maidservant in his dramatic picture *The Execution of Mary, Queen of Scots*.[14] Within weeks they both acknowledged 'an ensnaring of hearts'.[15] Maybe it was an instinct to recreate the family Madox Brown had recently lost. Choosing Elisabeth was a tangible, familial link to his dead mother and perhaps an unconscious imitation of that relationship. To the bereaved boy she embodied mother, sister and sweetheart in one.

They married on 3 April 1841, at the ancient parish church of Meopham in Kent, near the Bromley family home. Aged twenty-two, Elisabeth was slightly older than Madox Brown who was not quite twenty. The teenager looked so baby-faced that the vicar Mr Thompson enquired sceptically, 'Where's the bridegroom?'[16]

After the wedding, the couple made their first home in Paris, in order to extend Madox Brown's art studies. Intelligent and poised, Elisabeth was his ideal partner in Paris, well able to discuss art and literature. Both were sophisticated readers who equally enjoyed racy novels or serious plays.

One book they read was Laurence Sterne's *Sentimental Journey through France and Italy*, published in 1768. Hogarth had illustrated Sterne's notoriously bawdy *Tristram Shandy* and, in homage to Hogarth, the young artist made two drawings inspired by Sterne's amorous journey. His *Sterne and Maria Walking* (cat. 1) perfectly captures the author's lecherous intention as he gazes down protectively at 'poor Maria', all in white, tearful and deserted by her previous lover. Madox Brown and Elisabeth appreciated Sterne's roguish self-mockery as he pondered seduction. 'I am positive I have a soul; nor can all the books with which materialists have pestered the world ever convince me to the contrary.'[17]

When *The Last of England* was shown at the Pre-Raphaelite exhibition in Bloomsbury organised by Madox Brown in June 1857, the *Athenaeum* reviewer compared the picture to Hogarth. The compliment was particularly pleasing to Madox Brown who venerated the 'modern moral subjects' of the great realist. Later, when a club for like-minded exhibitors was founded in 1858 as an alternative to the stuffy Royal Academy, Madox Brown proposed it should be called the 'Hogarth', in honour of the painter he considered the 'originator of moral invention and drama in modern art' – principles identical with his own.[18]

Even as a young man he showed his range, from Sterne's off-beat humour to Shakespeare's most rigorous tragedy. In Paris with Elisabeth, Madox Brown made a series of powerful drawings illustrating *King Lear*.[19] He loved the theatre, especially Shakespeare, whose plays were increasingly attracting European artists. In 1828 the German artist, Moritz Retzsch, had produced a set of sixteen engravings, *Umrisse zu Hamlet*, in a linear 'outline style' which influenced Madox Brown. Then in 1843, a year before Madox Brown began to draw *King Lear*, Delacroix published thirteen dashingly Romantic lithographs illustrating *Hamlet*.

In his *Lear* drawings Madox Brown concentrated on the power struggles between characters: Lear against Cordelia, Goneril and Regan against Cordelia, Lear against Goneril and Regan. This gave his sketches narrative thrust and drama. With spare, energetic lines Madox Brown also pointed up profound thematic contrasts – youth against age, parent against child, insubordination against authority, female against male, weakness against strength, man against the elements, loving kindness against ruthlessness.

The artist showed the way we lived then, specifically in sixth-century Britain immediately after the departure of the Romans and, more universally, the way families live in every time and place. In the composed features of Elisabeth he found an implicit parallel with the resolute dignity of Cordelia who measures words so precisely:

> Unhappy that I am, I cannot heave
> My heart into my mouth: I love your Majesty
> According to my bond; no more nor less.[20]

Placed on the right of the picture, she is quite literally in the right, his youngest and best loved daughter. Madox Brown blocked his pictures with the instincts of a theatre director (cat. 2).

Cordelia would recur in Madox Brown's later works, part of his lifelong connection with *King Lear*, when a different face, Emma Hill's, would embody the symbolic virtue of Shakespeare's heroine. Each major relationship of his life answered a separate quest in his multi-faceted personality: his marriages with Elisabeth Bromley and later, Emma Hill, and his two intimate friendships, with artist Marie Spartali and poet Mathilde Blind.

Apart from Elisabeth Bromley, they were all, in their various ways, modern women. And even though Elisabeth was religious and traditional, as a couple she and Madox Brown were already exploring a more mutual, more modern form of marriage than the conventional model. He chose Elisabeth to satisfy his emotional and intellectual needs. He shared his deepest ambitions with her. 'It may be a kind of excitement, but I feel sure that in a few years I shall be known, and begin to be valued … God bless you, my dear Wife, and bless our child.'[21]

But Elisabeth's health was fragile. Her first child, a son, died aged just five days. He was the first of Madox Brown's three sons – and he lost them all. Eventually Elisabeth gave birth to Lucy in Paris in July 1843. Ominously recalling Caroline and Lyly's symptoms, Elisabeth developed tuberculosis. To alleviate her condition, the couple decided to leave for Italy. On the way south, in the art museum at Basle, Madox Brown had a life-defining experience when he saw the hyper-realistic pictures of Holbein. From then on he saw himself as a modern Holbein and set himself to transcribe directly from the visible world. Madox Brown 'really did initiate modern art. He seems to have been the first man in modern days … who began trying to paint what he saw.'[22] During the journey he also fell under the spell of early Italian artists, Giotto, Masaccio, Ghirlandaio, Leonardo and Luini. Once in Rome he met the German 'Nazarene' artists, Overbeck and Cornelius, continental precursors of the Pre-Raphaelites.

Rome was artistically stimulating but it did not cure Elisabeth. By early summer 1846, she had one wish, to get home to England to die. Aged twenty-seven, Elisabeth died in Madox Brown's arms, on 5 June 1846 in the post-chaise, as they crossed the Boulevard des Italiens in Paris. She was still pointing north, too weak to utter a word.[23]

Elisabeth left him with three-year-old Lucy, whom he placed with his late wife's relations in Kent while he worked frantically in London to support them both. Two major projects were *Oure Ladye of Saturday Night*[24] and *Wycliffe reading his Translation of the Bible to John of Gaunt*,[25] in a style that anticipated the Pre-Raphaelites. Meanwhile three younger artists, aged nineteen to twenty-one, John Everett Millais, William Holman Hunt and Dante Gabriel Rossetti discovered they shared a passion for early Italian artists. Inspired by the freshness and special transparency in pictures that predated Raphael, they founded in 1848 a protest movement against conventional Victorian painting, as epitomised by the Royal Academy. They were the three original members of the Pre-Raphaelite Brotherhood (PRB), soon expanded to seven. Dissatisfied with the Royal Academy Schools, Rossetti was looking for a teacher who shared his own ideals. In March 1848 he wrote to Madox Brown, 'personally quite unknown to him', expansively praising the older man's pictures and asking to become his pupil. Suspecting the letter was a practical joke, Madox Brown set off, equipped with a 'stout stick' to rouse Rossetti at 50 Charlotte Street. Rossetti assured him that both the praise and request for tuition were entirely genuine. Disarmed, Madox Brown accepted Rossetti as a student forthwith, refused remuneration, and made Rossetti 'his friend on the spot – a friend for that day … and a friend for life.'[26]

This was the beginning of Madox Brown's association with the Pre-Raphaelites, an association that was mutually influential long after the short-lived Brotherhood disbanded. Although 'from the first' he refused to join the PRB, arguing that 'coteries had in modern art no proper function',[27] he was perceived *in loco parentis*, often referred to as Father of the Pre-Raphaelites or even King of the Pre-Raphaelites. Identifying with their avant-garde style, he contributed a sonnet, a theoretical essay and one of his *Lear* pictures to the Brotherhood's arts magazine, *The Germ* (cat. 24).[28] Later he connected with a second wave of 'Pre-Raphaelites', notably Morris and Burne-Jones, and became a partner in 'The Firm' before an explosive falling-out. However, his friendship with Rossetti and the original Pre-Raphaelites, their devotion to labour-intensive pictures made on new principles, inspired some of Madox Brown's most memorable pictures.

Work left no time for any private life until one day late in 1848 when Madox Brown, a widower of twenty-seven, noted that 'a girl as loves me came in and disturbed me'. Emma Hill, aged nineteen, had just walked into his pictures and his life.[29]

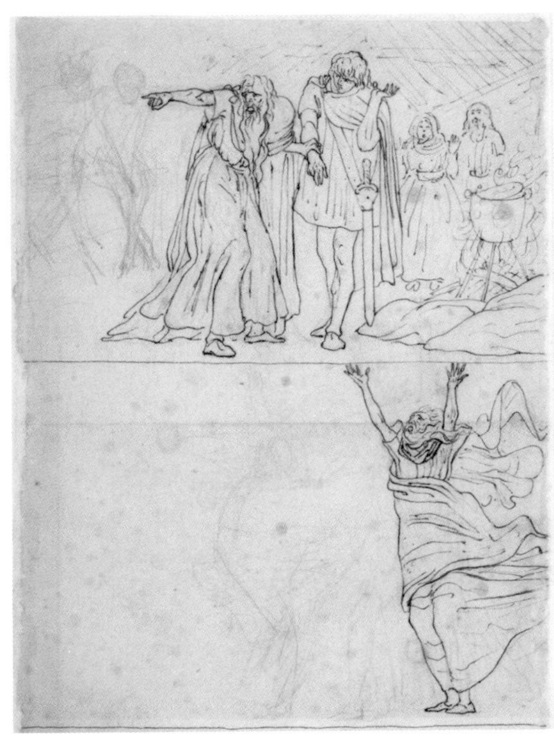

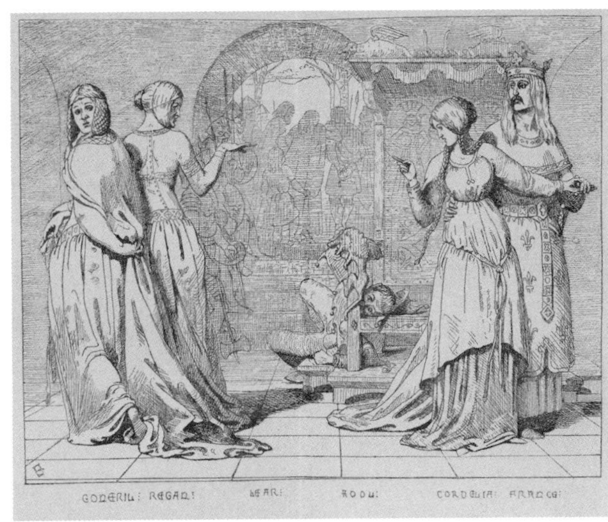
GONERILL REGANI   LEARI   RODUI   CORDELIAI FRANCOI

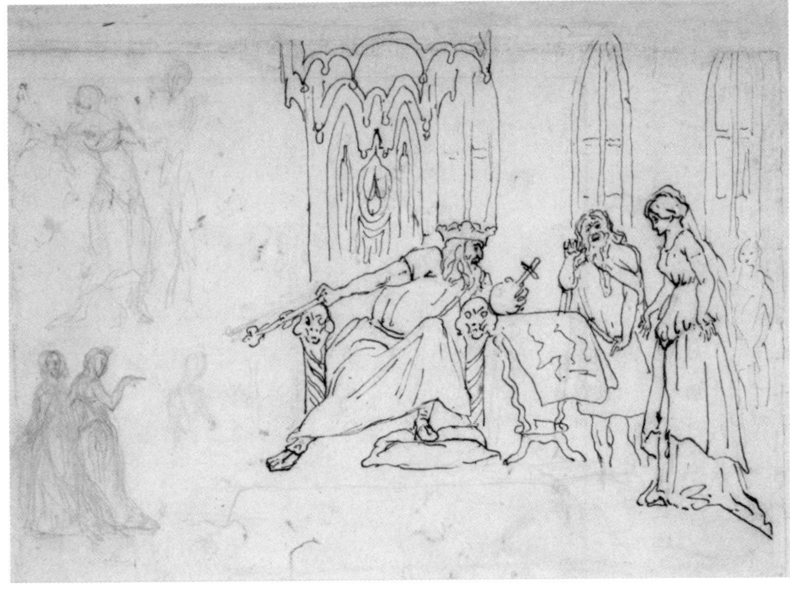

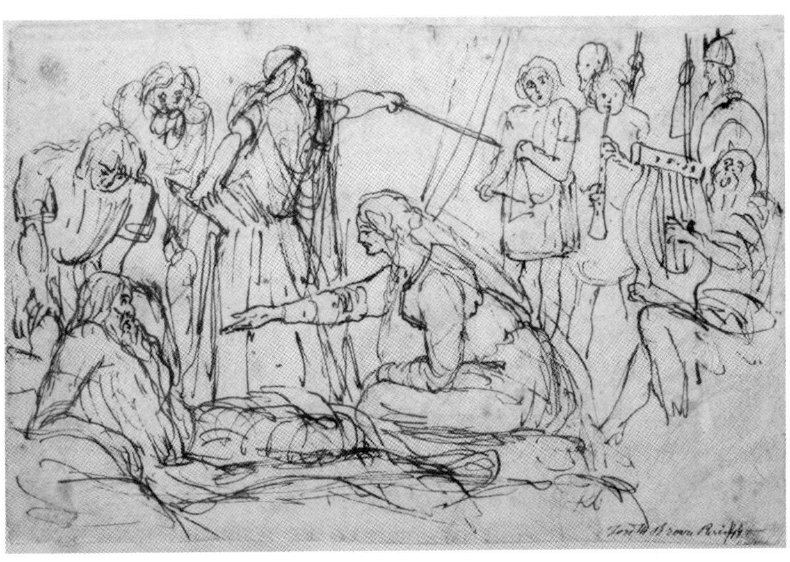

Emma was the opposite of Elisabeth Bromley: working class rather than middle class, unschooled not educated, robust rather than frail, blonde instead of sleekly dark. She had 'a pink complexion, regular features, and a fine abundance of beautiful yellow hair, the tint of harvest corn'.[30] In the studio Emma saw a young man who was 'good-looking as well as fine' with 'a face full of insight and purpose; thick straight brown hair, fair skin, bluish eyes, broad brow.'[31] The artist made a drawing of Emma's perfect head at Christmas 1848 when she modelled as Cordelia in *Cordelia at the Bedside of Lear*.[32] Now Emma's unspoilt beauty personified his ideal of female integrity. The face of an unlettered girl brought up on a farm had the innate nobility of Shakespeare's ancient British princess (cat. 22).

However, Madox Brown continued to visit Elisabeth's grave. Death was a natural component of Victorian lives. Slowly Elisabeth's impact faded, and with Emma trudging beside him up to Highgate cemetery, he turned back to life. His painting became more ambitious and confident. He allayed Emma's sense of social inferiority – 'without educational advantages' – by asking her to model for the most patrician, romantic and glamorous women in his pictures.

An early role was consort to the Black Prince in an imposing composition, *Chaucer at the Court of Edward III*, in which Emma modelled for the fair Maid of Kent, with braided hair, coronet and streaming red headdress.[33] With its ideal regularity Emma's face conveyed an almost universal appeal. She could morph into a princess but also embody Everywoman, as in *The Last of England*. From now on she would be his finest and most iconic model.

Throughout 1849 the couple rambled through the fields around north London with scant regard for Victorian sexual convention. At the end of the summer they ran off for a week together to the seaside resort of Ramsgate. Spontaneous and illicit, the affair was the total reverse of Madox Brown's bourgeois marriage to serious-minded Elisabeth. In extreme youth, he had conformed and complied; now in his late twenties he felt ready to live like a bohemian artist.

Madox Brown's feelings about women had been conditioned by love for his mother, his sister, and for Elisabeth. But in the studio he also dealt with women who modelled in the nude by day, and were probably prostitutes by night. Did he feel any confusion about which 'type' of womanhood fitted Emma best? Emma was still Miss Hill, with skin that 'resembled a peach', when their daughter Cathy was born in time for breakfast on 11 November 1850. She was such a fair, plump baby that they called her their 'hot roll as she arrived with the hot rolls' brought round by the baker.[34]

The early years of the liaison were tempestuous. Sometimes the tension simply could not hold – and it snapped in the early 1850s. Madox Brown suffered a depressive crisis. He contemplated suicide. He parted from Emma. He stopped writing his Painter's Diary for four years.

The idea for *The Last of England* came to Madox Brown when he was deeply depressed, so short of money or public recognition that he even considered emigrating to India. The lovers were living apart in planned disengagement. He was at Mrs Coates's lodgings in Hampstead, where he 'remained one year & nine months most of the time intensely miserable very hard up & a little mad'.[35] Although appointed head master of the North London Drawing School at £60 a year, the money never materialised. After banishment to Dover with Cathy during summer 1852, Emma returned to lodge just over Hampstead Heath in Highgate. From here she came to model for initial studies for the emigrant wife in *The Last of England* (cat. 29 and 30). And she posed on the most inhuman, sunless days for this authentically wintry picture. Madox Brown worked himself to exhaustion during early 1853 while Emma froze 'chiefly out of doors when the snow was lieing on the ground'.[36]

In a double way, Emma cemented his relationship to the Pre-Raphaelites. She modelled in his most Pre-Raphaelite pictures and, on a personal level, was close to Rossetti's girlfriend Lizzie Siddal. Their friendship probably dated back to childhood, when their two mothers were acquainted. The alliance with Emma 'was certainly the closest of Lizzie's intimacies'. In a parallel arc, Rossetti's greatest mutual male friendship of his life was with 'dear Bruno' – Madox Brown himself.[37]

Before and even after his eventual marriage to Emma on 5 April 1853, Madox Brown's state of mind veered dangerously. Yet, in spite of, or perhaps because of his erratic state, these first years of the 1850s were his *anni mirabili*. Between 1850 and 1854 he embarked on his most innovatory pictures, including *Waiting, Take Your Son, Sir!, An English Autumn Afternoon, The Last of England, Work* and *The Pretty Baa-Lambs*. With its teasing title, *The Pretty Baa-Lambs* disregarded the Victorian taste for clear narrative and instead anticipated the art of the Aesthetic Movement. He began this crystalline picture at Stockwell,

South London, during the long, hot summer of 1851. In a sun-filled landscape, a commanding Emma holds baby Cathy, among gambolling sheep. Madox Brown depicted every droplet of sweat on the sunburnt faces of this modern Madonna and Child. Meticulously he described the matted curls on the sheep – awkward and obstructive when brought daily to pose for the artist.

It was a landmark in modern European painting. Madox Brown was the first artist to show figures in a landscape, executed totally *en plein air*. This method of working predated not only the artists of the French Barbizon school such as Millet, but also Monet who painted his *Women in the Garden* in 1866–67.

Domestic relations remained volatile. The interdependent friendship between Emma and Lizzie began to have negative effects. Lizzie was addicted to laudanum and Emma took alcohol. Marriage to Emma, who retained her beauty until death, pitched Madox Brown alternately from extreme pleasure to livid despair. After Cathy, they had two more children, Oliver born 20 January 1855, and Arthur born 16 September 1856 (d. 21 July 1857). Emma's natural beauty continued to inspire her husband's most enduring images. Her physical appeal undiminished, she featured in his great commentary on the state of the nation, *Work*, and in his most erotic later pictures, *Romeo and Juliet*, *Byron's Dream* and *Down Stream* (cat. 47 and 48). But Emma drank more, suffered a debilitating miscarriage after baby Arthur's death in 1857 and often had fits of illness, perhaps due to epilepsy (cat. 50).

With much substantial work behind him, Madox Brown decided to hold an exhibition in 1865 at 196 Piccadilly. One-man shows by living artists were almost unprecedented in Victorian England. It was a daring and original venture, a personal retrospective, staging all his most important pictures, arranged like an autobiography. One hundred images, in cogent groupings, led the visitor inexorably forward to the heart of the show, to its centrepiece and *tour de force*. It was no less than the social mirror of Victorian England – the great canvas *Work*. In another 'first', he wrote a revealing, explanatory catalogue to guide visitors through the exhibition.[38] Gladstone himself made a surprise visit and shook Madox Brown by the hand.

The show and the gesture catapulted Madox Brown into the public arena. He became better known and for the first time enjoyed modest prosperity. He moved from the suburban village of Kentish Town to bohemian Fitzrovia. Here he threw brilliant parties, hosted animated debates and even séances. Admirers considered him the handsomest man in London and the best conversationalist. Whistler came and met 'the most wonderful people, Swinburne, anarchists, poets, and musicians, all kinds and sorts, and in an inner room Rossetti and Mrs. Morris sitting side by side in state, being worshipped'. And among the party visitors were two exotic young women: Greek artist, Marie Spartali, and German-Jewish poet, Mathilde Blind.

These two women fulfilled different exciting and intellectual needs that Emma could not meet. Marie came to Madox Brown in the 1860s as a student, and during the intensity of his passion for teaching, for making things clear, he found that he was falling in love with his pupil. It was unrequited but Marie's tact enabled them to sustain a friendship for the rest of his life. After Marie married William Stillman, a sensationally unsuitable American widower in 1871, Mathilde entered his life on a long-term basis. They shared deep interests in literature, history and radical politics. Mathilde was the more equal love he had longed for, ever since he lost Elisabeth in his twenties.

In 1878 Madox Brown accepted a commission from Manchester Corporation to paint twelve murals in the Town Hall, celebrating the history of 'Cottonopolis', a mighty industrial city.[39] He saw it as the culmination of his career, a public validation of his life's work and a permanent monument. He undertook it in the spirit of a modern Veronese, the Renaissance painter who had celebrated civic Venice, and added his own special humour to the project. For *The Expulsion of the Danes*, he needed a real piglet to trip up the heels of a magnificent figure in the painting. During an organ recital in the Town Hall, the farmer suddenly smuggled in his piglet. Madox Brown's bright eyes glittered as he retold the story. The organist was 'playing some exquisitely soft sacred music, with his great audience breathless before him, anxious to lose no vibration.' Madox Brown remained hidden inside his special painting tent, 'all alone – alone with a pig!' Suddenly 'the thrilling strains so touched whatever passes as sentiment in the porcine nature that the pig began to squeak and grunt and howl, and had to be carried bodily out of the place.'[40]

Mathilde joined them when he and Emma moved to Manchester in 1880. The triangle was soon untenable and Mathilde moved out to lodgings nearby. When he moved back to London, they repeated the domestic geography, with Mathilde installed locally in Hampstead. But he felt guilty about Emma and as she deteriorated at the end of the 1880s, he found himself rediscovering his love for her. 'He was terribly unhappy when she died [in October 1890.] He used to sit alone in the studio for hours together, doing no work at all,' recalled granddaughter Juliet. 'In the evening he used to wander up and down and in and out from room to room, as if he were looking everywhere to try and find my grandmother.'[41]

Madox Brown died three years later. 'When I went out I saw the placards, "Death of F.M.B.", and I stood and stared at them. I didn't cry because I couldn't believe that the dead man was really my dear grandpapa, who had always been there in the studio winding himself up and down in the screw-chair, and calling me "little pigeon", and loving me.'[42]

Reports of Madox Brown's death were copied nationally and internationally from London to Edinburgh, from Dublin to Cardiff, from Paris to New York. Obituaries and the world's assessment followed. Some saw him as other-worldly. 'He painted, not for money, or even for fame, but for art's sake.'[43] Others saw him as a modern man, 'A Captain of the Advance.'[44]

The funeral took place in the unconsecrated section of St Pancras Cemetery at 12.30 on Wednesday 11 October. The coffin was polished elm with brass fittings, covered with wreaths and inscribed simply, 'Ford Madox Brown. Born in Calais, 16th April 1821. Died in London, 6th Oct., 1893.' Sixteen carriages followed the hearse drawn by two horses. Many family members, friends and representatives from Manchester Corporation convened at the graveside.[45] *The Daily Graphic* reported the unusual procedure. 'As soon as the mourners had gathered round under the shadow of a fine sycamore, of which the leaves have just faded into a beautiful golden brown, the coffin was

lowered.' Then American free-thinker, Moncure Conway, delivered a moving and entirely secular address. Many newspapers described Mathilde Blind's beautiful foliage wreath with a 'line from Blake woven in gold on a ribbon of black silk: – "Death is the mercy of eternity".'[46] In fact, Mathilde had deliberately revised Blake's gnomic words from *Milton*. The original line reads 'Time is the mercy of eternity.' Mathilde's reworking, while still ambiguous, presumably hints at the agnosticism she shared with the artist. Neither Mathilde nor Madox Brown envisaged an afterlife. In a curious pre-Freudian slip, several newspapers noted Mathilde's name incorrectly as 'Mathilde Brown'.[47]

Today Madox Brown's grave lies hidden behind bushes and brambles in a remote part of the cemetery. It is distorted by the growth of a huge ash tree which has pushed the headstone forward at a rakish angle. The grave itself is almost sunk into the earth and the foot stone is also skewed and half-buried in the ground. A few steps away in a more accessible position is an elegant monument to Mathilde Blind, carved from Carrara marble by Edouard Lanteri. It shows Mathilde as a classical goddess, presiding over two graceful female figures, Philosophy and Poetry. Cut beneath her name is the same line she had chosen for Madox Brown's wreath – DEATH IS THE MERCY OF ETERNITY.

Just before his last illness, Madox Brown called on another granddaughter, Helen Rossetti, nearly fourteen. 'Oh Nellie … I'm going for a little walk in the Park. Come with me.' So off they stepped together, Madox Brown in his Inverness cape and top hat, down Ormonde Terrace, across the Albert Road, over the bridge across the Regent's canal, straight into the setting sun. 'Never shall I forget that sun nor the vision of grandpapa walking as it seemed straight into it – opaque and glowing and unnaturally big. I had the vision that Grandpapa could not stop, bound to walk on for ever into the setting sun.'[48]

1. A commission intended for presentation to the nation. Ford M. Hueffer, *Ford Madox Brown: A Record of his Life and Work* (London, Longmans, Green and Co., 1896), pp. 395–96, 444 (hereafter *Hueffer*, 1896).

2. I am grateful to Dr Elspeth Macdonald for the modern diagnosis of FMB's cause of death.

3. Accounts of FMB's final days from contemporary newspaper reports and from William Michael Rossetti, *Some Reminiscences*, 2 vols (London, Brown, Langham, 1906), I, p. 526 (hereafter *W. M. Rossetti)*, and Juliet Soskice, *Chapters from Childhood* (London, Selwyn & Blount, 1921), pp. 68–73 (hereafter *Soskice*).

4. *The World*, in its 'Celebrities at Home' series, 11 October 1893. FMB had

been interviewed for this just before he was taken ill.

5. Lucy Madox Rossetti, 'Ford Madox Brown', *The Magazine of Art* (XIII, 1890), pp. 289–96.

6. Both memories from Ford Madox Brown's letter to Henry Boddington, 25 March 1889, University of British Columbia, Rare Books and Special Collections, Angeli-Dennis Collection, 5–10.

7. Dante Gabriel Rossetti to Louisa, Lady Ashburton, 8 June 1871, *The Correspondence of Dante Gabriel Rossetti*, ed. William E. Fredeman , 9 vols (Cambridge, D. S. Brewer, 2002–8), V. 71.66.1.

8. Lady Lever Art Gallery, Port Sunlight, Merseyside.

9. One of the murals at Manchester Town Hall.

10. *Hueffer*, 1896, pp. 16–17.

11. Ibid., p. 357.

12. Ibid., p. 376. After Casey's death, Madox Brown transferred his efforts to Mrs Casey for whom he raised a fund of £32. £32 in 1886 represents approximately £2,400 today. (Information from www.measuringworth.com.)

13. New entry on FMB by Tim Barringer in the *Dictionary of National Biography*, 2004.

14. *The Execution of Mary, Queen of Scots* survives in a substantial but smaller version than the original (now lost) at the Whitworth Art Gallery, Manchester. The study of Elisabeth Bromley's head is at the Ashmolean Museum, Oxford.

15. Helen Rossetti Angeli, *Dante Gabriel Rossetti: His Friends and Enemies* (London, Hamish Hamilton, 1949), p. 26 (hereafter *Angeli*).

16. Ibid., p. 27.

17. Laurence Sterne, *A Sentimental Journey*, this edition (London, Cassell, 1911), p. 135.

18. *W. M. Rossetti*, I, p. 224.

19. Extensive drawings by FMB of *King Lear* are at the Whitworth Art Gallery, Manchester.

20. *King Lear*, Act I, sc. i, 91–93.

21. FMB's letter to 'My dearest Lizz', [?]18 May 1845, from William Michael Rossetti, *Præraphaelite Diaries and Letters* (London, Hurst and Blackett, 1900), pp. 59–60.

22. Ford Madox Hueffer, *The Pre-Raphaelite Brotherhood* (London, Duckworth, 1907), p. 21.

23. Lucy Madox Rossetti, 'Ford Madox Brown', *The Magazine of Art*, 13 (1890), pp. 289–96, 291.

24. Also known as *Oure Ladye of Good Children*, 1847, Tate Britain.

25. 1847, Bradford Art Gallery.

26. William Michael Rossetti, *Dante Gabriel Rossetti: His Family Letters with a Memoir*, 2 vols (London, Ellis and Elvey, 1895), I, p. 118 (hereafter *DGRFLM*).

27. Theodore Watts-Dunton, *Old Familiar Faces* (London, Herbert Jenkins, 1916), p. 73.

28. Four issues, 1850, reproduced in *The Germ* (Oxford, Ashmolean Museum, 1992).

29. *Diary of Ford Madox Brown*, ed. Virginia Surtees (New Haven and London, Yale University Press, 1981), p. 56 (hereafter *Diary*).

30. *W. M. Rossetti*, I, p. 137.

31. *DGRFLM*, I, p. 118.

32. Tate Britain.

33. Art Gallery of New South Wales, Sydney, and another version at Tate Britain.

34. Details from two unpublished documents written by Cathy Madox Brown Hueffer for her grandson, Frank Soskice, 'Jottings with a shaky pen', dated August 1922, Private Collection, and 'A Retrospect', undated, House of Lords Record Office, Stow Hill Papers: STH/BH/2/3–6.

35. *Diary*, p. 78, retrospective entry 16 August 1854, referring to summer 1852.

36. *Diary*, p. 80, retrospective entry 16 August 1854, referring to early 1853.

37. *Angeli*, p. 188.

38. Reproduced in Kenneth Bendiner, *The Art of Ford Madox Brown* (University Park, PA: Pennsylvania State University Press, 1998), Appendix 3.

39. For discussion of the murals see Julian Treuherz, 'Ford Madox Brown and the Manchester murals', Chapter 7 in *Art and Architecture in Victorian Manchester* (Manchester, Manchester University Press, 1985).

40. *Yorkshire Daily Post*, 7 October 1893, quoting a profile of Ford Madox Brown by Mrs Alexander (Anne Elizabeth) Ireland previously published in the *Yorkshire Weekly Post*, July 1892.

41. *Soskice*, p. 44.

42. Ibid., p. 73.

43. *The Times*, 7 October 1893.

44. *Pall Mall Budget*, 19 October 1893, p. 1641, also carried by the *Galignani Messenger*, Paris, 15 October 1893.

45. Details from the *Birmingham Daily Gazette*, 12 October 1893.

46. *The Daily Graphic*, 12 October 1893.

47. *Birmingham Daily Post*, 12 October 1893, *The Globe*, 12 October 1893, *The Morning Post*, 12 October 1893, *The Citizen*, 14 October 1893.

48. Notes on FMB by Helen Rossetti Angeli from the Fredeman Family Collection.

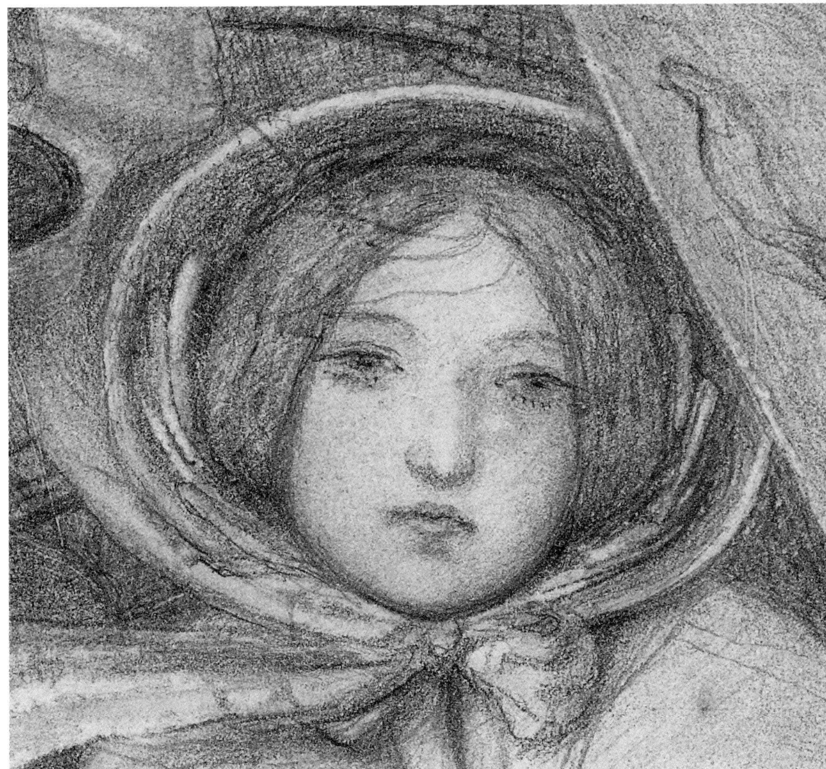

The Last of England: Cartoon, 1852 (cat. 30, detail of Emma Hill)

The Effects of Industry: Ford Madox Brown and Artistic Identities in Victorian Britain

TIM BARRINGER

We still have no fixed image of Ford Madox Brown. The creator of *Work* and *The Last of England*, Brown has nonetheless remained a shadowy presence in art history. Gainsborough's verdict on Reynolds – 'Damn him, how various he is' – might equally apply to Brown: as difficult to sum up as to pin down, his work is marked by an unmistakable, edgy originality. His personality, too, is vividly recognizable: uncompromising, harsh, witty, yet deeply emotional; easily wounded and yet passionately committed to the reform and reformation of art and of society.

During five decades of unceasing artistic activity, Brown occupied a range of different positions, subtly shifting his identity and the style in which he painted to accord with (and sometimes to protest against) the changing times. He explored a wide repertoire of tropes of artistic identity, never settling easily into one or other of them. Unlike his contemporaries, John Everett Millais and Frederic Leighton, he did not become a staunch member of the establishment, but nor did he follow William Holman Hunt by turning Pre-Raphaelitism from a rebellious creed into a rigid orthodoxy. Paradoxes abound. French-born and Belgian-trained, Brown was the most English of artists, a fierce nationalist, a devotee of William Hogarth and a leading light in the Hogarth Club. Usually described as a Pre-Raphaelite, he was (as the title of this publication attests) never a member of the Pre-Raphaelite Brotherhood. His later career found him in less familiar guises – as a pioneering Aesthete, an innovative designer of furniture and a path-breaking socialist. Above all, throughout his life Brown confronted the problem of what it meant to be an artist in the railway age – of how to register visually the historical meanings of urban and suburban modernity. Whether creating a grand tableau of the court of Edward III, minutely transcribing the social fabric of everyday life in *Work*, designing stained-glass windows for churches, teaching artisans to draw, running a soup kitchen, or painting murals charting the development of Manchester on the walls of its Town Hall, Brown was determined and persistent in his engagement with the problems of the modern.

While Ford Madox Brown was constantly renegotiating his identity as an artist across many media, he was also deeply engaged with the question of masculinity: what it meant to be a man in Victorian society. Few who see the gloomy and troubled visage of the male protagonist of *The Last of England* realise that this face is the artist's own (cat. 32). Yet while the image purports to be both a generalised account of the historical phenomenon of emigration at mid-century, and a specific portrayal of Thomas Woolner, the Pre-Raphaelite sculptor who left to seek his fortune in Australia, *The Last of England* ultimately represents Madox Brown's own despairing response to the critical rejection and market failure of his work. It represents a crisis not only of Brown's own personal psyche but one that could, potentially, afflict all Victorian middle-class men. Brown's negotiation of his own position, as an artist and as a man, is therefore paradigmatic of broader trends in Victorian culture.

The Artist as Scholar

Ford Madox Brown's unorthodox and anti-establishment leanings, as well as a sense that the world was against him, were prefigured in his background. His grandfather, John Brown (1735–1788), was the son of a Scottish labourer whose career as a mould-breaking medical doctor was marked by hostility to social superiors and professional peers. The doctor's second son, Ford Brown, at one time purser on the ship HMS *Arethusa*, retired after the Napoleonic Wars. Financial stringencies forced Ford and Caroline Brown to seek inexpensive lodgings in Calais, and it was these reduced circumstances that marked Ford Madox Brown's childhood. Brown's diary, which survives from a later period in his life, is filled with anxieties about money and professional status

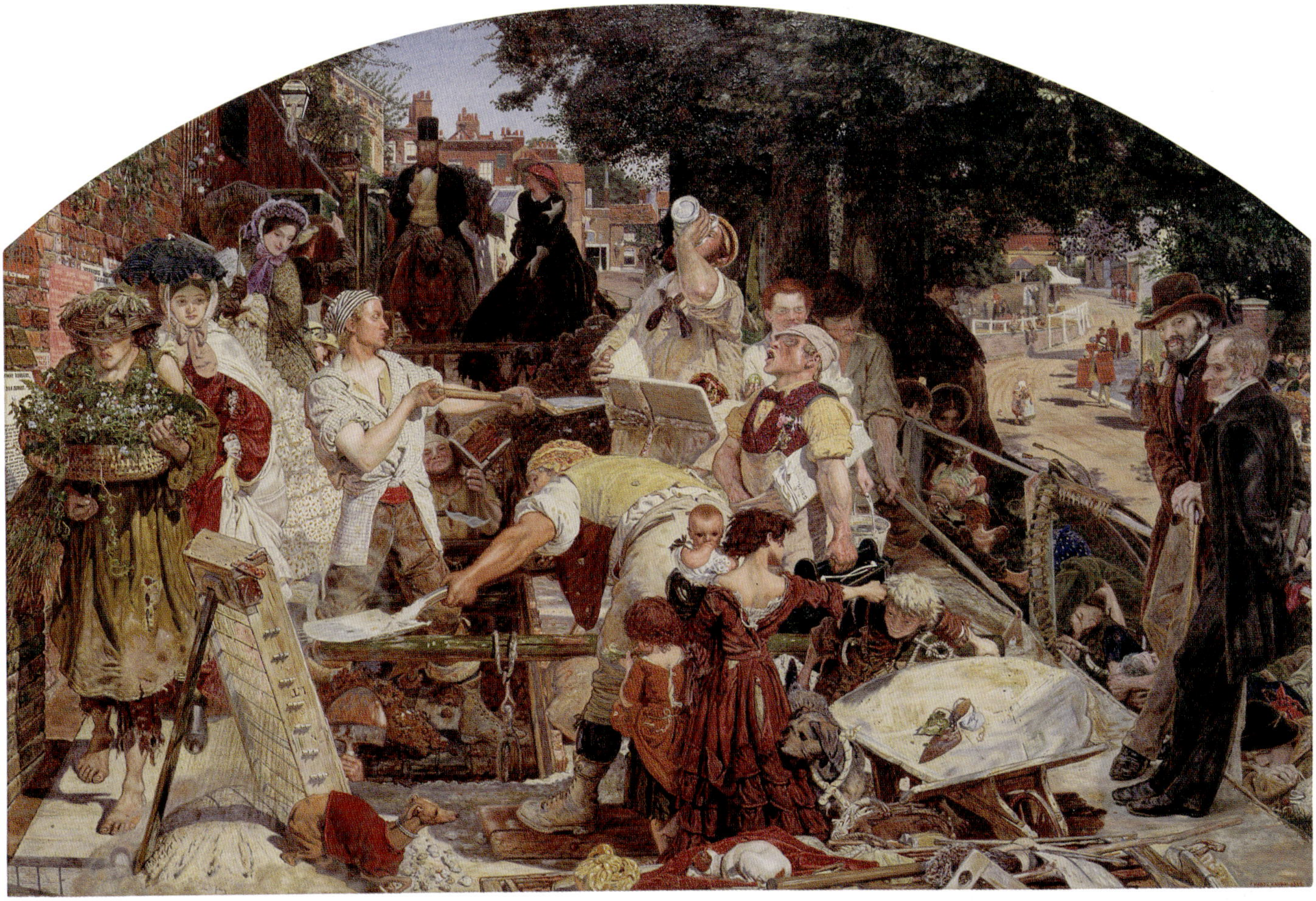

ABOVE: *Work,*
commissioned 1852,
finished 1863 (cat. 39)

RIGHT: *Portrait: Thomas
Carlyle,* c. 1859 (cat. 38)

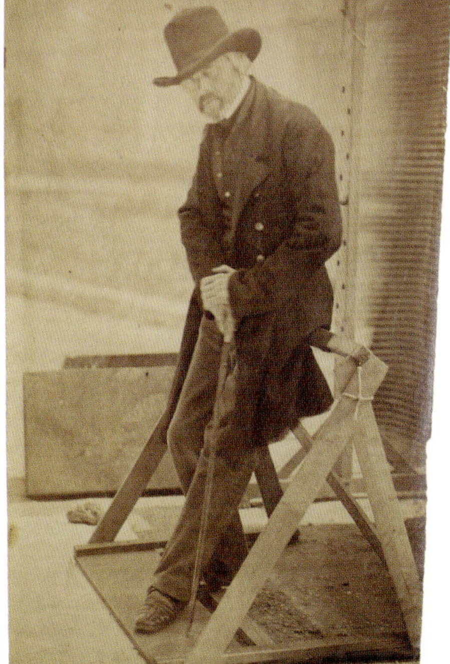

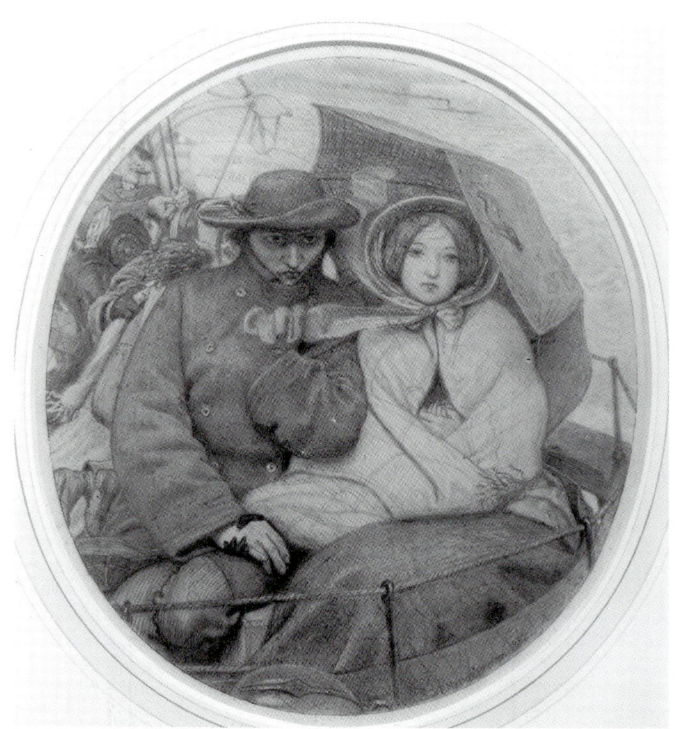

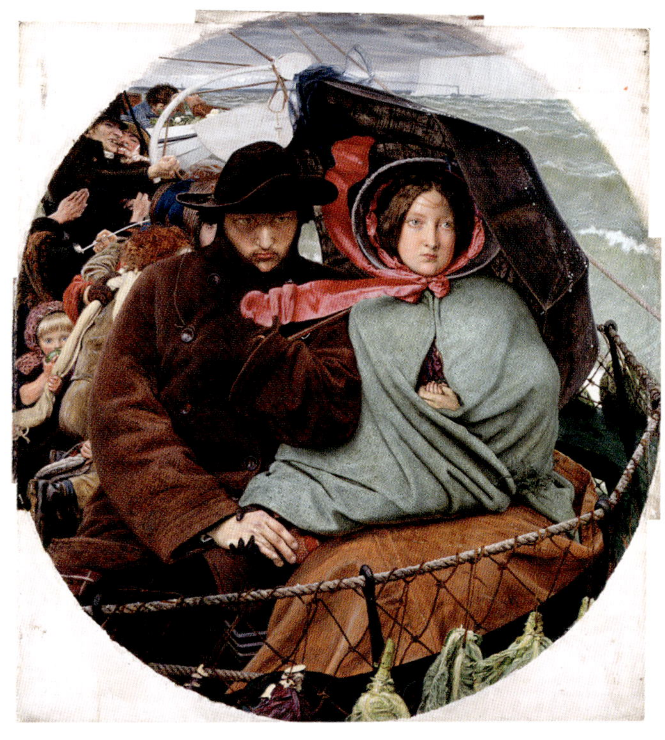

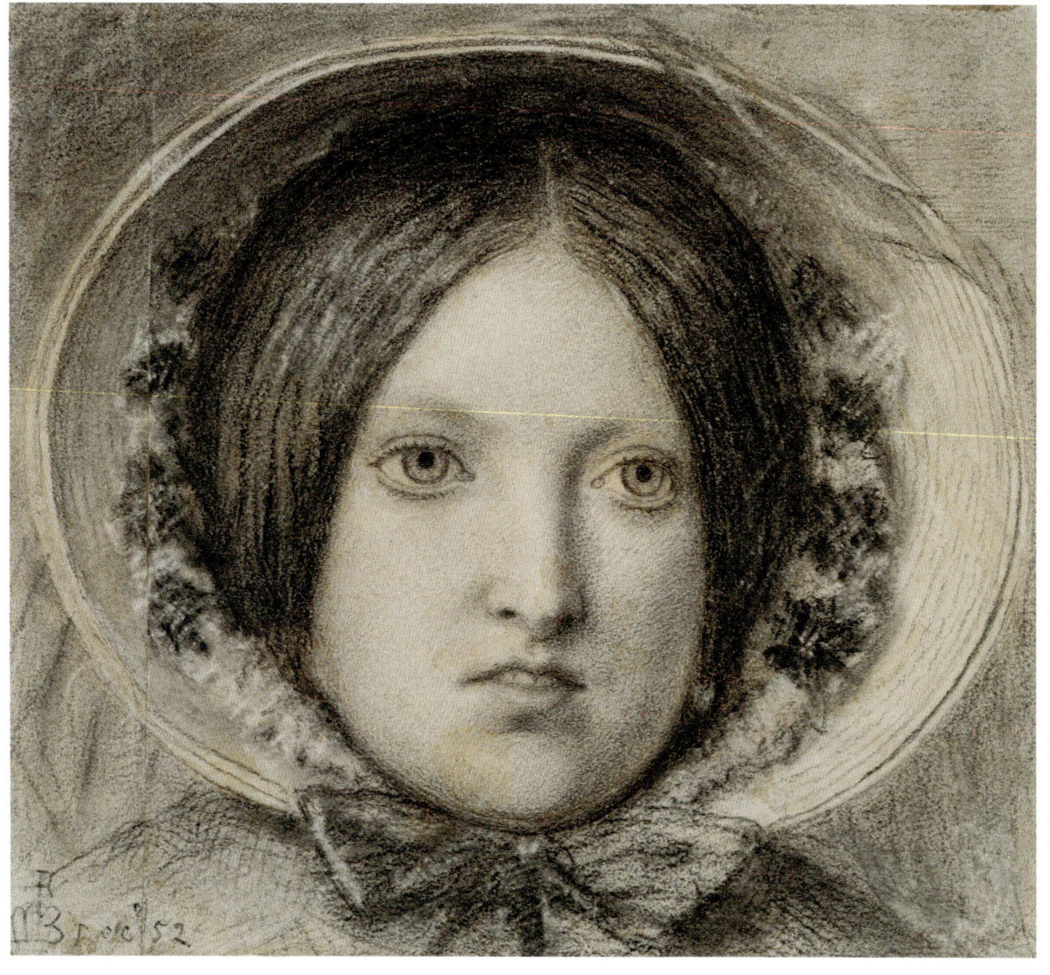

ABOVE LEFT: *The Last of England: Cartoon*, 1852 (cat. 30)

ABOVE: *The Last of England*, 1852–55 (cat. 32)

LEFT: *The Last of England: Portrait of Emma Hill*, 1852 (cat. 29)

RIGHT: *Head Study of Emma Hill (later Mrs Madox Brown)*, 1848 (cat. 22)

BELOW: *Sketch of Mrs Madox Brown (née Emma Hill)*, 1854 (cat. 33)

BELOW RIGHT: *Portrait of Emma Hill*, 1852 (cat. 28)

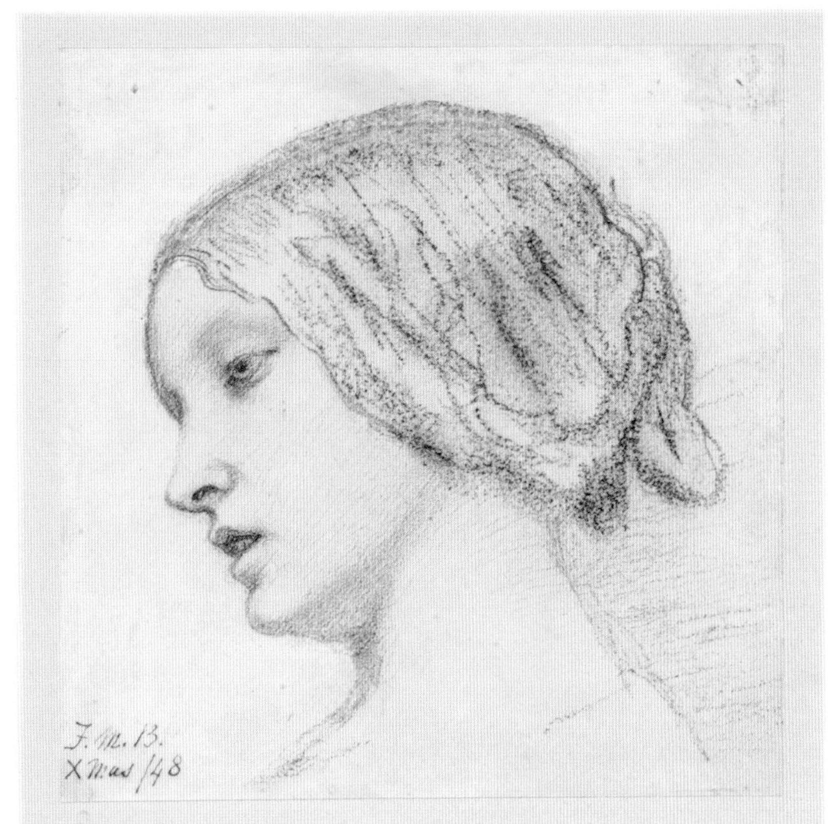

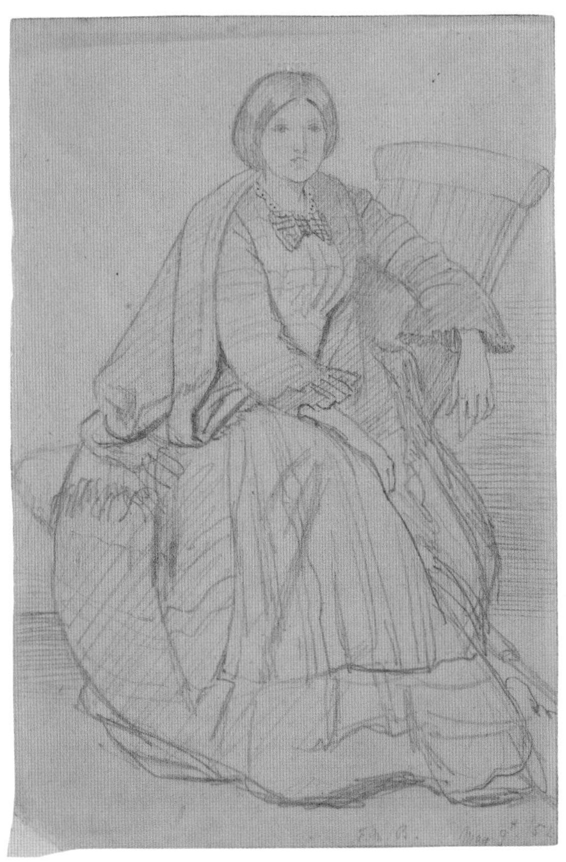

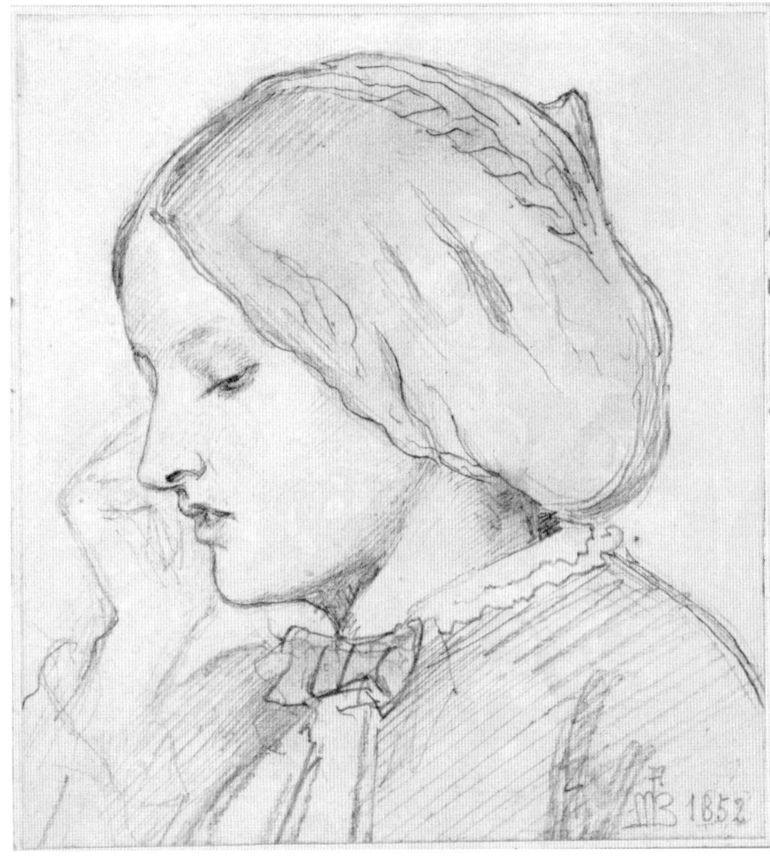

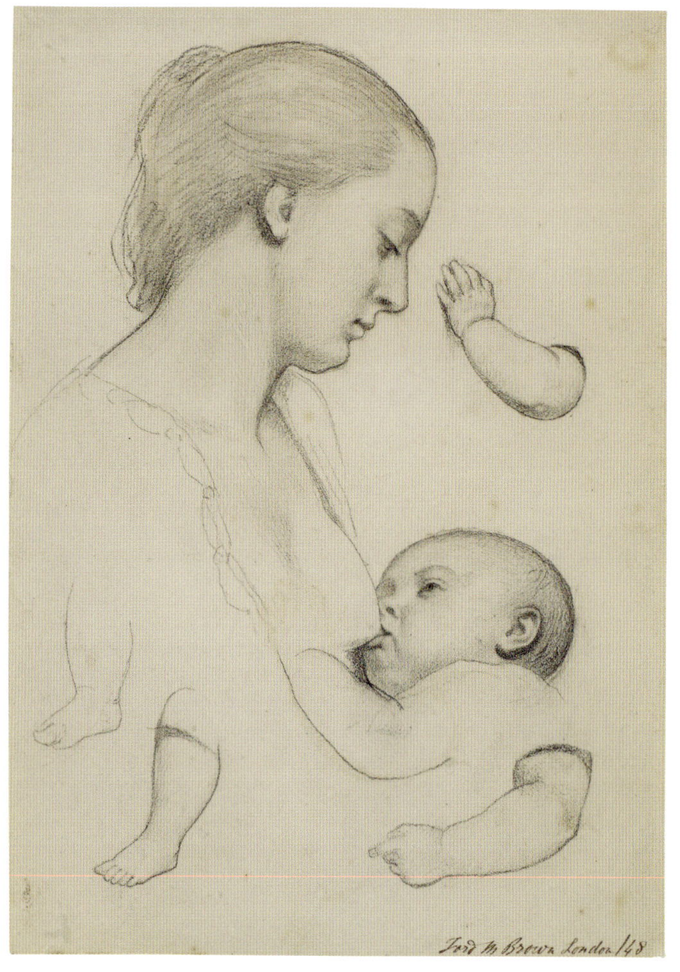

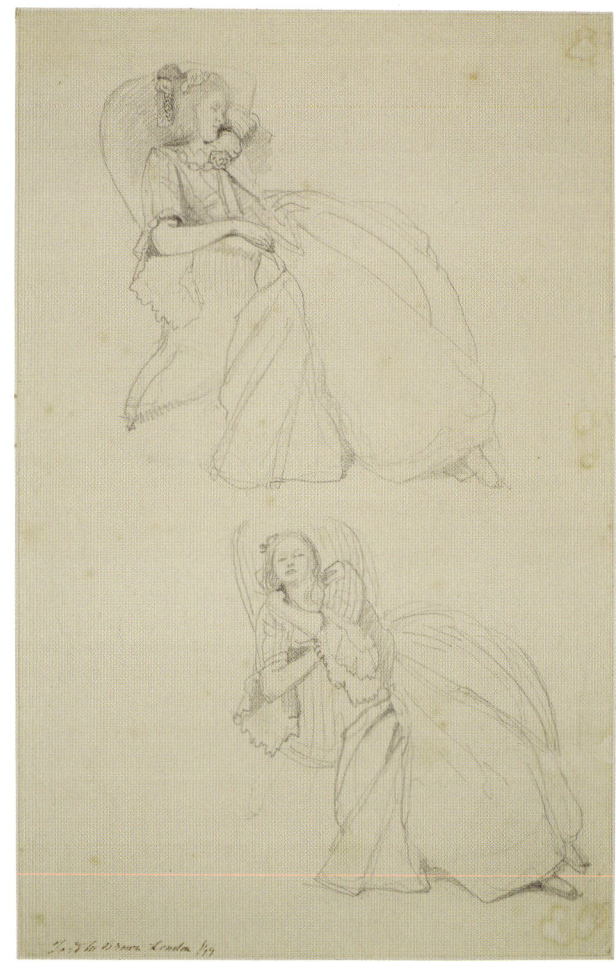

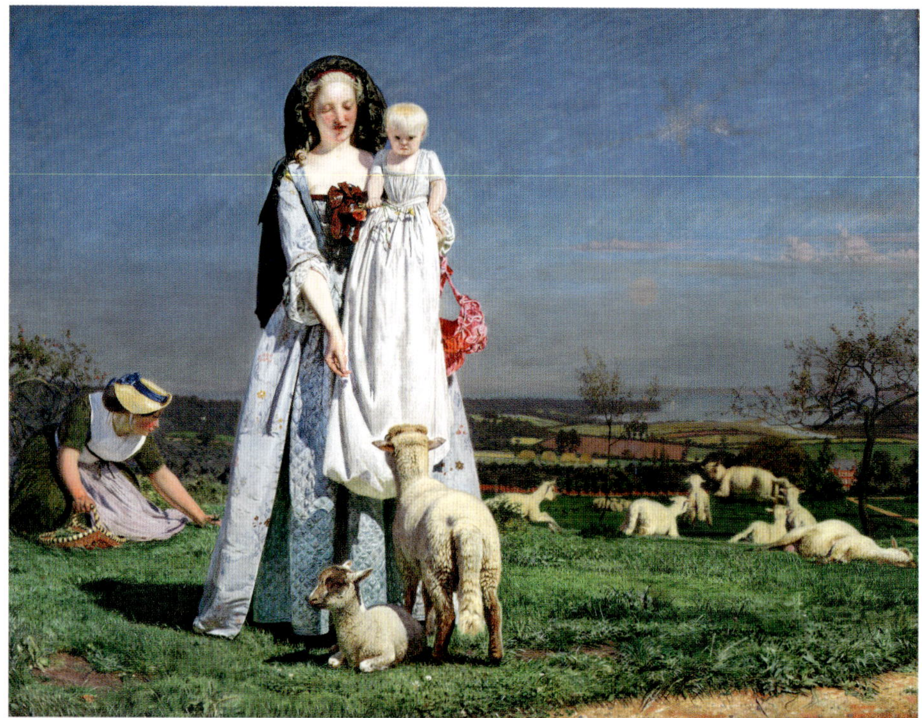

ABOVE LEFT: *The Infant's Repast: Study of Mother and Child with separate Arm and Leg Studies of the Child*, 1848 (cat. 20)

ABOVE: *Young Woman in eighteenth-century Costume: Two Studies*, 1849 (cat. 23)

LEFT: *The Pretty Baa-Lambs*, 1851–59 (cat. 27)

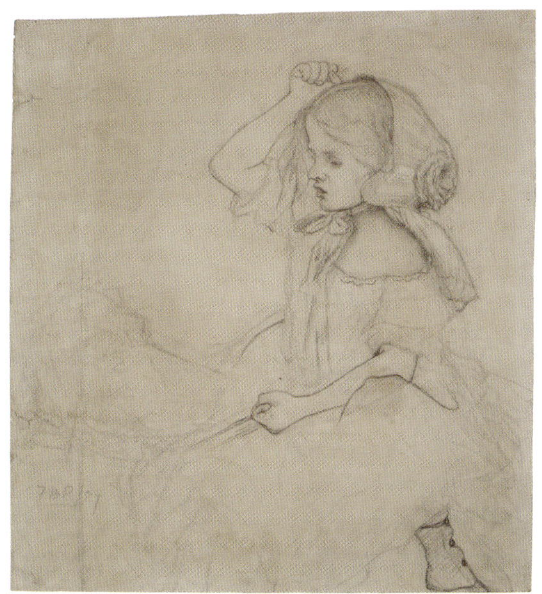

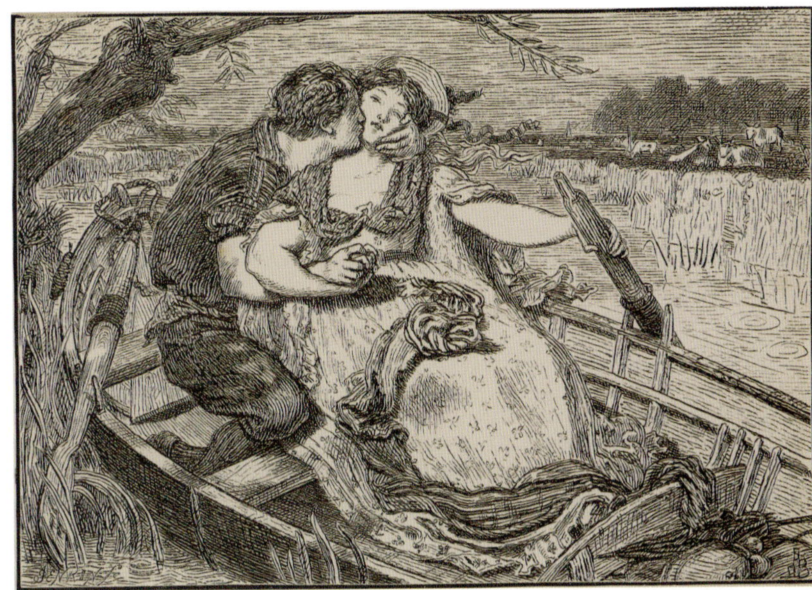

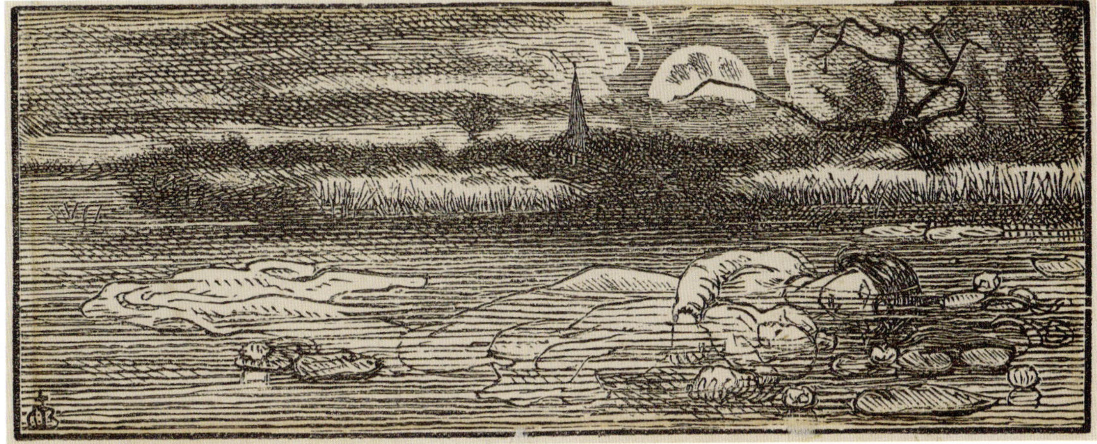

ABOVE: *Stages of Cruelty: Study for the Child (Catherine Madox Brown)*, 1857 (cat. 37)

ABOVE RIGHT: *Down Stream (Last Year's First of May)*, pub. 1871 (cat. 47)

RIGHT: *Down Stream (This Year's First of June)*, pub. 1871 (cat. 48)

BELOW RIGHT: *An English Autumn Afternoon*, 1852–53, 1855 (cat. 31)

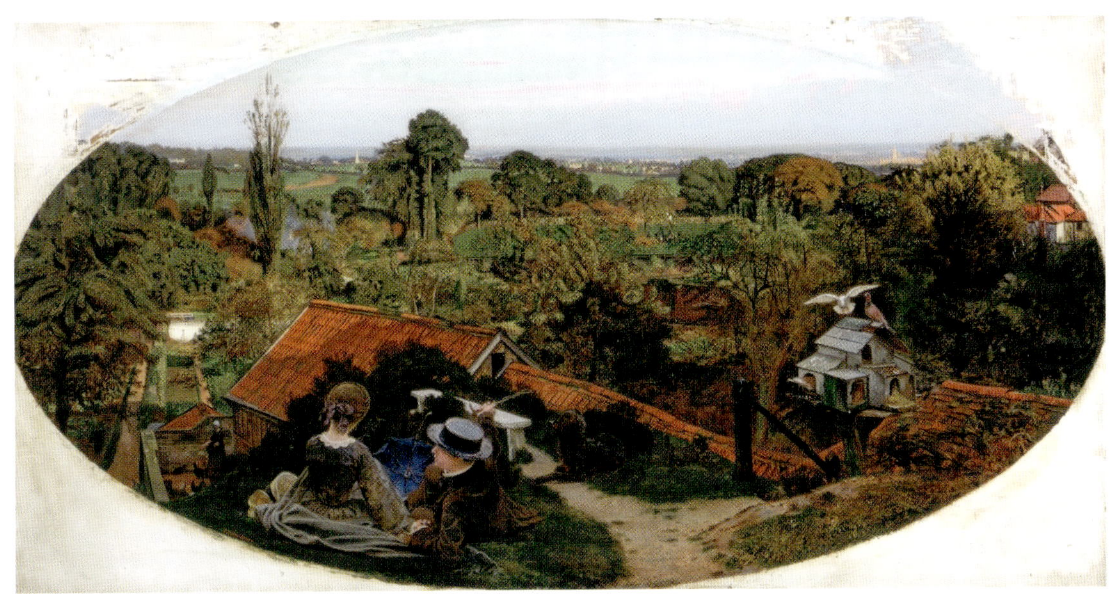

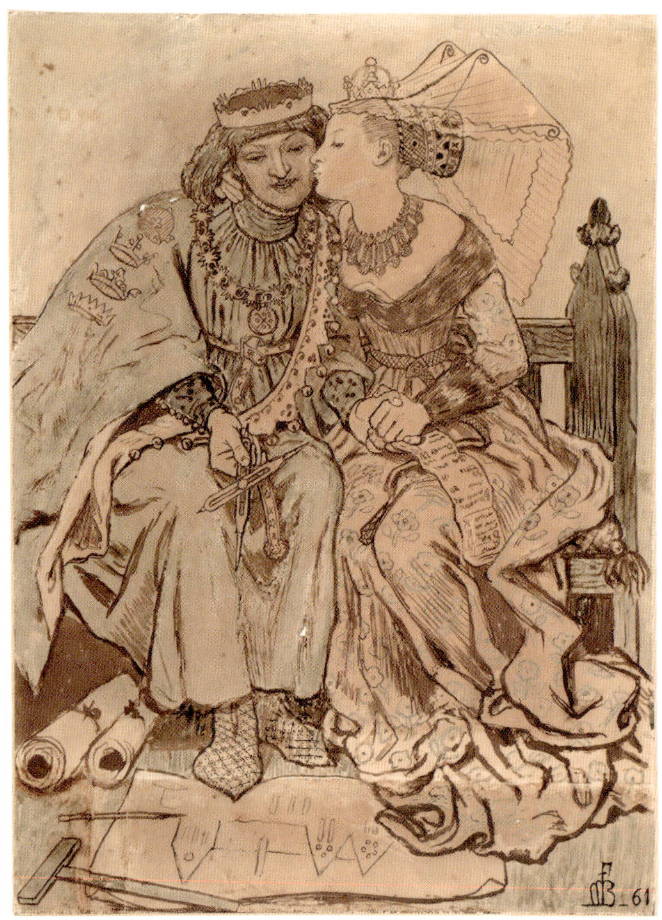

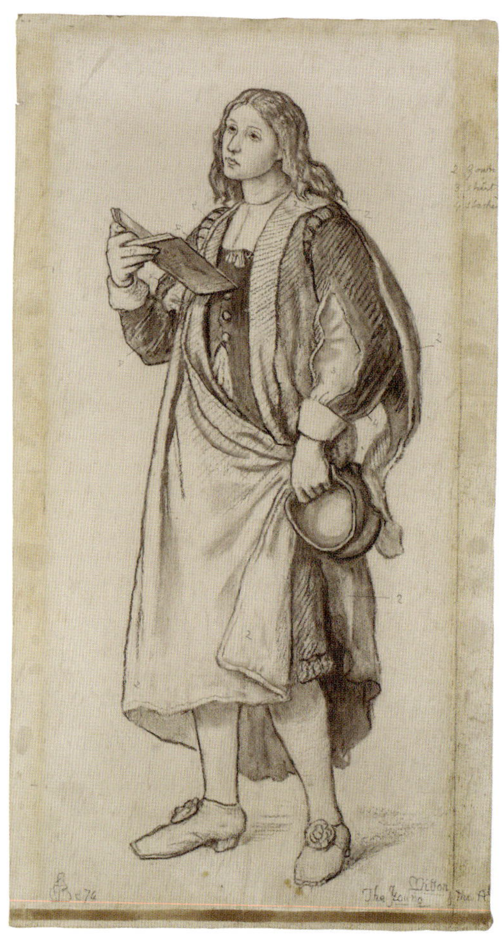

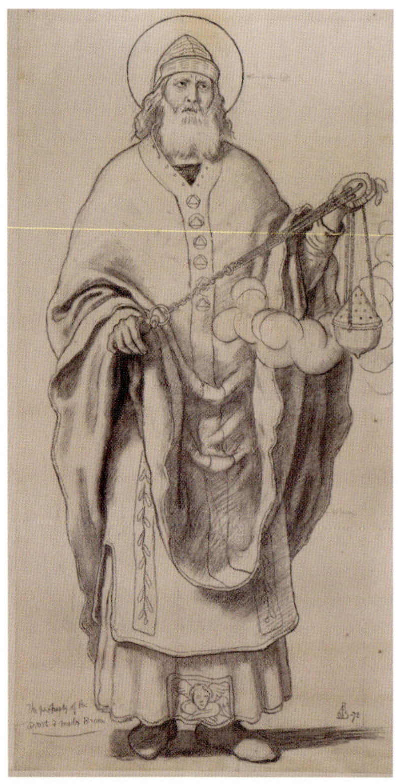

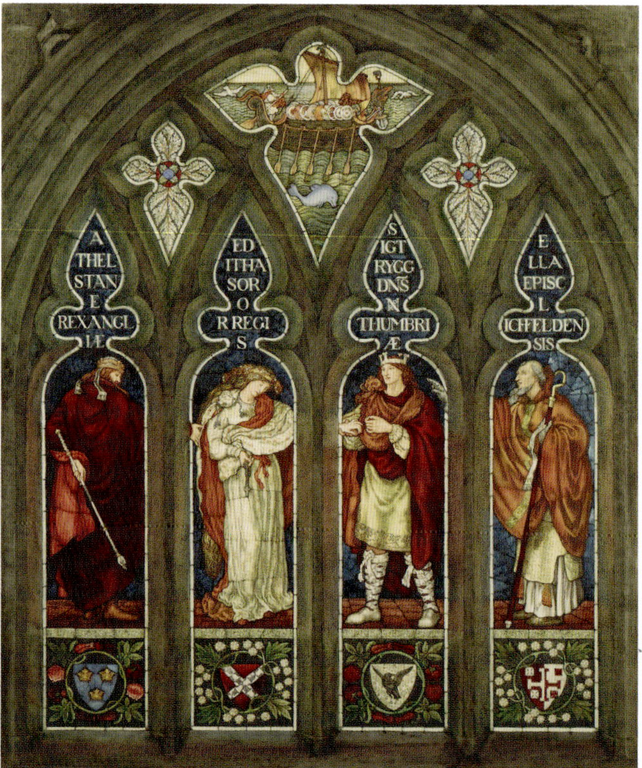

ABOVE LEFT: *Study for King René's Honeymoon: Architecture*, 1861 (cat. 40)

ABOVE: *Stained Glass Design: Cartoon for the Young Milton*, 1874 (cat. 52)

FAR LEFT: *Stained Glass Design: Cartoon for Zachariah, The High Priest*, 1872 (cat. 49)

LEFT: *Stained Glass Design: The Marriage of Editha with Sigtrygg, King of Northumbria*, 1909, copy by T. M. Rooke (cat. 55)

RIGHT: *Chaucer at the Court of Edward III: Eight early Studies of Figures and Hands*, 1845 (cat. 8)

BELOW: *Chaucer at the Court of Edward III: Drapery Study for Robert Burns*, 1848 (cat. 18)

BELOW RIGHT: *Chaucer at the Court of Edward III: Head of an old Woman*, 1851 (cat. 25)

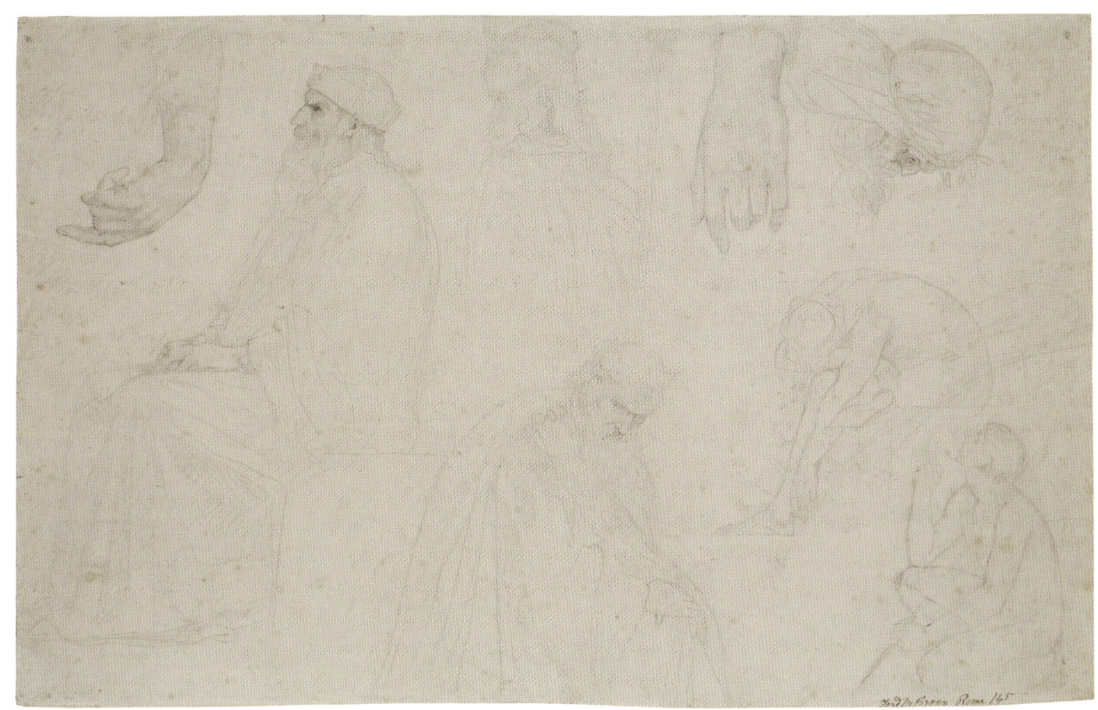

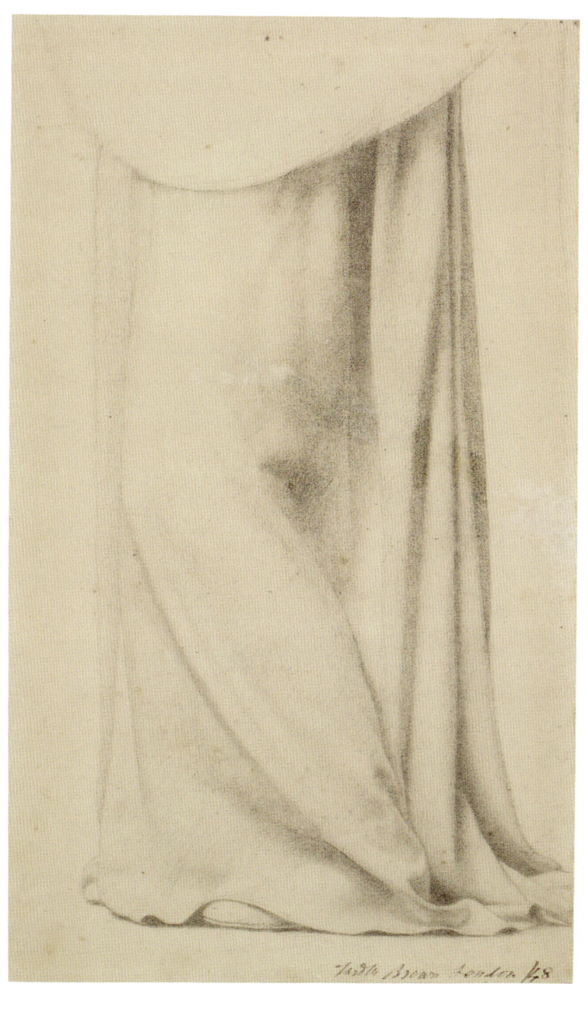

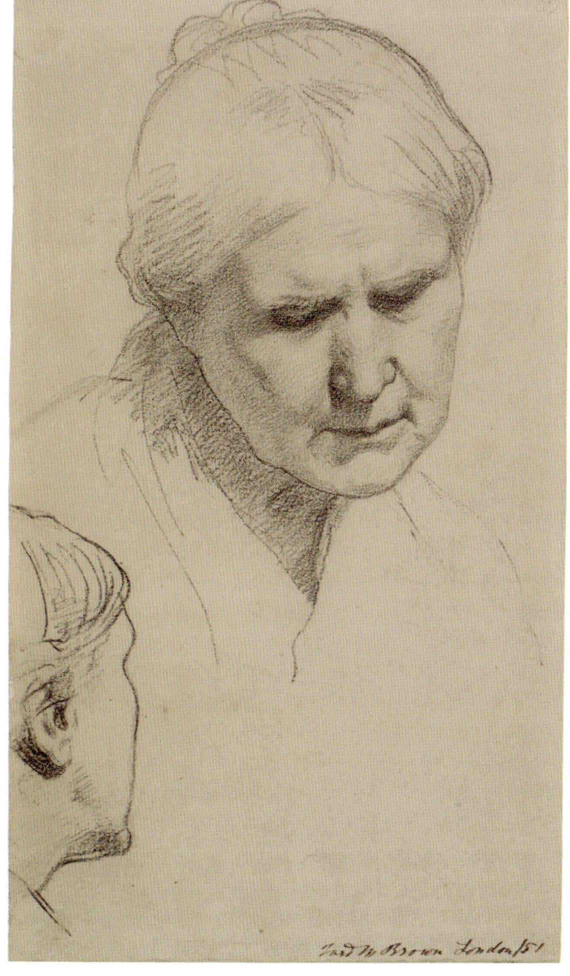

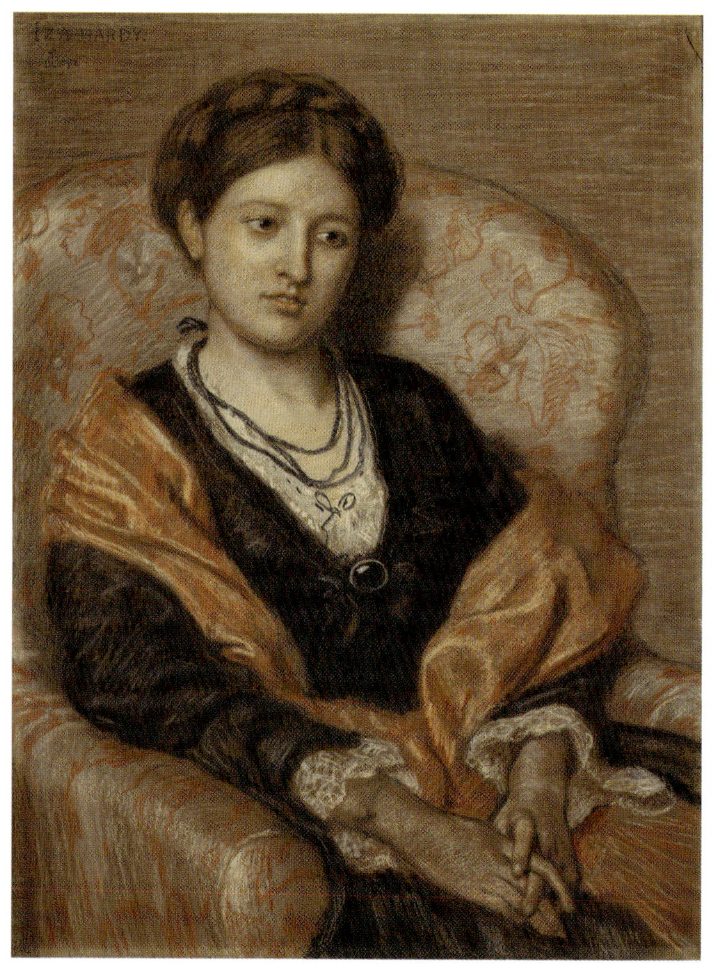

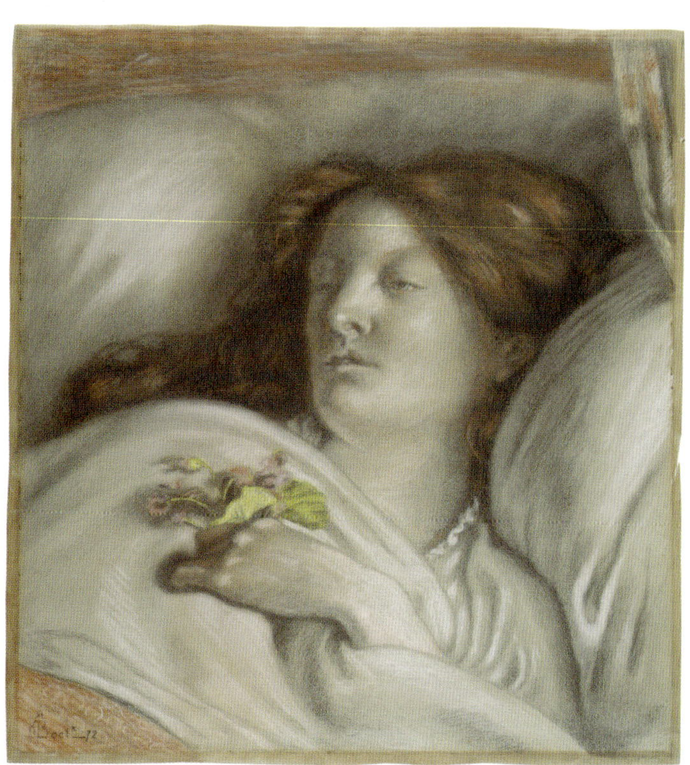

ABOVE: *Portrait of Miss Iza Duffus Hardy,* 1872 (cat. 51)

LEFT: *Convalescent: Portrait of Emma Madox Brown,* 1872 (cat. 50)

which might ultimately derive from the insecurity of these early years.

The boy displayed a precocious aptitude for drawing and his father moved the family to Bruges in 1835 in order to facilitate the younger Ford's artistic education. At fourteen he began his studies under Albert Gregorius (1774–1853) and later transferred to the Academy in Ghent to study under another of David's pupils, Pieter van Hanselaer (1786–1862). These early masters introduced Brown to the practice of history painting, in which drawing occupied a central role, and to the laborious routine of building up a multi-figure composition through sketches, cartoons and compositional studies. Each figure was carefully drawn, first nude, then clothed, often in poses echoing the classical sculptures that had been exactly copied as the very first stage of the student's education. That Brown learned much from these early studies is evident from his article 'On the Mechanism of a Historical Picture', published in the second edition of the Pre-Raphaelite journal *The Germ* in 1850.[1] Yet Brown never seems to have been entirely at ease with the favoured style of Gregorius and Hanselaer – a rather formulaic, hard-edged neoclassicism.

A move to Antwerp in 1837 to study with Gustave, Baron Wappers (1803–1874), however, was decisive for Brown's artistic development and for his understanding of the artist's role in society. His parents returned to London, allowing Brown to enjoy a bohemian lifestyle at the Pot d'Etain lodging house, where he struck up a friendship with the Irish artist Daniel Casey (cat. 21, B122). Brown's portraits of Casey date from 1848, and are perhaps inscribed with something of the seriousness of purpose felt by the two from an early age. Evident in Brown's slow, searing scrutiny of his friend's face is both technical accomplishment and moral purpose. During his time in Antwerp, Brown acquired from Wappers a technique and intellectual rigour far in advance of that available to his contemporaries at the Royal Academy Schools in London. Wappers's Rubensian painterliness affected Brown less than his belief that history painting should engage with contemporary social, moral and political issues.

The Painter of History for the Modern Age

There followed a period in Paris where Brown hoped to benefit from the French system of state patronage for history painters. Brown's firm sense of the public mission of art was shared by few British artists or patrons, despite the strictures of Reynolds's *Discourses* and the public rhetoric of the Royal Academy. The reliance of British art on the free market for its survival was always a provocation for Brown and he never achieved financial success to compare with that of his contemporaries William Powell Frith or John Everett Millais.

The announcement in 1843 of an annual competition to select designs for frescoes to decorate the new Palace of Westminster indicated a rare source of patronage for history painting in England, offering the kind of public commission to which Brown aspired. The competition was the brainchild of Prince Albert, whose ambition was to emulate the great public decorative schemes executed by Nazarene painters such as Peter Cornelius in Munich and Berlin. In 1844 Madox Brown submitted to the Westminster competition a dramatic large cartoon of *The Body of Harold Brought before William*, which survives in fragments (Camberwell School of Art). The powerful drawings for this work, and more especially those for its successor, *The Spirit of Justice* (1844–45), announced Madox Brown's maturity as an artist, the latter notable for their bold clarity of utterance (B132–B142). Yet Brown was unsuccessful in both competitions, and indeed he received no national patronage from the state throughout his career. It is entirely typical of Brown that his sardonic portrayal of the Normans in *The Body of Harold Brought before William* – implying a critique of the aristocracy, many of whom could trace their ancestry back to the Conqueror's supporters – may have offended the jury; a more likely cause for its failure, however, was its refusal to conform to pictorial orthodoxy. Brown's figures were attenuated for dramatic effect and the composition gives an overwrought, mannered impression: Harold's lifeless body is wildly elongated while William glowers menacingly at the apex of a complex pile of bodies. English taste at this time was better served by the decorative symmetry and clarity of William Dyce's Raphaelesque compositions, and it was Dyce and Daniel Maclise who received the bulk of the Parliamentary commissions.

Undeterred, Brown persevered with historical subjects, eventually creating a monumental upright canvas depicting *Chaucer at the Court of Edward III* (Art Gallery of New South Wales, Sydney), which was finished and exhibited at the Royal Academy in the year of the Great Exhibition, 1851. This was the zenith of the machine age. The iron and glass Crystal Palace, the innovative prefabricated structure designed by Joseph Paxton to house the exhibition, was immediately recognised as a keynote structure of commercial modernity – and was condemned as such by the leading art critic of the day, John Ruskin. Brown's elaborate painting, concerning itself with a distant moment in medieval history, was given the full – and pedantic – title: *Geoffrey Chaucer Reading the 'Legend of Custance' to Edward III and his Court, at the Palace of Sheen, on the Anniversary of the Black Prince's Forty-Fifth Birthday*. It might seem to constitute a complete rejection of what Charles Dickens called the 'steam-whistle party', advocates of technology and industrialisation. Yet this painting also stands at the meeting point of several key developments in British art of the nineteenth century. It represents one of the finest painted contributions to the Gothic Revival, the Romantic return to medieval art which produced Pugin's now iconic Houses of Parliament at Westminster. It speaks, too, of the creative dialogue between British and German art, too little acknowledged by twentieth-century historians. And it is a key work in the emergence of that most idiosyncratic and powerful of Victorian art movements, Pre-Raphaelitism, announcing the return of a Hogarthian, satirical sensibility which became one of the keynotes of the era.

Brown derived the subject from Sir James Mackintosh's *History of England* (published serially from 1830). As he recalled in his diary, a passage on Geoffrey Chaucer, 'at once fixed me, I immediately saw visions of Chaucer reading his poems to knights & Ladyes fair, to the king & court amid air & sun shine'.[2] Chaucer, for Madox Brown, represented not only the origin of English literature, but a remarkably vibrant and accessible figure: 'Spelling, and a few minor proprieties apart, after a lapse of five hundred years, his delicate sense of naturalistic beauty and his practical turn of thought ... comes to us as naturally as the last volume we hail from the press.'[3] *Chaucer at the Court of Edward III* is a highly original historical composition, bathed in real sunlight, and set against a precisely rendered naturalistic landscape. The clarity, individual definition and local colour of each object gives the painting's surface a kaleidoscopic dizziness as fabrics and features compete for the viewer's attention. The careful individualisation of each face confirms that every figure was painted from an individual model.

The First Pre-Raphaelite?

These were the stylistic hallmarks of the Pre-Raphaelite Brotherhood, founded in 1848 by seven young men, led by William Holman Hunt, John Everett Millais and Dante Gabriel Rossetti. Significantly junior to, and notably more callow than Brown, they intended to revive English painting by abandoning academic convention and, like painters before Raphael (or so they thought), turning to the direct and unflinching representation of nature. Their choice of a collective group identity partook both of the spirit of revolution that gripped Europe in 1848, and also something of the schoolboy prank. The homosocial bonds that held the group together and the willingness to submerge the individual within a group identity were alien to the aloof and frequently troubled Brown, who was very much his own man.

The pressing question, of course, is whether the stylistic traits that we now identify as 'Pre-Raphaelite' were in fact originally developed by Brown, or whether, as most critics have assumed, he was influenced by the younger artists, and modified *Chaucer* to conform to their project. Was he an 'unofficial' Pre-Raphaelite, or in fact the first Pre-Raphaelite? William Holman Hunt put forward in his self-serving but influential memoir *Pre-Raphaelitism and the Pre-Raphaelite Brotherhood* (written in 1905) the idea that he, Rossetti and Millais – on the eve of founding the PRB – were dismissive of their elder's efforts and that he cravenly adopted their favoured manner. In fact, however, the young Pre-Raphaelites were in awe of Brown, whose intellectual and practical experience, and whose personal gravitas, far outweighed their own. Although he may have been asked to do so, Brown never joined the Brotherhood.

As if defending himself against the accusation of being a follower of the Pre-Raphaelites, Brown recalled in the catalogue to his one-man exhibition in 1865 that *Chaucer* was 'the first in which I endeavoured to carry out the notion, long *before conceived*, of treating light and shade absolutely, as it exists at any one moment, instead of approximately, or in generalised style. Sunlight a bit too bright, such as is pleasant to sit in out of doors, is here depicted.'[4] He was working on an historical composition as if it were painted from life. This is the exact opposite of the form of history painting proposed by Reynolds, or indeed by Brown's own Davidian tutors in Belgium, in which figures must be idealised and generalised, and compositions should pay homage to the great works of the old masters. Sharp and scientific, painted in a style wholly modern, *Chaucer* is an image of history entirely in keeping with the spirit of the Great Exhibition. So with this work – conceived in 1845, begun in 1847 but completed only in 1851 – was Brown the instigator, or merely a follower of this crucial trend? Our answer can never be a certain one, and the fact that Brown retouched the work in 1856 adds a further layer of uncertainty. Nonetheless, the diary entry of 1847 referring to the 'king & court amid air & sun shine' adds crucial support to Brown's assertion of his intentions to paint the work in this style from the beginning; but of course we can never know what it would have looked like had he never seen a Pre-Raphaelite painting.

The Artist as Naturalist

Whether or not Brown invented the Pre-Raphaelite style, his exercises in painting minutely from nature are consummate examples of the genre. Brown turned suddenly to landscape painting in the early 1850s, when he produced a series of views striking for their rejection of the picturesque and sublime subject matter typical of English Romantic landscape painters. Instead, Brown meticulously chronicled nondescript stretches of landscape often found within walking distance of his various residences in North London, at Hendon, Finchley and Hampstead. He scrutinises the urban hinterland, revealing its strange beauty in one of the masterpieces of nineteenth-century painting, *An English Autumn Afternoon*, begun in a period of extraordinary creative energy in 1852 (cat. 31). The painting was intended as an experiment in seeing, its oval shape drawing attention to the optical process, perhaps even alluding to the shape of the eye. The artist here is all-seeing; on the one hand a scientific apparatus conveying empirical truth, and on the other a poetic visionary finding value and pathos in the quotidian world which others would miss. Madox Brown wrote in his 1865 exhibition catalogue:

> The smoke of London is seen rising half way above the fantastic shaped, small distant cumuli, which accompany particularly fine weather …. The time is 3PM., when late in October the shadows already lie long, and the sun's rays (coming from behind us in this work) are preternaturally glowing, as in rivalry of the foliage.[5]

The artist (unlike the camera) can record both the natural and the preternatural, the optical and the spiritual, effect and affect. The landscape is not merely one of botanical, climatic and topographical facts: it is a social landscape, full of human life, and replete, also, with personal associations for Brown. The view is from the back window of an upper floor of a house in which Brown lodged in Hampstead High Street, and looks north east towards the neighbouring suburb of Highgate, the home of the working-class woman Emma Hill, whom he secretly married at St Dunstan-in-the-West, London, on 5 April 1853 in the presence only of Rossetti and another artist friend, Thomas Seddon. The foreground passages of *An English Autumn Afternoon* are essential to the overall meaning of the painting, providing, in the two figures, middle-class viewers wholly modern in their behaviour, with whom the viewer can identify. They are, Brown tells us, 'peculiarly English … hardly lovers, more boy and girl, neighbours and friends'.[6] Their presence together is a symbol of English modernity and social informality. The informal couple are enjoying the suburban idyll: the young man gestures towards the view, catching the last of the low sunlight, which his companion is admiring. The duck-egg blue of the sky – in a virtuoso passage – can be seen reflected in the high sheen of the man's hat.

The painting is a striking example of Brown's refusal to adopt the familiar compositional devices that artists such as Constable and Turner had used to maintain order and structure. Constable's 'naturalist' paintings make extensive use of inherited conventions such as *repoussoir* trees at one side of the composition which frame a central vista with a low horizon. Madox Brown's high, flat horizon is bereft of vertical elements.

An English Autumn Afternoon was too much for John Ruskin, who, it is clear, disliked Brown's gruff manner and his refusal to court favour with the critic. A vivid passage in Brown's diary from 13 July 1855 describing a tea party at Rossetti's house reveals the personal animosity between Brown and Ruskin, whom the artist observed,

> talking divers nonsense about art, hurriedly in shrill flippant tones – I answer him civilly – then resume my coat & prepare to leave. Suddenly upon this he sais 'Mr Brown will you tell me why you chose such a very ugly subject for your last picture [*An English Autumn Afternoon*] … it was a pitty for there was some <u>nice</u> painting in it.' I … being satisfied that he meant impertinence, replied contemptuously 'Because it lay out of a back window' & turning on my heel took my hat & wished Gabriel goodbuy.[7]

This mutual personal animosity was to cost Brown dear: Ruskin turned his back on Brown and directed patrons to support Rossetti and Millais instead. The true source of Ruskin's rage, however, was Brown's rejection of the legacy of landscape painting which Ruskin's idol Turner, for all his radicalism, had embraced. Though Ruskin had advised young artists to 'go to nature … selecting nothing, rejecting nothing, and scorning nothing', he was horrified when Madox Brown did exactly that.

Brown acknowledged his own role explicitly in the luminescent *Walton-on-the-Naze*, completed in 1860 (Birmingham

Museums and Art Gallery). Affectionately holding the hand of his wife, a respectable middle-class man (an image of Brown himself) expounds on the beauties of the scene. Through Brown's intervention as interpreter, the urban hinterland is transformed into a place of limitless visual delight. *Walton-on-the-Naze* is the most extreme of Brown's anti-picturesque statements: the natural landscape is compromised by modernity; agriculture, shipping and building have colonised every inch of the terrain. Groups of angular modern buildings, probably hotels and boarding houses, jarring to picturesque taste, are seen on the horizon. Each one is scrutinised with a steely intensity. The landscape is a catalogue of individual objects and features – windmill, rainbow, ship, figures, corn stooks, fieldmouse, union flag – each seen in perfect focus and with its own local colour. Yet, as with *An English Autumn Afternoon*, it is also a meditation on national identity, another aspect of the Englishness which Brown had poignantly captured in the evening light over Hampstead.

The Artist as Social Critic

In the 1850s Brown turned the same rigorous attention to modern society as to landscape. While genre painting had been prominent throughout the preceding decades in the hands of masterly narrative painters such as David Wilkie, William Mulready, and Richard Redgrave, Brown was unique in his attempt to merge close observation of modern life with the larger ambitions previously reserved for history painting. His iconic roundel, *The Last of England*, was, as the artist explained, 'in the strictest sense historical. It treats of the great emigration movement which attained its culminating point in 1852'[8] (cat. 32). The immediate stimulus was the departure of Thomas Woolner, the sculptor among the Pre-Raphaelite Brothers, for the goldfields of Australia. Brown laboured on *The Last of England* for so long – three years from 1852 to 1855 – that by the time of its completion Woolner was back in England, his dreams of making a fortune shattered. Perhaps it is for this reason that Brown replaced the text 'White Horse Line of Australia', which appears in the 1852 cartoon stenciled on the lifeboat just above the emigrant's head (cat. 30), with the name 'Eldorado', the mythical lost city of gold in the final oil version completed in 1855. Woolner and his wife were, of course, not available for the lengthy period of sitting as a model which Madox Brown's obsessive realism demanded for *The Last of England*; rather, under-lining the personal significance of the image, Madox Brown

drew the main figures from himself and his wife Emma, the latter in particular a portrait of an individual woman, which achieves an uncanny verisimilitude. This all the more apparent in the superb drawing of Emma for *The Last of England*, probably executed while she was sitting outside in the garden, in order to produce just the right effect of 'outdoor light without sun' and a pinched pallor in the skin (cat. 29, front cover).[9]

Brown signalled the seriousness of his intentions by grouping the figures into an oval, almost circular shape, refer-encing the tondo forms of the Renaissance. These frequently portrayed the Holy Family or the Virgin and Child, as in the famous Michelangelo marble tondo in the collection of the Royal Academy in London. The image of the wife and mother here clearly alludes to the iconography of the Virgin Mary, her bonnet suggesting a halo and her gaze turned heav-enward, although in anguish rather than ecstasy. This pointed allusion to a highly esteemed iconographic precedent raised the status of the subject to one of global significance.

Meanwhile, the subsidiary figures form a Hogarthian – or perhaps Dickensian– sideshow revealing the seedier side of modern life. These emigrants must travel together, their iden-tities piled up one upon the other, their personal space and dignity threatened by the chaotic conditions on board ship. Careful looking will untangle the identities of these folk, and their reasons for emigrating to Australia. The lower middle classes are represented (Brown tells us) by 'an honest family of the green-grocer kind'. The father is signified only by his rounded brown hat and his long china pipe; his life in England has collapsed after the death of his wife, and he seeks a new start in the colonies, taking his children with him. His daughter bites balefully into an apple, Eve-like. More signifi-cant is the grotesque figure, behind the greengrocer, of a gap-toothed drunkard who 'shakes his fist with curses at the land of his birth, as though that were answerable for his want of success'.[10] Forced to travel with her son, on whom she depends, is his old mother, whose gnarled hands express her distaste at his unpatriotic diatribe. The masculine identities on offer here have all been tested to destruction by the economic and social strains of work in the modern age. Only emigration offers a second – and a last – chance for these characters.

The painting is thus both specific and general: intended as an analysis of the causes of emigration and of its impact on the members of each social class. It is a painted treatise, the equivalent of the critical essay on social subjects (such as Thomas Carlyle's 'Signs of the Times').[11] When the painting was exhibited in 1865, the artist published a commentary which greatly assists in interpreting the work's more general implications. Yet the painting also reflects in very specific ways on Brown's own circumstances, and a crisis concerning his particular artistic identity. The two central figures – Brown/Woolner and his wife – are, clearly, middle-class, well-dressed and respectable. Yet (in Brown's words) they are 'depressed enough in means, to have to put up with the discomforts and humiliations incident to a vessel "all in one class"'.[12] Clearly the man has failed in his profession; he 'broods bitterly over blighted hopes'.[13] *The Last of England* was painted at a moment when the artist declared himself to be 'intensely miserable very hard up & a little mad' and talked of leaving in desperation for India.[14] The male body, swathed in a greatcoat, is reduced to hand and head, emblems of the power of manual labour and the intellect, the two means by which a man can earn a living. This would be the key theme of Brown's greatest painting.[15]

The Artist as Labourer

In *Work*, Brown created a modern history painting in which he laid out with unprecedented sophistication the question of the role and meaning of labour in modern society and the place of the artist within that scheme (cat. 39). Crucial for Madox Brown's thinking on the issue was *Past and Present* (1843) by Thomas Carlyle, who himself appears in the right foreground of the painting. *Past and Present* declared that 'there is a perennial nobleness, and even sacredness, in work' and argued that in labour was revealed the inner character or moral worth of a man.[16] In Madox Brown's *Work*, labour conquers all and is a celebration of ideal masculinity and the healthy body. The visual logic of the painting is very complex, but the essence of it is the organisation of social types into hierarchies. The most obvious one is from the rich at the top to the poor at the bottom. At the apex of the composition is an MP, probably a member of the gentry, if not the younger son of an aristocrat, who, Madox Brown informs us in his published catalogue, is worth £10,000 a year. We should beware of this shadowy man, however, who occupies the same position as the swarthy William in *The Body of Harold*. In the centre of the composition, by contrast, is a group of navvies, catching the full force of the July sun which reflects harshly from their bared forearms. These mighty working men, digging a trench to accommodate a new fresh water supply in Hampstead, emerge as heroes around whom the composition is built. Taken together with the biblical quota-

tions on the frame, and the altarpiece-like shape of the painting, the direct glare of sunlight can be understood as a metaphor for the divine grace bestowed by work, as described by Carlyle.

A further antithesis in the painting sets the masculine in opposition to the feminine. *Work* glorifies the physique of the working men: the muscular navvy shovelling soil was described by Brown as being 'in the pride of manly health and beauty'.[17] The antithesis of this working, masculine central group, is found to the left of the composition where two women appear, heavily draped and conventionally feminine in appearance, and the tragic, shifty figure of a flowerseller who for Brown represents the 'ragged wretch who has never been taught to work'[18]: this crucial absence results in a loss of masculinity.

But what then of the artist, who does not appear in *Work*, and who is in these terms no match for that 'potent agent of civilization', the navvy? An earlier watercolour version of *Work* (Manchester Art Gallery) shows a sketchily depicted figure in the place later to be occupied by Carlyle and the churchman F. D. Maurice, which can be identified from Brown's diary as representing an 'artist'.[19] Hand against his mouth, perhaps in the gesture of a thinker, but more likely holding a cigar, this daydreaming figure is the epitome of self-regarding nonchalance. Brown's diary reveals an obsession with his own labour; he recorded each day the hours spent, relishing in calculating '7 hours per diem *pure work*', hotly insisting, as if contradicting some inner interlocutor, 'I only put down the time I actually work at art, not the time lost in preparations.'[20] Yet just as often he agonised about his 'degrading idleness' or 'fearful Idleness self abasement & disgust'.[21] These are the anxieties written on the face of the emigrant, composite of the 'manly' men, Madox Brown and Woolner, in *The Last of England*. Madox Brown's justification of his own labour as an artist was ultimately achieved through the very manifest presence of his work in applying paint to canvas, the hard work that went into painting. Contemporary critics, however, perceived the signs of this extensive and extended labour in the surface of the painting and in its conceptual structure, and one even believed that:

> Mr Ford Madox Brown in his very cleverly-painted picture intended to illustrate the dignity of labour, appeals quite as eloquently in his own behalf to show the effects of industry as in that of the robust type he presents and describes as 'the British excavator or *navvy*'....[22]

Absent in body but present as the work's creator through hard labour, Brown himself, so the painting argues, combined the manly virtues of the navvy with the intellectual penetration of a Carlyle.

The Artist as Aesthete

By the time Brown held his major one-man show in 1865, with *Work* at its centre, avant-garde artists in London were pioneering new ways of conceiving the role of art. The Aesthetic Movement, as it came to be known, was a loose-knit phenomenon whose central tenet was that beauty, rather than truth in a scientific, empirical spirit, should lie at the heart of aesthetics. Art was no longer about campaigning for change or registering the momentous social and epistemological shifts in modern culture: rather, the new creed was 'art for art's sake' (a translation of Charles Baudelaire's 'l'art pour l'art'). The impact of these ideas on painting and drawing was to emphasise formal elements, to base compositions around an ideal of musical harmony, rather than on social problems or historical themes. James Abbott McNeill Whistler and Albert Moore, in particular, stressed the formal value of colour schemes, in which white was a keynote. Brown's contribution to this tendency is a remarkable pastel drawing, *Convalescent: Portrait of Emma Madox Brown* (cat. 50), a symphony in off-white, which utilises a very narrow palette of colours and captures the yellow-green of Emma's pale skin during a feverish illness. No longer the respectable wife and helpmeet of the mid-Victorian canvases, Emma now resembles Rossetti's voluptuous models of the 1860s, Fanny Cornforth and Jane Morris.

Brown's work in the 1860s shifted to adopt more decorative forms, and often richer, deeper colours. Aestheticism brought forth a new construction of artistic identity, in which the artist would cultivate an outsider position, assuming the pose of a bohemian (in the case of Dante Gabriel Rossetti) or a dandy and provocateur (in the case of Whistler). Brown's 1877 *Self-Portrait* (Fogg Art Museum, Harvard University) stands alongside works of Frederic Leighton and Whistler as a consummate Aesthetic portrait. The subtle harmonies of the burnished golds, browns and blacks of the colour scheme and a new sensitivity to texture have replaced the fierce, interrogatory realism of Brown's earlier work. Suggestive of Aesthetic taste is the tooled and painted leather screen bearing decorative motifs of Eastern origin, parallel to the picture plane. The screen formed part of Brown's home or studio furnishings, which, like those of Whistler and Rossetti, were notably eclectic. Brown, however, was never entirely happy with much that the Aesthetic Movement stood for, and though he remained friendly with Rossetti throughout the latter's life, he was never comfortable with the bohemian ménage surrounding Rossetti at Tudor House, Chelsea, nor with the withdrawal of the artist from social and political commitment.

The Artist as Designer

One strand of Aestheticism was a continuation and extension of the Pre-Raphaelite interest in matters medieval. Brown's early fresco designs had mined a rich vein of Gothic association and he was sympathetic to this later medievalist development. Aesthetic medievalism was pioneered by Rossetti, in his watercolours of the late 1850s, and more systematically explored by Edward Burne-Jones and William Morris, who together spearheaded a radically new approach to design which combined the Aesthetic Movement's formal values with a commitment to skilled manual labour and pre-industrial working practices. In 1861 Brown became a founding member of Morris, Marshall, Faulkner & Co. designers of furniture, textiles and stained glass, headed by William Morris. Brown contributed innovative designs, though the extent of his involvement remains questionable. He is now widely credited with the design of Morris & Co.'s 'Sussex' range, which brilliantly combines a folk-like simplicity with a modernity of form that has won it the distinction of being the earliest work of art (1865) to be displayed in New York's Museum of Modern Art.

Among the firm's earliest commissions was the decoration of an oak cabinet which had been designed by the architect, artist and administrator John Pollard Seddon, to house his architectural drawings. This work represented a buoyant collaboration between Brown, Rossetti, Burne-Jones and Morris. Brown's design for the panel *King René's Honeymoon: Architecture* (cat. 40) already encapsulates many of the keynote gestures of Brown's later style: an emphasis on pattern and design; swirling, calligraphic lines; strangely foreshortened faces; and an awkward eroticism. The idea of collaborative labour, a return to the Renaissance 'workshop' was a powerful alternative to models of artistic identity born of Romanticism. Yet Brown was ultimately a loner, and the resonance of his King René image was such that Brown translated it into more conventional media redolent of the artist as individual, producing an oil painting and two watercolours, as well as two other designs, one for a stained-glass panel.

The Artist and Society

Unlike Rossetti, Brown did not withdraw from public life in later years, and in 1878, thanks to the lobbying of the Manchester painter Frederic Shields, and the collector Charles Rowley, he received the major civic commission which had eluded him hitherto. He was asked to provide wall paintings for the great hall of Alfred Waterhouse's Gothic Town Hall in Manchester. The subjects, taken from the history of Manchester, were selected by a committee of local worthies, and some of Brown's own suggestions – such as the politically charged *Peterloo Massacre, 1819* – were rejected. Anxious to avoid the technical flaws which had plagued the earlier Westminster frescoes, Brown revisited the scene of his own artistic formation, Antwerp, in 1875 and 1877, in order to examine Baron Leys's celebrated works in the medium. Exaggerated posture and gesture characterise Brown's triumphantly inventive though somewhat uneven series of compositions.

In one of the Manchester murals, *Romans Building a Fort at Mancenion* (1880), the unfairness of the distinction between the overlords and the labourers – between Romans and the conquered Britons – is made explicit, and is noted in Brown's interpretative notes. It is not hard to see an allusion to the class divisions of industrial Britain, a theme present by analogy in Brown's paintings even before *Work*, such as *Christ Washing Peter's Feet* (1852, Tate) and even *The Spirit of Justice* cartoon. Between 1879 and 1887, Brown lived largely in Manchester, where in addition to work on the frescoes, his interest in social issues grew. Horrified by the suffering caused by unemployment, in 1886 he formed a labour bureau. He also employed Joe Waddington, an out-of-work joiner, who made up Brown's design for a Workman's Chest of Drawers, which was exhibited at the Manchester Jubilee Exhibition of 1887. Brown also designed the massive images of labouring figures which adorned the exhibition building, though these made no decisive political statement. Brown never endorsed revolutionary socialism, as Morris did, and did not look back to the medieval period as an idyllic riposte to the present day. Rather, he embraced the industrial world – claiming even to find great beauty in the modern industrial metropolis – but took small practical steps to obviate its inequalities. He did not, then, see the artist as a revolutionary, but as an interpreter of modern society.

Conclusion

Brown's contribution to the history of nineteenth-century art has been profoundly undervalued. A unique and profound talent, he was neither a conformist nor a bohemian, but a man of moral seriousness and brilliant intellect, whose visual inventiveness never waned in five decades of creativity. Trained in academic methods by the most rigorous of masters, he never ceased to interrogate his own practices, and he never became merely representative of a tendency – even the tendency he himself has a good claim to have founded: Pre-Raphaelitism. Brown's work, deeply rooted in history and tradition, and yet always urgently modern, is, like the man himself, difficult. Yet among his work are some of the most penetrating and fully achieved masterpieces in nineteenth-century art.

1   Reprinted in *The Germ: The Literary Magazine of the Pre-Raphaelites*, ed. Andrea Rose (Oxford, Ashmolean Museum, 1992), pp. 70–73.

2   Virginia Surtees, ed., *The Diary of Ford Madox Brown* (New Haven and London, Yale University Press, 1981), p. 1 (hereafter *Diary*). The diary entry was written retrospectively on 4 September 1847.

3   Ford Madox Brown, *The Exhibition of Work and Other Paintings by Ford Madox Brown*, 1865 (hereafter *Work*, 1865). Reprinted in Kenneth Bendiner, *The Art of Ford Madox Brown* (University Park, PA, Pennsylvania State University Press, 1998), pp. 132–33.

4   *Work*, 1865, p. 4, repr. *Bendiner*, p. 132, my italics.

5   *Work*, 1865, pp. 7, 8, repr. *Bendiner*, p. 136.

6   *Work*, 1865, p. 8, repr. *Bendiner*, p. 136.

7   *Diary*, p. 144.

8   *Work*, 1865, p. 8, repr. *Bendiner*, p. 136.

9   *Diary*, p. 80.

10 *Work*, 1865, p. 8, repr. *Bendiner*, p. 137.

11 Thomas Carlyle, 'Signs of the Times', *Edinburgh Review*, 1829; reproduced at http://www.victorianweb.org/authors/carlyle/signs1.html.

12 *Work*, 1865, p. 8.

13 Ibid.

14 *Diary*, p. 78.

15 For a full discussion, see Tim Barringer, *Men at Work: Art and Labour in Victorian Britain* (New Haven, CT, Yale University Press, 1995), ch. 1.

16 Thomas Carlyle, *Past and Present* (London, Everyman, 1912), p. 189.

17 *Work*, 1865, p. 27.

18 Ibid.

19 See *The Pre-Raphaelites*, ed. Leslie Parris (London, Tate Gallery, 1984), p. 258.

20 *Diary*, 1865, p. 94.

21 *Diary*, 1865, p. 102.

22 *The Builder*, 18 March 1865, p. 186.

Forgotten Images:
The Illustrations of Ford Madox Brown

L A U R A   M a c C U L L O C H

In Ford Madox Brown's mind his first attempt at illustrating was not a success. He was asked to produce an illustration for the third volume of the Pre-Raphaelite magazine *The Germ* published in March 1850 (cat. 24). Years later he recalled the circumstances of his commission:

> I was hurriedly appealed to one day to supply, at shortest notice, an etching. D. G. Rossetti having with uncontrollable [peevishness] drawn his etching-point across his copper-plate just as he had completed it – leaving of course the magazine in the lurch for the coming Saturday issue. I like a good-natured fool, supplied the deficiency on this short notice, & did no small injury to my reputation, I have often thought.[1]

As the basis of the design he used one of a series of pen-and-ink drawings of scenes from *King Lear* made in 1844 whist living in Paris (Whitworth Art Gallery, University of Manchester). He chose to work up the scene in which Cordelia leaves her sisters Goneril and Regan but because of his inexperience in etching, the vitality and rawness of the earlier pen-and-ink drawing are lost, the poses of the figures have become stilted and the contrasts of light and dark which he sought are almost non-existent.[2] He was so disappointed with the finished product that he made his signature illegible and wrote in his diary, 'the Etching for the Germ … cost me 31.6 & brought me in nothing'.[3] Thus at a time when Brown was desperate for paying commissions and a healthy artistic reputation, his unfruitful first printed illustration was a costly disappointment to him. Yet despite his unhappiness with the final etching the members of the Pre-Raphaelite Brotherhood (PRB) were evidently pleased with it; William Michael Rossetti composed a poem to accompany it; they made sure Brown's name appeared on the contents page; and it was given a fold-out at the front of the magazine rather than the usual single page allotted to other *Germ* contributors.

In fact, in 1853 Brown reused the composition of the etching for a painted sketch which he later sold to his usual dealer, D. T. White, for £10 (now in a private collection). Despite his disappointment with the illustration he needed to find a way of making it pay in order to justify the amount spent on its production. By replicating the composition in oil he was able to recoup some of his losses.

Brown's diary reveals that in 1854 his interest was rekindled. He experimented with different types of graphic techniques and worked on three separate compositions. In summarising his achievements for the year so far he wrote:

> [Spent] 10 days on a lithograph of Winandermere [sic] (a failure), nearly a month on an etching of King Lear, yet unfinished, 6 days on a Lythotint of "Baby" (a failure).[4]

Ford Madox Hueffer, Brown's grandson and biographer, discussed his grandfather's experiments to reproduce his painting *Windermere* as a lithograph:

> Chromo-lithography was at that date by no means the vulgarised commercial process it subsequently became, and at every stage of his career Madox Brown took a lively, almost naïve, interest in the various improvements and refinements in mechanical reproductive processes. The present one would not seem to have afforded him much satisfaction. Of it only five copies were printed, and then the stone was rubbed out. Subsequently four of the lithographs were destroyed, the remaining one, after having been coloured in body colour, being presented some years subsequently to John Marshall, the surgeon.[5]

Like the etching for *The Germ*, these printed compositions did not satisfy him and it is easy to see how scholars have come to focus on Brown's negative attitude towards illustration. However, he persevered and in the mid-1850s produced the first of several notable designs.

A number of Brown's commissions for illustrations came from his friendship with the Pre-Raphaelites. Indeed it was through Dante Gabriel Rossetti's connections that he got his second published assignment. In his diary entry for 4 March 1856, Brown recorded: 'Came home and found Dalziel here with a note from Rossetti, wants me to do him a Prisoner of Chilon [sic] on wood'.[6] George and Edward Dalziel were the leading reproductive wood-engravers in England in the second half of the nineteenth century. The illustration for Byron's poem *The Prisoner of Chillon* was for the anthology *The Poets of the Nineteenth Century* edited by R. A. Willmott and published by Routledge in 1857 (cat. 36).[7] The poem is the gloomy tale of the Swiss patriot François de Bonivard and his brothers who are held captive in a dungeon by the Duke of Savoy. Chained to separate pillars with little light able to reach them, one by one the brothers die until the narrator is left alone. For this project Brown chose to depict what happened after the death of the middle brother. He illustrated the lines:

> He died and they unlocked his chain,
> And scoop'd for him a shallow grave
> Even from the cold earth of our cave,
> I begg'd them as a boon to lay
> His corpse in dust whereon the day
> Might shine – it was a foolish thought,
> But then within my brain it wrought,
> That even in death his freeborn breast
> In such a dungeon could not rest.
> I might have spared my idle prayer –
> They coldly laugh'd, and laid him there:
> The flat and turfless earth above
> The being we so much did love
> His empty chain above it leant,
> Such murder's fitting monument.[8]

Rossetti may well have recommended Brown, knowing that he had a passion for Byron's work and that he had previously used an earlier scene from the poem as the subject for an 1843 painting (now in Manchester Art Gallery).[9]

Brown's lack of confidence in producing illustrations for reproduction was still evident five years after his first attempt for *The Germ*. On the day he wrote to Edward Dalziel to agree to undertake the illustration, a frustrated note in his diary lamented that, 'in the evng I designed [for *Prisoner of Chillon*] but could absolutely do nothing. I kept thinking of Gilbert & his great facility'.[10] The artist he admired was Sir John Gilbert (1817–1897), a prolific illustrator who had recently produced the designs for an edition of *Longfellow's Poems* (1855), published by Routledge and engraved by the Dalziel brothers. Brown had visited the Dalziels on 5 March and borrowed a copy of *Longfellow's Poems*. When he agreed to accept the commission he wrote to them enclosing the book and commenting that 'the bearer will return the volume of "Longfellow", which I have looked through with great delight; and I think it bears honourable testimony to the high excellence which wood engraving has attained in this country'.[11]

As well as a copy of the printed illustration, the Birmingham collection holds two of the drawings Brown made for *The Prisoner of Chillon*: an early compositional sketch and a detailed study of a corpse (cat. 34 and 35). Brown noted in his diary the vast amount of time and effort he put into the project; this included two long visits to University College Hospital, where his friend Dr John Marshall supplied him with a cadaver to draw.[12] The sheer number of hours he put into the commission highlights how Brown, like the other Pre-Raphaelites, 'placed illustration on a level with [his] paintings' and 'emphasized creative integrity and hard work in all areas'.[13] Unfortunately for Brown, although his attention to detail helped him produce a remarkable design, giving him a reputation as a competent illustrator, by itself the commission was not financially rewarding.

In order to make his work as an illustrator pay he developed his earlier money-making strategy. Having come up with a successful composition for an illustration, Brown used this to gain commissions for the same design in watercolour or oil. This was to be a strategy he followed for the next twenty years, significantly linking his work as an illustrator with his work as a painter. Brown received only £8 from the Dalziels for the illustration itself, but in 1858 he was commissioned by the Pre-Raphaelite patron Thomas Plint to paint a vivid watercolour version of *The Prisoner of Chillon* for thirty guineas, almost four times as much as he had originally received (Yale Center for British Art, New Haven).[14] For this commission Brown used the tiny brushstrokes and stippling technique associated with Rossetti's watercolours, revealing the close links between their work at the time.

Brown's experience of designing for the Dalziels produced in him a much more optimistic view of illustration. As the brothers noted in their memoirs, Brown, 'subsequently, on seeing the volume, *The Poets of the Nineteenth Century*, … wrote:

> Let me take this opportunity of expressing my admiration of the work you last brought out, and the drawings by [Thomas] Dalziel in particular, which are most poetic and took us by surprise, although whether yours or your brother's I as yet, know not. The Millais are admirable, both as regards him and the engraver.[15]

Of all those in the inner circle of Pre-Raphaelites, John Everett Millais was by far the most successful illustrator.[16] In comparison to Brown, Rossetti and Holman Hunt, his output was staggering. This must have been largely due to his ability to produce extraordinarily good illustrations, for magazines and books, in a relatively short time, unlike Brown and Rossetti who appear to have agonised over each design. Some of Millais's most beautiful illustrations were for the Moxon edition of Tennyson's *Poems*. Both Hunt and Rossetti were involved with the project but Brown was not invited to contribute. Brown recorded seeing some of Millais's designs in his diary, and his remarks reveal that his approach to the text was often more literal than that of the younger Pre-Raphaelites. On 20 April 1856 he wrote:

> Wednesday last I finished the drawing on wood of the P. of Chillon having worked at it pretty regularly …. I saw [Millais] at Lewards on Monday, showed me proofs of a Dozen wood cuts he had done, most of them very beautifully drawn & full of beauties but scarcely illustrations from Tennisson [sic].[17]

Whereas Brown's designs clearly illustrate the text and include minute details to enhance the reader's understanding of it, both Rossetti and Millais, to a lesser extent, liked to 'allegorize off [their] own hook', creating designs that used the text merely as a springboard for their artistic visions.[18] Despite Millais's ease of execution, Rossetti 'drove Moxon near to distraction, was dilatory in [the] execution [of his five designs and] troublesome to Dalziel the engraver' and Millais championed Brown as a replacement artist.[19] On the same night as Brown admired Millais's designs, he noted in his diary that Millais 'proposed that he should get Moxon to give me some to do, which might considerably modifie any opinion adverse to the merits of his [illustrations]'.[20] It

appears that Millais did approach Moxon, for two weeks later Brown records:

> Met Millais … N.B. Millais told me that he had got Moxon to give me the designs for Tennisson [sic] which were for Rossetti as he would never do them. Ergo Briccum est. Of course I will not take Gabriels [sic] work without his concent.[21]

Rossetti must have objected to this plan as Brown did not design any illustrations for the Moxon Tennyson.

Brown's next illustration project was also connected with the Dalziels. One of the brothers' leading strategies was to commission contemporary artists to illustrate the books on which they were working. From 1863, Brown and a number of other artists including Holman Hunt, Frederick Sandys and Simeon Solomon were approached by the brothers to design illustrations for a 'Bible Gallery'.[22] This was to rival the highly successful German edition of *The Bible in Pictures* by Julius Schnorr von Carolsfeld (Leipzig, 1852; English edition from 1855) but the Dalziels were unable to get their version published until 1881, and it ended up a commercial failure. Despite the long delay in publishing, Brown, like most of the artists involved in the project, actually designed his illustrations between 1863 and 1865. He was commissioned to do three: *Joseph's Coat*, *Elijah and the Widow's Son* and *The Death of Eglon* (cat. 53 and 54, B62). These illustrations certainly impressed the Dalziels, who wrote in their memoirs:

> Of Ford Madox Brown's three contributions we have chosen 'Elijah and the Widow's Son', as being not only an original conception of the subject, but perhaps one of the most beautiful specimens of manipulative skill he ever produced. He called it an etching, and so it was to all intents, it being perfectly pure line work. Although more beautiful, it is in no way finer than 'Joseph's Coat', or 'The Death of Eglon'.[23]

As with his two previous illustrations, Brown used these designs as the basis for several paintings. He sold several versions of both *Joseph's Coat* and *Elijah and the Widow's Son* but never worked *The Death of Eglon* into a painting. His granddaughter Helen Maria Madox Rossetti's defence of this illustration perhaps explains its lack of popularity:

> Most people feel a strong inclination to laugh at the figure of Eglon, engulfed in the arm chair of ease; but to

RIGHT: *The Prisoner of Chillon: Study of a Corpse*, 1856 (cat. 34)

BELOW: *The Prisoner of Chillon: Compositional Sketch*, pub. 1856 (cat. 35)

BELOW RIGHT: *The Prisoner of Chillon*, 1857 (cat. 36)

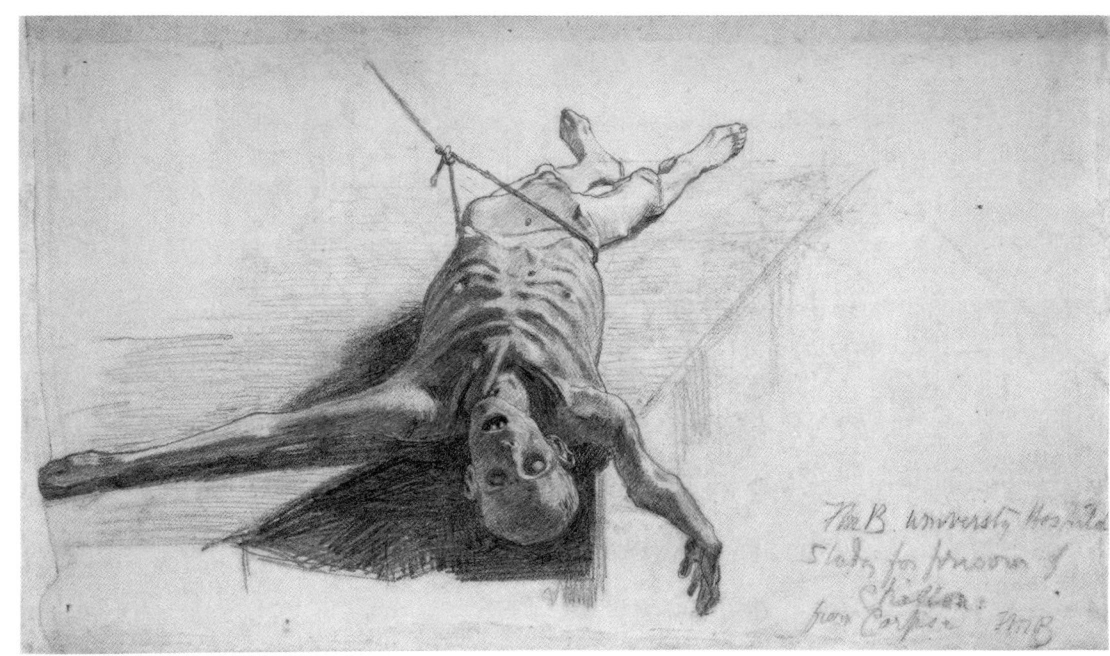

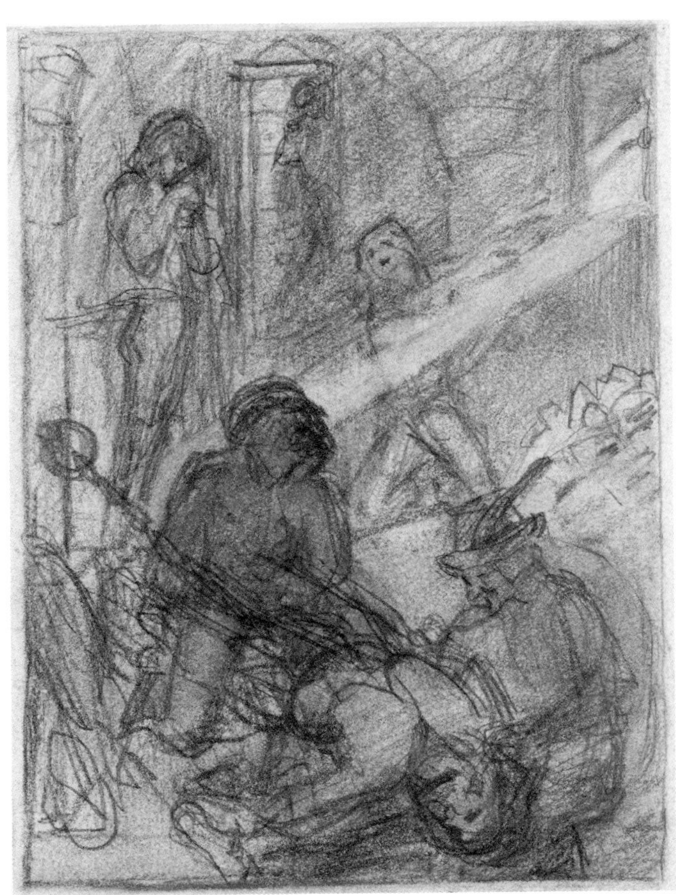

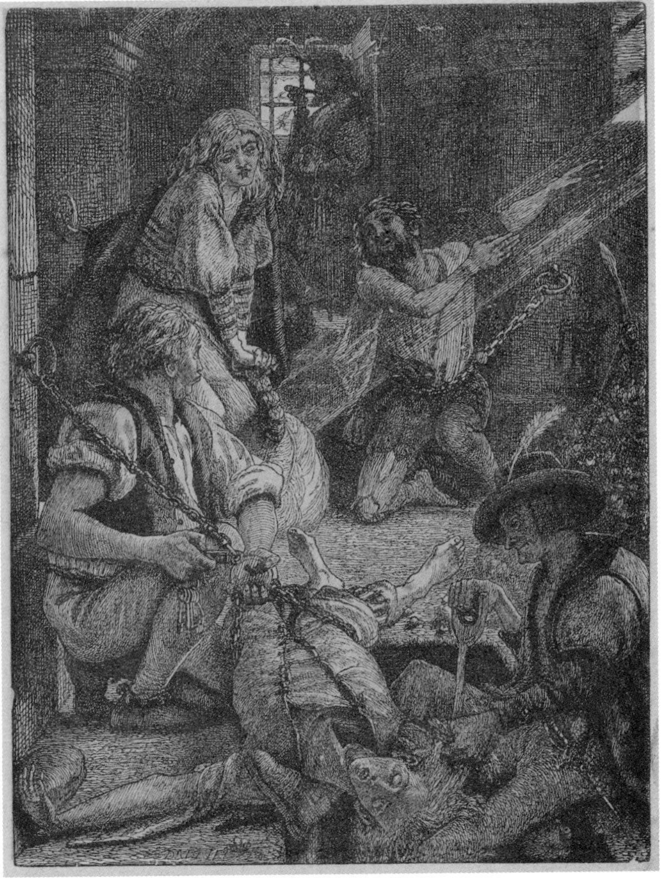

my mind, no artist of any age or country could have depicted more powerfully or more contemptuously sensuality run to ignominious fat, nor the fury of patriotic revenge more vividly than in the on-rushing figure of Ehud.[24]

Brown found other ways in which to make his designs pay. In the 1860s he was one of the head designers for Morris, Marshall, Faulkner & Co., the firm he helped set up with Morris, Rossetti and Burne-Jones, among others. He applied his money-making strategies to the stained glass and tile compositions he created for the company, and sought other ways in which to make the time he spent on them pay. As a letter from the designer John Leighton reveals, book illustration became a way for Brown to reuse previous decorative compositions. Leighton was superintending *Lyra Germanica*, an anthology of German hymns translated into English. The religious nature of the book suited the compositions Brown had produced for Morris, Marshall, Faulkner & Co. which were largely stained glass cartoons for churches. He wrote to Brown:

> The 'Sower' seems to me as if it would be useful 'as you sow so shall you reap'. It would be quite safe to do the Isaac I could use that in 50 places as an emblem of 'Faith' but the others I should have to fit in & that will take time. – I think you are wise to touch your cartoon & allow them to be copied on wood. Messrs Longmans only want the design on the wood – & the cartoons would be of greater value from having been in a livre de Luxe as a known work & commissions continually come out of those books. I suppose we begin with the Isaac to see how it comes by this method – if the result is happy all will be well.[25]

In the end only three of Brown's compositions were used, but Brown apparently thought that having his work published would generate commissions. For this project he worked with three different engravers: Joseph Swain (1820–1909) engraved his small, simple design for *Abraham and Isaac* (B92), Thomas Bolton was responsible for engraving *The Entombment* (cat. 46) and the Dalziel brothers worked on *He that Soweth*.

Birmingham Museums and Art Gallery holds the final drawing for the most splendid of the three designs, *The Entombment* (cat. 45), which accompanied the lines:

> O Blessed Rock!
> Soon grant Thy flock
> To see Thy Sabbath morning!
> Strife and pain will all be past
> When that day is dawning.

This was most likely made on Leighton's insistence because a later letter from him asks Brown to supply drawings to be either photographed or etched onto the block.[26] It is only on close inspection that Brown's highly worked image reveals itself as a drawing – one made very much with the engraver in mind – rather than a print. Brown worked up two versions of *The Entombment* in watercolour and sold one of them to Henry Boddington for £200 along with the pen-and-ink drawing for £12 (this watercolour is now in the National Gallery of Victoria, Melbourne). In these versions he extended the scene on the right to include a view of Calvary, a flock of sheep, and a woman and a little boy watching the burial. Frederick Leyland also bought a version in oil for £210 which, according to Hueffer, was begun in 1867 (Walker Art Gallery, Liverpool). Thus he had managed to use his original stained glass cartoon many times, making more from each commission.

He that Soweth had originally been a design for a tile produced by Morris, Marshall, Faulkner & Co. who were employed to restore the hall of Queens' College, Cambridge, between 1864 and 1873. The tiles surround the great fireplace and depict the months of the year; Brown's design was for November.[27] The close relationship between artist and engraver is highlighted by a letter Brown sent to the Dalziel brothers during the process of reproducing the original illustration. It also gives a sense of the attention to detail that Brown brought to his engraved illustration. Once Brown had finished drawing on the woodblock it was engraved and then a hand-pulled proof was made which he could view and correct. It appears that after the second set of proofs had been produced, Brown was still not satisfied and there were several exacting corrections he wanted to be made:

> I should have liked to call upon you with respect to the few touches which the block in question shall require, but I have found it impossible to make time – I must therefore try to explain by letter – but first I must say that the whole work is much improved & if the touching now required prove successful I shall inform the publishers that I am quite satisfied.

The clouds are still too dark … in execution & the rain too heavy and uniform. This being in contravention with the text illustrated, is important. The clouds should be rounded off well or I should say softened off well at their edges & one or 2 of them left darker than the rest – & some hard jerky lines under them <u>running across the rain</u> be cut away. The rain lightened where the flat-white is. As to the face & hair –.1st there is a spot of light too much on the right eye-brow (left as we look at it) as this interferes with the drawing of the head I have by f. white corrected it into the end of a lock of hair coming over it. – This I did … for the first proof but as it was unexplained it seems to have been looked upon as an accident of my brush & not cut away therefore – but you will now see that the touch of white very much improves the drawing of the head.[28]

Brown's next illustration project was born of his long-standing passion for the work of Byron. In 1870 Moxon published a complete volume of the works of Byron.[29] Brown provided six illustrations and his son Oliver, a budding artist, designed a further two.[30] These illustrations were all reproduced by steel engraving by Herbert Bourne (1820–1885). From letters at the Victoria and Albert Museum written by Bertrand Payne, the man in charge of the project, it appears Brown was originally asked to provide all eight designs himself and that the book was to be part of a reasonably priced series. However, Brown was unable to design his eight illustrations quickly enough, Oliver had to design two and the book was ultimately published separately, edited by William Michael Rossetti. It was altogether a much more costly volume but one which led to many commissions for Brown. Almost all of Brown's designs were later worked up into paintings in oil or watercolour, including three versions of *The Finding of Don Juan by Haidee*, one of which is in the Birmingham collection.[31]

After his etching for *The Germ*, Brown undertook only two other illustrations for periodicals. *The Traveller* was published in *Once a Week* in 1869 (no. 161) and engraved by Joseph Swain. According to Hueffer it was based on Victor Hugo's poem of the same name, 'about a traveller who rides through a village at nightfall when all the world besides is resting,' but the illustration was not accompanied by Brown's translation of the poem as Hueffer mistakenly believed.[32] Keeping to his entrepreneurial strategy Brown made two versions of *The Traveller*, a watercolour, which according to

accounts was painted in 1867 and sold to E. Ellis; and an oil version begun in 1868 but not finished until 1884 when sold to Henry Boddington.[33]

In 1871 Brown made his last illustration for a periodical. He produced two designs to illustrate Rossetti's poem 'Down Stream' which was published in the short-lived liberal magazine *Dark Blue* (cat. 47 and 48). The poem tells the sad tale of a young woman seduced on a boating trip on the first of May. She becomes pregnant but is abandoned by her seducer and in desperation kills herself and her child on the first of June the following year. Brown illustrated the start of the poem, with the seducer roughly caressing a robust, young woman in a rowing boat, and the moonlit conclusion with a thin Ophelia-like figure floating amidst water lilies, clutching her baby. The most arresting element of these two illustrations is the marked contrast between the woman at the moment of and after her fall. The buxom woman in the first illustration becomes a delicate, wan figure in the tailpiece, thus matching the pathos of the poem.

These designs mark the start of the final phase of Brown's illustrations. From this date until his death in 1893 he made illustrations only for his family and close literary friends. He was always noted for his keenness to help others further their careers and it was often through his illustrations that he felt best able to do so. Significantly, Brown was no longer concerned with making his work as an illustrator pay and did not reproduce these later designs in any other media, having gained a strong artistic reputation and a far greater number of patrons. In 1873 he designed the cover for Oliver's first novel *Gabriel Denver*, hoping to add kudos to his son's fledgling literary career.[34] The following year he also designed the cover for *Richard Wagner and the Music of the Future* by his son-in-law, the music critic Franz Hueffer.[35] In 1876, following Oliver's death, Brown etched two portraits of him for each volume of the published collection of his literary works: *Dwale Bluth: Hebditch's Legacy and Other Literary Remains of Oliver Madox Brown*.[36] These very personal portraits show Oliver at the age of four and as a young man.

Brown was keen to help his literary friends and associates. In 1889 he designed the title page of Grace Black's *A Beggar and other Fantasies* published by the writer Edward Garnett (1868–1937), who later introduced Brown's grandson, Ford Madox Hueffer, to Joseph Conrad.[37] For several years Brown had been a close friend of Mathilde Blind, a literary figure with feminist leanings. In 1891 he designed the title page for her book of stories *Dramas in Miniature*.[38] This time he used an existing chalk drawing of Emma in bed recovering from an illness, *Convalescent: Portrait of Emma Madox Brown* (cat. 50), as the basis for the illustration rather than producing a subsequent version as had previously been his practice. In 1892 Ford Madox Hueffer published his first two books, fairy stories called *The Brown Owl* and *The Feather*.[39] Brown designed two illustrations for *The Brown Owl* and one for *The Feather*, all reproduced – like the illustration for *Dramas in Miniature* – using the new method of photo-engraving which began to replace wood engraving as the medium of choice in the printing world.

Ford Madox Brown's work as an illustrator has previously been seen as a short-lived, unprofitable sideline in his career as a painter.[40] Nevertheless, despite Brown's early frustration and lack of confidence in creating designs for publication, he gained a significant reputation as an illustrator as well as inventing a strategy which allowed him to make money from this area of his work without compromising his artistic values. In the last twenty years of his life, when he no longer required his illustrations to make money, he continued to use his skills as an illustrator to further the careers of those close to him. Viewed within the context of the explosion of illustration in the mid-nineteenth century, the designs Brown produced in the 1850s and 60s, such as *The Prisoner of Chillon* and *Joseph's Coat*, can be seen as leaders in their field along with those of Millais and Rossetti.

1. Letter from Ford Madox Brown to Mr Ireland, 9 March 1891, Princeton University. This is a particularly interesting letter as Brown states his position vis-à-vis the Pre-Raphaelite Brotherhood, claiming that 'for the sake of accuracy I would like it to be known that I was never in any way responsible for, as a partner in the speculation [*The Germ*]. I was never in fact a member of the renowned P. R. B. (who used to shout out these cabalistic initials under one another's windows at night) nor was I a shareholder in their magazine. I was only a friend very much interested in their lively ways & novel doctrines & not considering myself anything but a painter' (ibid.).
2. Birmingham Museum and Art Gallery (BMAG) holds a sketch for another scene, *Lear questioning Cordelia* (cat. 2), which has pencil sketches for the figures of Goneril and Regan found in both the Whitworth drawing and the etching.
3. Virginia Surtees, ed., *The Diary of Ford Madox Brown* (New Haven and London, Yale University Press, 1981), p. 72 (hereafter *Diary*).
4. Ibid., pp. 80, 82. *Winandermere* was Brown's alternative name for his small landscape painting *Windermere*.
5. Ford Madox Hueffer, *Ford Madox Brown: A Record of his Life and Work* (London, Longmans, Green and Co., 1896), p. 92 (hereafter *Hueffer*, 1896).
6. *Diary*, p. 165.
7. Rev. R. A. Willmott, ed., *The Poets of the Nineteenth Century* (London, George Routledge and Co., 1857).
8. Lord Byron, *The Poetical Works of Lord Byron* (London, John Murray, 1857), p. 252.
9. Brown painted five early scenes from poems by Byron (*The Giaour's Confession, Manfred in the Chamois Hunter's Hut, Manfred on the Jungfrau, Parisina* and another version of *The Prisoner of Chillon*). He also included him as one of the great English poets in the triptych *The Seeds and Fruits of English Poetry*, which became *Chaucer at the Court of Edward III*. The earlier painting shows the influence on Brown of both Delacroix's interest in Byron, and Fuseli's Gothic depictions of captive men.
10. *Diary*, p. 166, 6 March 1856.
11. George and Edward Dalziel, *The Brothers Dalziel. A Record of Work in Conjunction with many of the Most Distinguished Artists of the Period 1840–1890* (London, Methuen and Co., 1901), p. 120. Brown's diary notes that during his visit to the Dalziels on 5 March he was shown 'Millais' wood cuts of Tennison [*sic*]' (*Diary*, p. 166). In correspondence with the author, Paul Goldman pointed out that the Dalziels' memoirs are not completely reliable: 'They sometimes get the dates of their own books wrong and they are notoriously boastful about themselves.'
12. See cat. 36.
13. Gregory R. Suriano, *The British Pre-Raphaelite Illustrators* (Newcastle, DE, and London, Oak Knoll Press and the British Library, 2005), p. 39.
14. Thomas Plint was an industrialist from Leeds. He also commissioned Brown's painting *Work* (Manchester Art Gallery).
15. *The Brothers Dalziel*, p. 122. Thomas was one of George and Edward's brothers.
16. See Paul Goldman, *John Everett Millais: Illustrator and Narrator*, exh. cat., BMAG, 2004.
17. *Diary*, p. 169.
18. A letter dated 23 January 1855 quoted in Forrest Reid, *Illustrators of the Sixties* (London, Faber & Gwyer, 1928), pp. 31–32.
19. *Diary*, 8 May 1856, p. 172.
20. Ibid., p. 169.
21. Ibid., p. 172. Surtees notes that 'Rossetti … extorted £5 more for each design than was given to the other contributors'.
22. George and Edward Dalziel, *Dalziels' Bible Gallery* (London, George Routledge & Sons, 1881).
23. Ibid., p. 252.
24. Helen M. Madox Rossetti, *Ford Madox Brown* (London, De La More Press, 1902), p. 14.
25. Letter from John Leighton to Ford Madox Brown, 20 June 1866, V&A. John Leighton worked as an illustrator but was most well known as a designer of bindings.
26. Letter from John Leighton to Ford Madox Brown, 16 July 1866, V&A.
27. Duncan Robinson and Stephen Wildman, *Morris and Company in Cambridge*, exh. cat., Fitzwilliam Museum, Cambridge, 1980, pp. 27–28.
28. Letter from Ford Madox Brown to the Dalziel brothers, 7 April 1867, Princeton University.
29. Lord Byron, *Poems* (London, Edward Moxon, 1870).
30. All of Brown's children helped him in his studio. Lucy and Cathy were very competent artists and exhibited their work.
31. The other two versions are at the National Gallery of Victoria, Melbourne, and the Musée d'Orsay, Paris.
32. *Hueffer*, 1896, p. 229.
33. Ibid., p. 441. Both versions are now at Manchester Art Gallery.
34. Oliver Madox Brown, *Gabriel Denver* (London, Smith, Elder & Co., 1873). Oliver Madox Brown died the following year from peritonitis and septicaemia aged nineteen. The novel contained no illustrations except the one Brown designed for the front cover.
35. Franz Hueffer, *Richard Wagner and the Music of the Future* (London, Chapman & Hall, 1874).
36. Oliver Madox Brown, *Dwale Bluth: Hebditch's Legacy and Other Literary Remains of Oliver Madox Brown*, 2 vols (London, Tinsley Brothers, 1876).
37. Grace Black, *A Beggar and other Fantasies* (Holmswood, Edward Garnett, 1889). Garnett also used the design for a bookplate. Ford Madox Hueffer later changed his name to Ford Madox Ford and became a successful novelist.
38. Mathilde Blind, *Dramas in Miniature* (London, Chatto and Windus, 1891).
39. Ford Madox Hueffer, *The Brown Owl: A Fairy Story* and *The Feather* both published in London by T. F. Unwin in 1892.
40. The most notable recent example is Paul Goldman, who states that Rossetti 'produced just ten and [Brown] fewer than 20 images in total, and both artists abandoned illustration early in their careers' (*John Everett Millais: Illustrator and Narrator*, BMAG, 2004, p. 8). Though Rossetti gave up illustrating early on, as has been shown, Brown continued to design illustrations until a year before his death.

Exhibits

The catalogue entries are set out in the following sequence: catalogue number, title of work, medium, size in millimetres (height before width), literature (Lit.) and exhibition (Exh.) references, and finally provenance details with the Birmingham Museums and Art Gallery accession number. It should be noted that the original format of the accession number, as set out in *Whitley*, has been reversed to facilitate computer compatibility, so for example 670'1906 has become 1906P670 and so on. Birmingham Museums and Art Gallery is abbreviated to BMAG and Literature sources have been limited to two page references, with the abbreviation ff. indicating further page references.

Unless otherwise stated, the exhibits were purchased from Charles Fairfax Murray and presented by subscribers in 1906.

Abbreviations

Exh. – Exhibitions; Insc. – Inscriptions; Lit. – Literature; Prov. – Provenance

b.- bottom; bl. – bottom left; br. – bottom right; bc. – bottom centre; tl. – top left; tr. – top right; cl. – centre left; cr. – centre right; i. – image; p. – paper, s. – sight

Abbreviated References

***Work*, 1865** *The Exhibition of Work, and other Paintings, by Ford Madox Brown, at The Gallery, 191 Piccadilly, London, 1865*

***Sale Catalogue*, 1894** *A Catalogue of the House & Decorative Furniture, Works of Art, Books & Effects belonging to the Distinguished Painter Ford Madox Brown, which will be sold by Mr T. G. Wharton* (No. 1, St Edmund's Terrace, Regent's Park, 29–31 May 1894)

Hueffer Ford M. Hueffer, *Ford Madox Brown: A Record of his Life and Work* (London, Longmans, Green and Co., 1896)

***Grafton*, 1897** *Exhibition of the Works of Ford Madox Brown, held at the Grafton Galleries, London, 1897*

***Gleeson White*, 1897** Gleeson White, *English Illustration: 'The Sixties' 1855–70* (London, Archibald Constable and Co., 1897)

***George and Edward Dalziel*, 1901** George and Edward Dalziel, *The Brothers Dalziel. A Record of Work in Conjunction with many of the Most Distinguished Artists of the Period 1840–1890* (London, Methuen and Co., 1901)

W. M. Rossetti William Michael Rossetti, *Some Reminiscences of William Michael Rossetti* (London, Brown, Langham & Co. Ltd., 1906)

***Manchester*, 1911** *Loan Exhibition of Works by Ford Madox Brown and the Pre-Raphaelites* (City Art Gallery, Manchester, Autumn 1911)

***National Gallery British Art*, 1911–12** *The National Gallery British Art Loan Collection of Works by English Pre-Raphaelite Painters* (National Gallery British Art (Tate Gallery) December 1911 – March 1912)

***Twelve Pre-Raphaelite Drawings*, 1925** *Twelve English Pre-Raphaelite Drawings, reproduced from the Originals in the City of Birmingham Museum and Art Gallery; selected and with foreword by Sir Whitworth Wallis* (London, Methuen, 1925)

Reid Forrest Reid, *Illustrators of the Sixties* (London, Faber and Gwyer, 1928)

***Brussels*, 1929** *Exposition Rétrospective de Peinture Anglaise (XVIIe et XVIXe)* (Musée Moderne, Brussels, 1929)

Whitley A. E. Whitley, *City of Birmingham Museum & Art Gallery, Catalogue of the permanent Collection of Drawings in Pen, Pencil, Charcoal and Chalk, etc., including Cartoons for Stained Glass* (Derby, Bemrose & Sons, 1939)

***Aberystwyth*, 1956** *Paintings and Drawings by British Artists from the City of Birmingham* (National Library of Wales, Aberystwyth, 1956)

***Ford Madox Brown*, 1964** Mary Bennett, *Ford Madox Brown* (Walker Art Gallery, Liverpool, 1964)

Sewter A. Charles Sewter, *The Stained Glass of William Morris and his Circle* (New Haven and London, published for the Paul Mellon Centre for Studies in British Art by Yale University Press, 2 vols, 1975)

Rabin Lucy Rabin, *Ford Madox Brown and the Pre-Raphaelite History-Picture* (New York and London, Garland Publishing, 1978)

Andrea Rose, 1981 Andrea Rose, *Pre-Raphaelite Portraits* (Oxford Illustrated Press, 1981)

Diary *The Diary of Ford Madox Brown*, ed. Virginia Surtees (New Haven and London, published for the Paul Mellon Centre for Studies in British Art by Yale University Press, 1981)

The Pre-Raphaelites, 1984 *The Pre-Raphaelites*, ed. Leslie Parris (Tate Gallery, London, 1984)

Hong Kong, 1984 Richard Lockett, *Pre-Raphaelite Art from Birmingham Museums and Art Gallery* (Hong Kong Museum of Art, 1984)

Bennett, 1988 Mary Bennett, *Artists of the Pre-Raphaelite Circle: The First Generation, Catalogue of Works in the Walker Art Gallery, Lady Lever Art Gallery and Sudley Gallery* (Walker Art Gallery, Liverpool, 1988)

Casteras, 1991 Susan Casteras, *Pocket Cathedrals: Pre-Raphaelite Book Illustration* (New Haven, CT, Yale Centre for British Art, 1991)

Newman and Watkinson Teresa Newman and Ray Watkinson, *Ford Madox Brown and the Pre-Raphaelite Circle* (London, Chatto & Windus, 1991)

BMAG, 1991 Stephen Wildman, *British Watercolours from 1750–1900 from Birmingham* (Tokyo Station Gallery, 1991)

Rooke, BMAG, 1992 *'Faithful and Able': The Architectural Watercolours of T. M. Rooke (1842–1942)* (BMAG, 1992)

Rooke, Sheffield, 1993 *Works by Thomas Matthews Rooke 1842–1942: The Collections of Birmingham Museums and Art Gallery and the Ruskin Gallery (Collection of the Guild of St George), Sheffield* (Ruskin Gallery, Sheffield, 1993)

Visions Stephen Wildman, *Visions of Love and Life, Pre-Raphaelite Art from the Birmingham Collection, England* (Alexandria, VA, Art Services International, 1995–96)

Goldman Paul Goldman, *Victorian Illustration: The Pre-Raphaelites, The Idyllic School and The High Victorians* (London, Lund Humphries, 1996 and 2004)

Engen Rodney Engen, *Pre-Raphaelite Prints* (London, Lund Humphries, 1995)

Bendiner Kenneth Bendiner, *The Art of Ford Madox Brown* (University Park, PA, Pennsylvania State University Press, 1998)

Prettejohn, 2000 Elizabeth Prettejohn, *The Art of the Pre-Raphaelites* (London, Tate Publishing, 2000)

Suriano Gregory R. Suriano, *The British Pre-Raphaelite Illustrators* (Newcastle, DE, and London, Oak Knoll Press and the British Library, 2005)

Barringer, 2005 Tim Barringer, *Men at Work: Art and Leisure in Victorian Britain* (New Haven, CT, and London, published for the Paul Mellon Centre for Studies in British Art by Yale University Press, 2005)

Bennett Mary Bennett, Catalogue of the complete works of Ford Madox Brown, to be published by Yale University Press, forthcoming

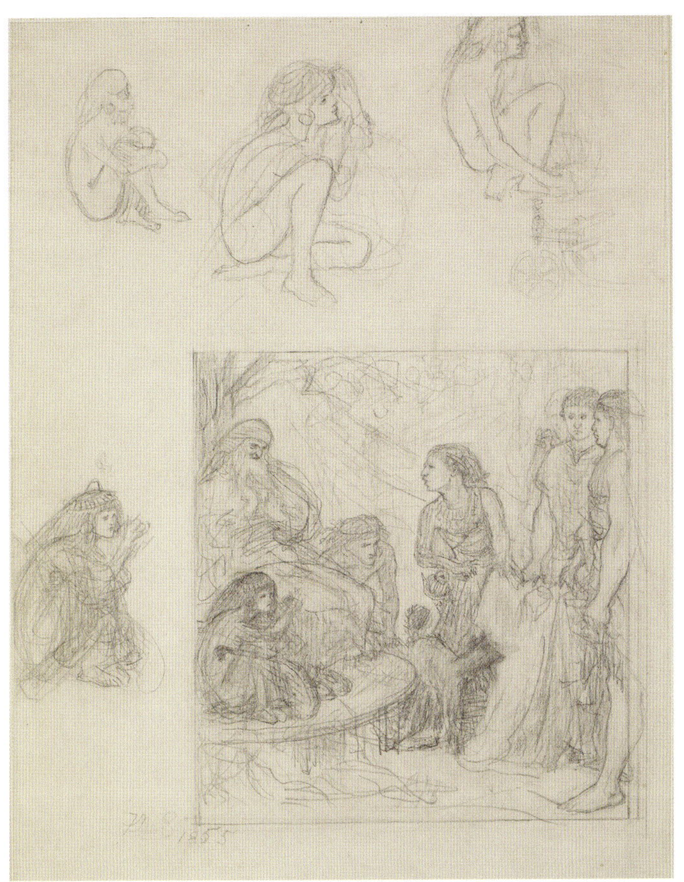

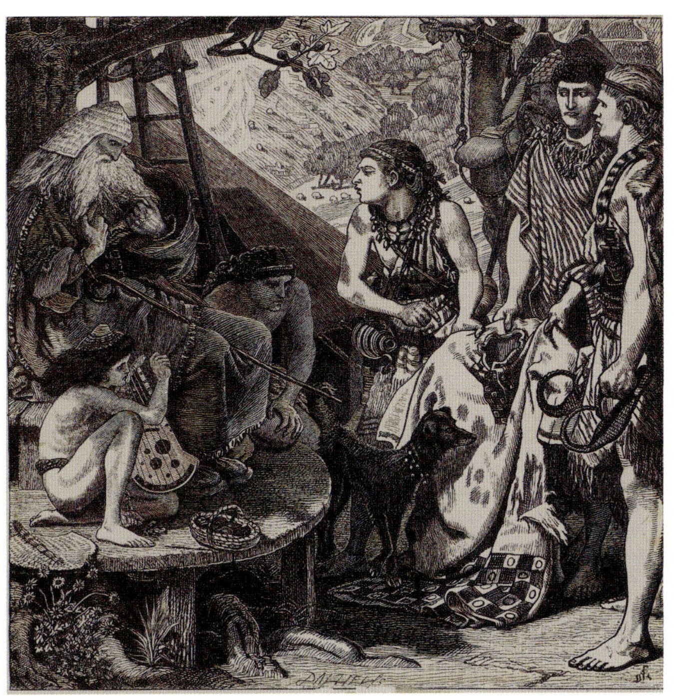

ABOVE: *Dalziels' Bible Gallery: Joseph's Coat: Compositional Sketch and Four Studies for Jacob's Granddaughter*, 1863–65 (cat. 43)

ABOVE RIGHT: *Dalziels' Bible Gallery: Joseph's Coat*, pub. 1881 (cat. 54)

RIGHT: *Dalziels' Bible Gallery: Elijah and the Widow's Son*, pub. 1881 (cat. 53)

FAR RIGHT: *Elijah and the Widow's Son*, 1864 (cat. 42)

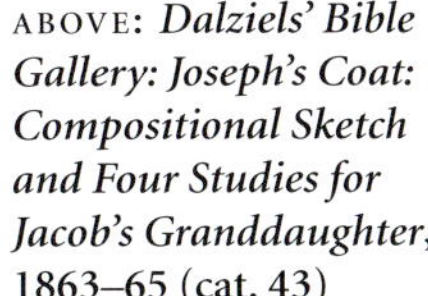

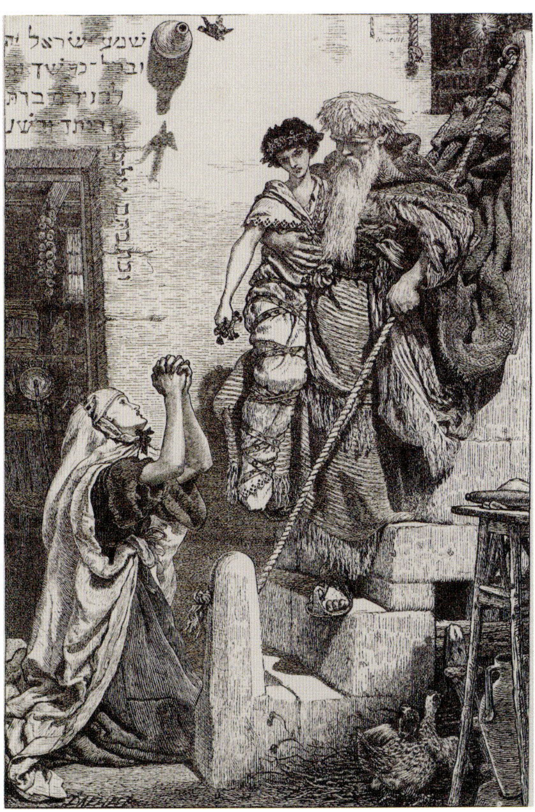

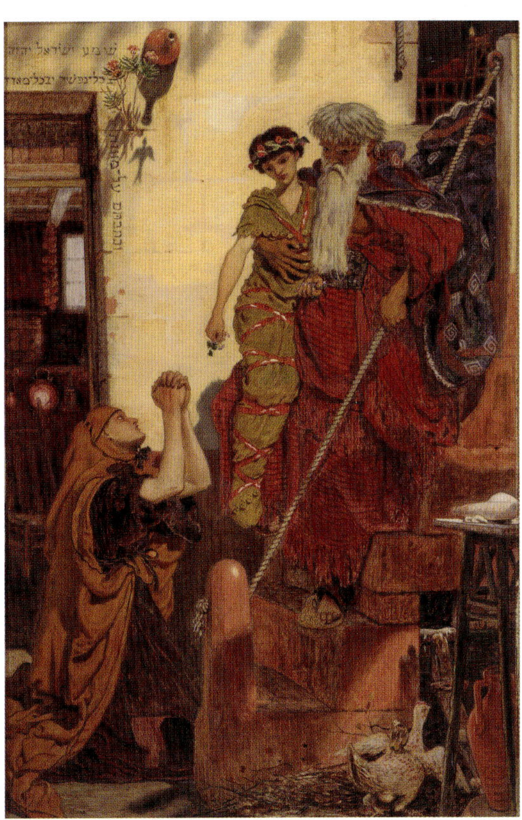

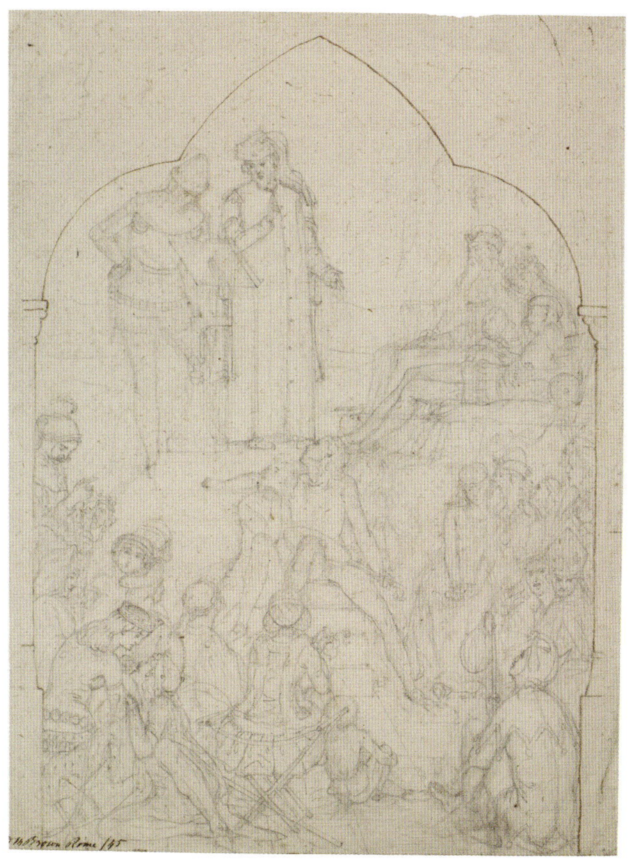

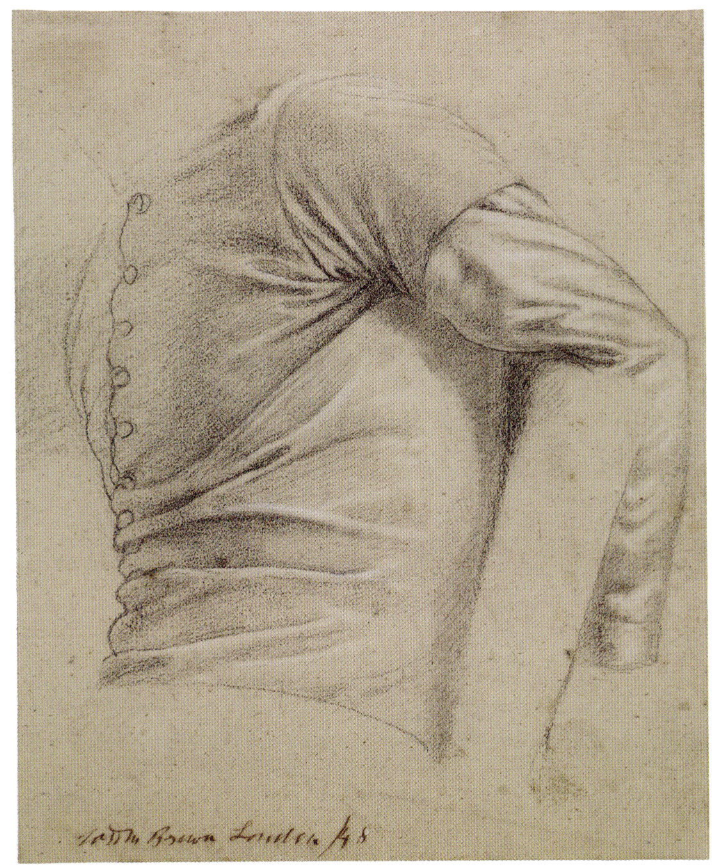

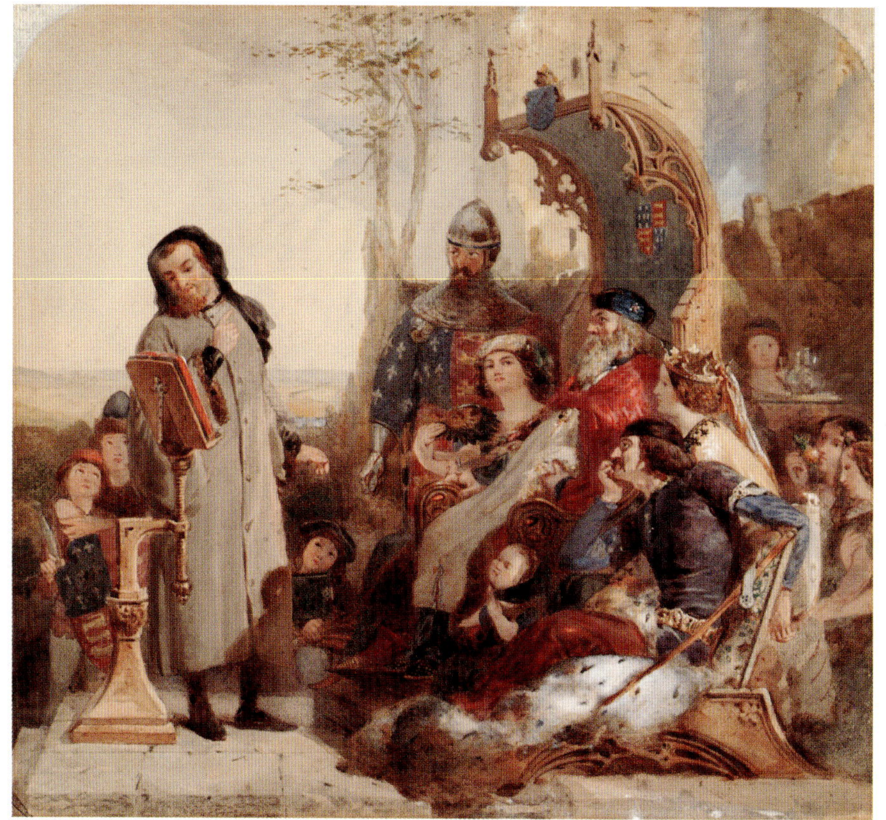

ABOVE LEFT: *Chaucer at the Court of Edward III: Early compositional Study*, 1845 (cat. 7)

ABOVE: *Chaucer at the Court of Edward III: Drapery Study for the Black Prince*, 1848 (cat. 19)

LEFT: *Chaucer at the Court of Edward III: Watercolour Version*, c. 1851 (cat. 26)

RIGHT: *Costume Studies: French and Italian thirteenth- and fourteenth-century Costumes*, 1845 (cat. 6)

BELOW: *Chaucer at the Court of Edward III: Study of a Man in medieval Hood*, 1847 (cat. 12)

BELOW RIGHT: *List of historical Names and Dates over Sketches of King Alfred*, 1844–50 (cat. 5)

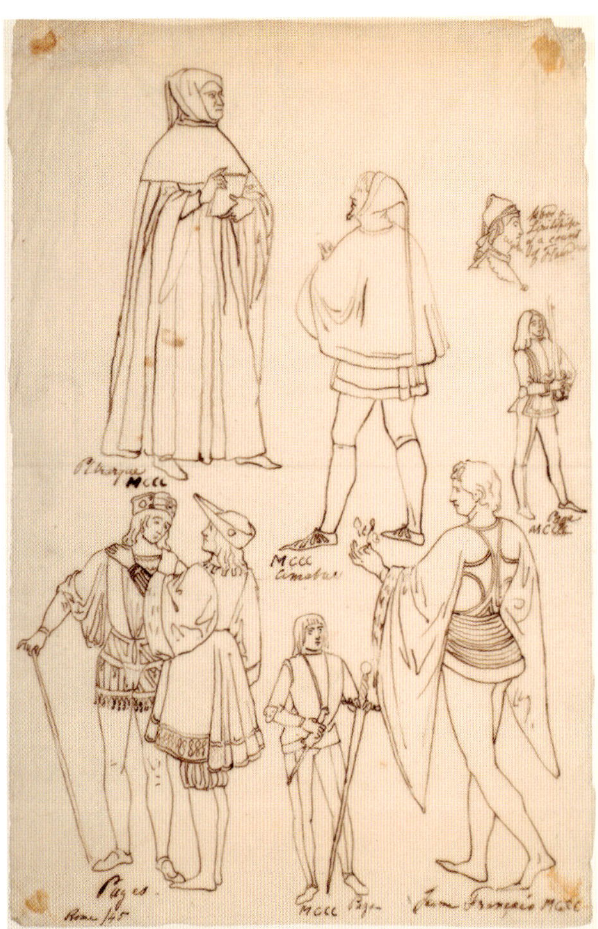

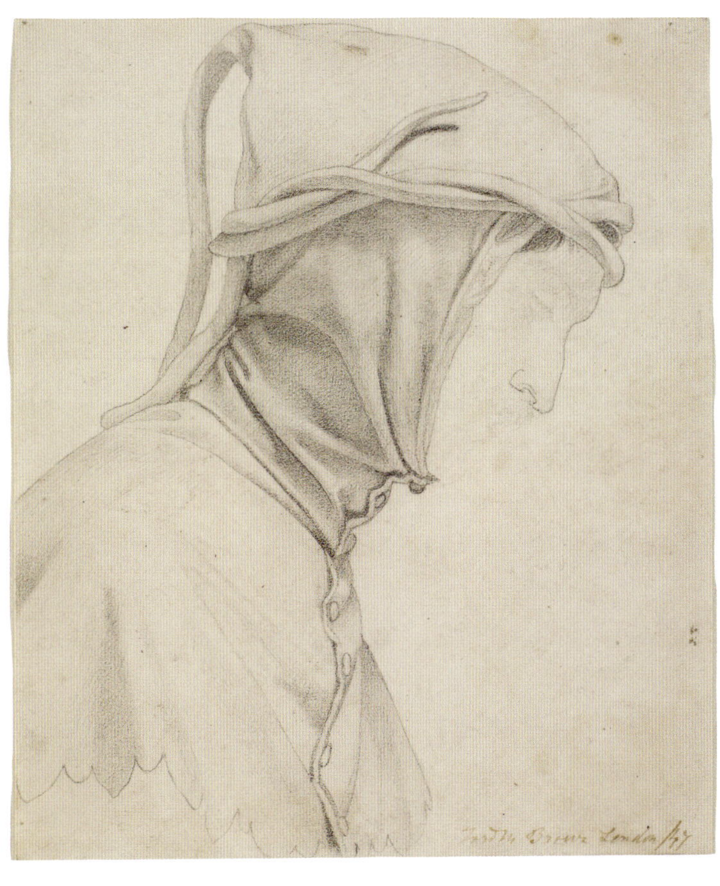

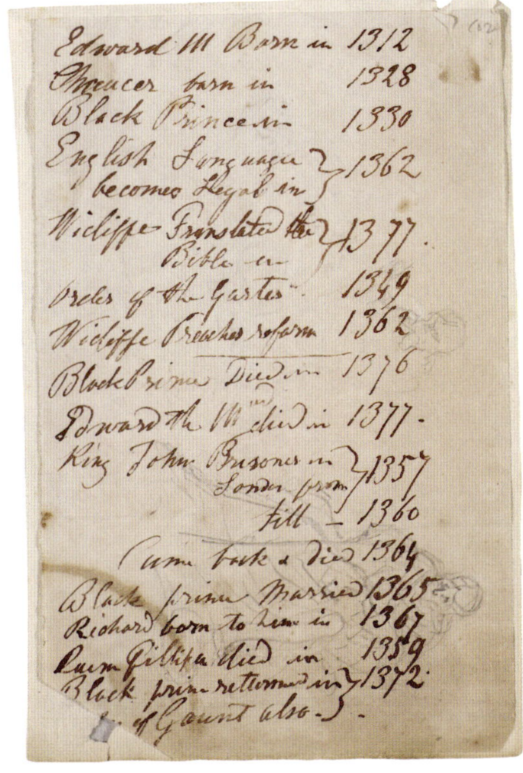

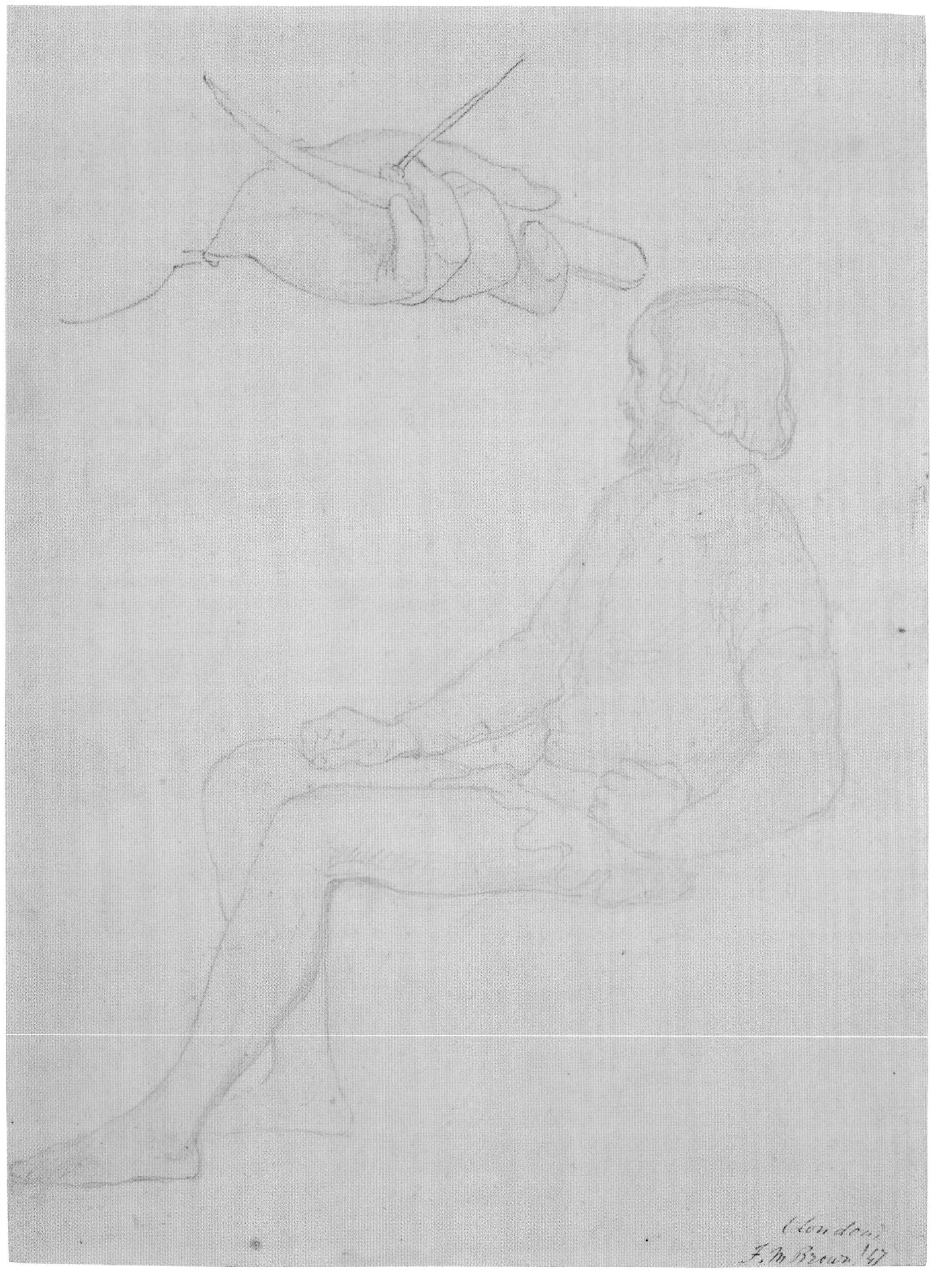

LEFT: *Wycliffe reading his Translation of the Bible: Study of John of Gaunt and Chaucer's left Hand,* 1847 (cat. 16)

OPPOSITE PAGE:
Wycliffe reading his Translation of the Bible: Studies of Hands for John of Gaunt and Gower, 1847 (cat. 17)

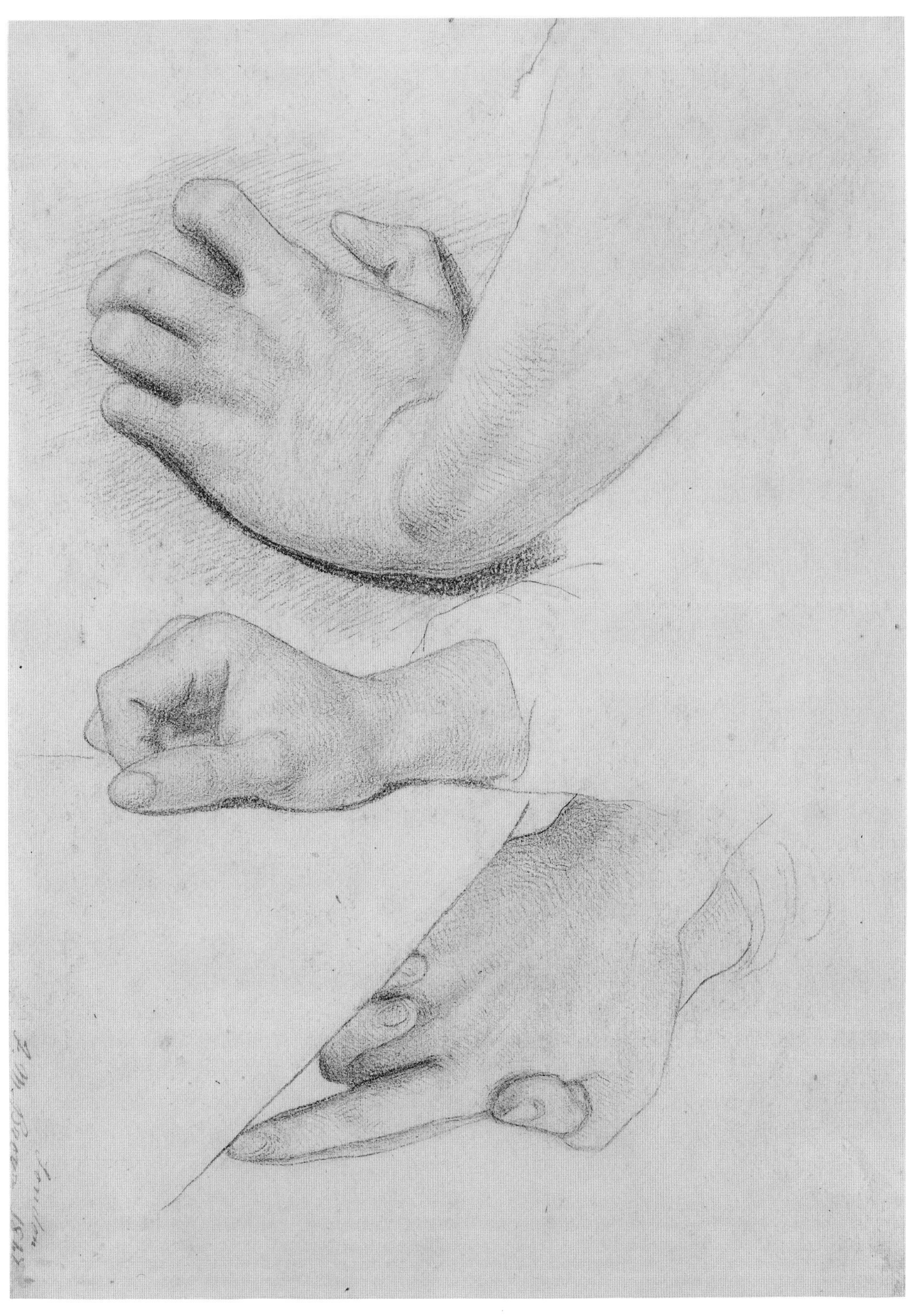

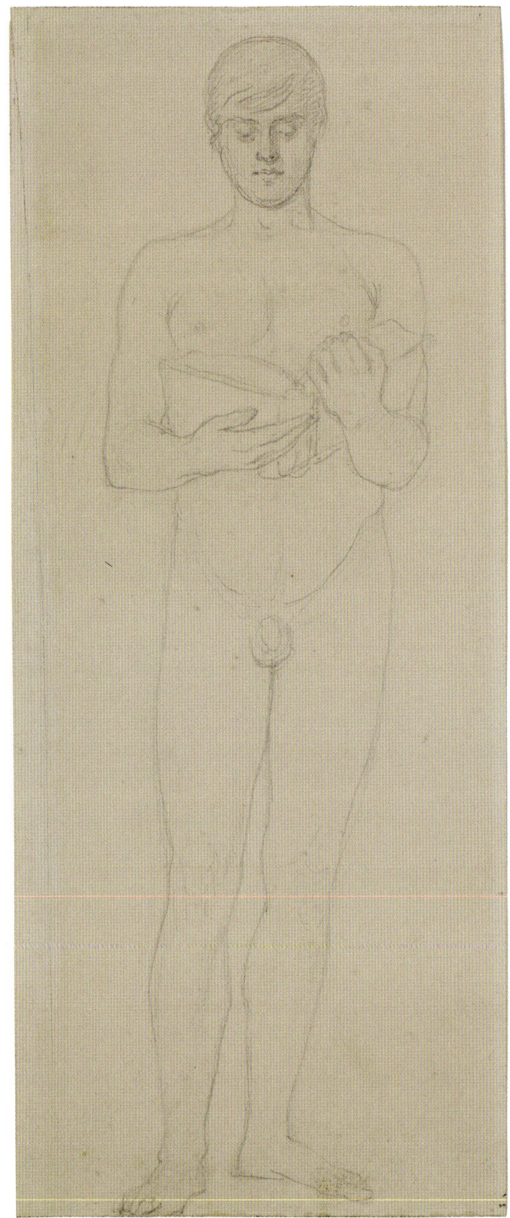

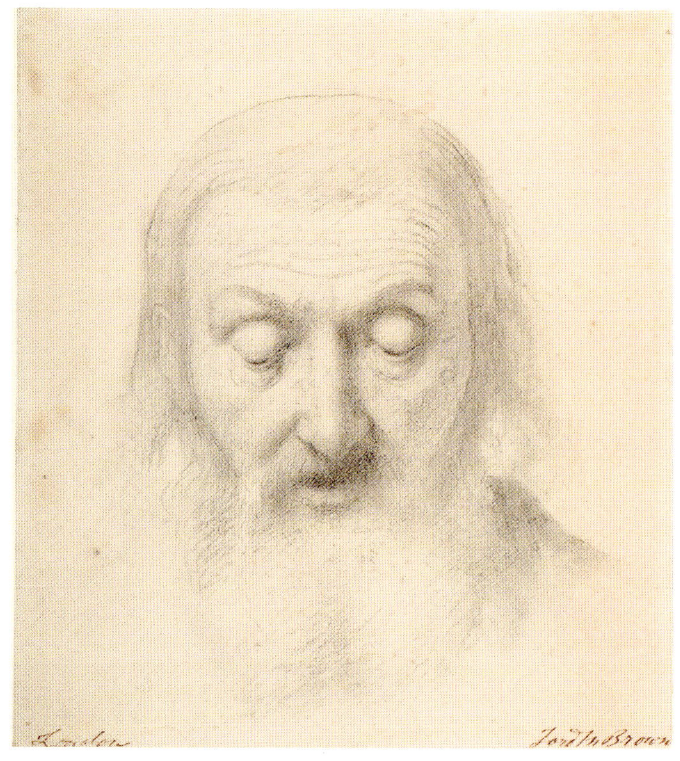

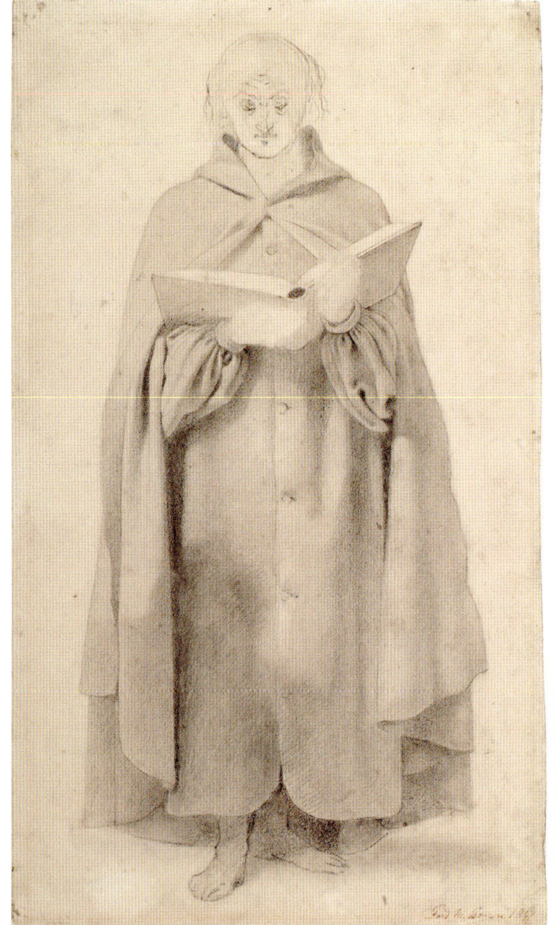

ABOVE LEFT: *Wycliffe reading his Translation of the Bible: Nude Study of Wycliffe*, 1847 (cat. 13)

ABOVE: *Wycliffe reading his Translation of the Bible: Head of Wycliffe*, 1847 (cat. 15)

LEFT: *Wycliffe reading his Translation of the Bible: Drapery Study of Wycliffe*, 1847 (cat. 14)

RIGHT: *Academic Study of a nude Man with Moustache and Arms folded*, 1846–49 (cat. 11)

BELOW: *Chaucer at the Court of Edward III: Nude Studies for Figures of Byron, Burns and Shakespeare*, 1845 (cat. 9)

BELOW RIGHT: *Study of a Statue of the 'Discobolus'*, 1845 (cat. 10)

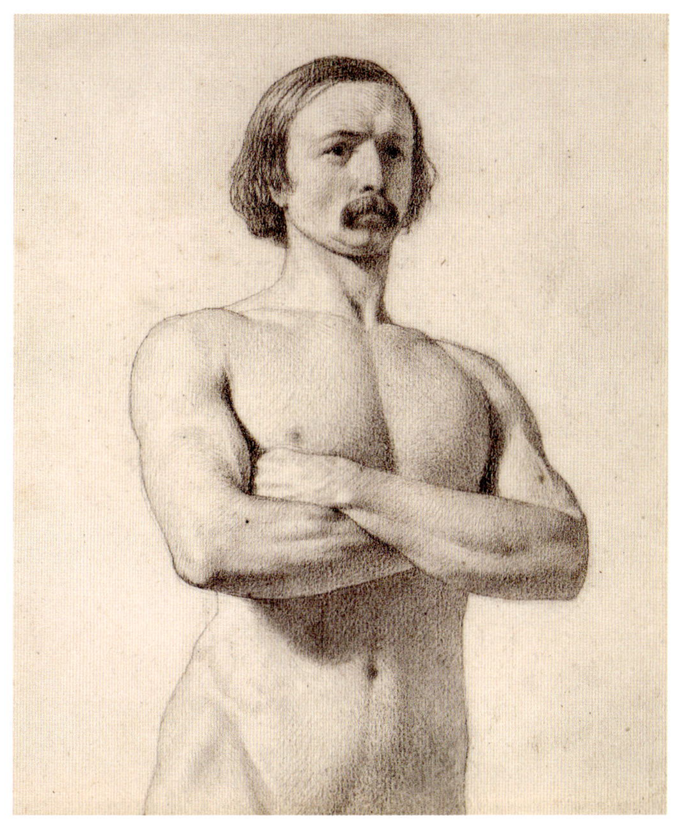

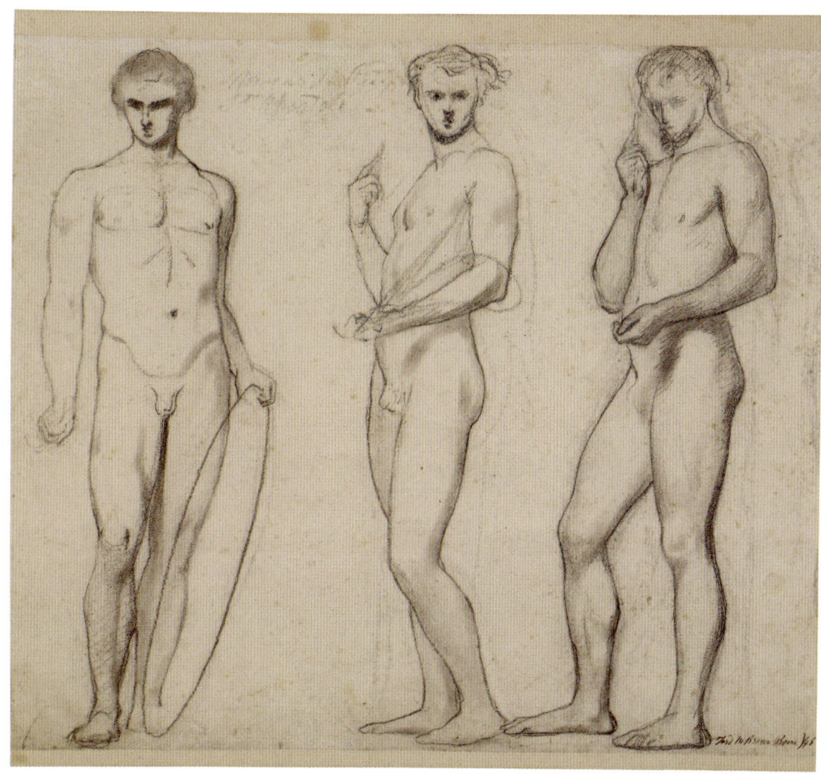

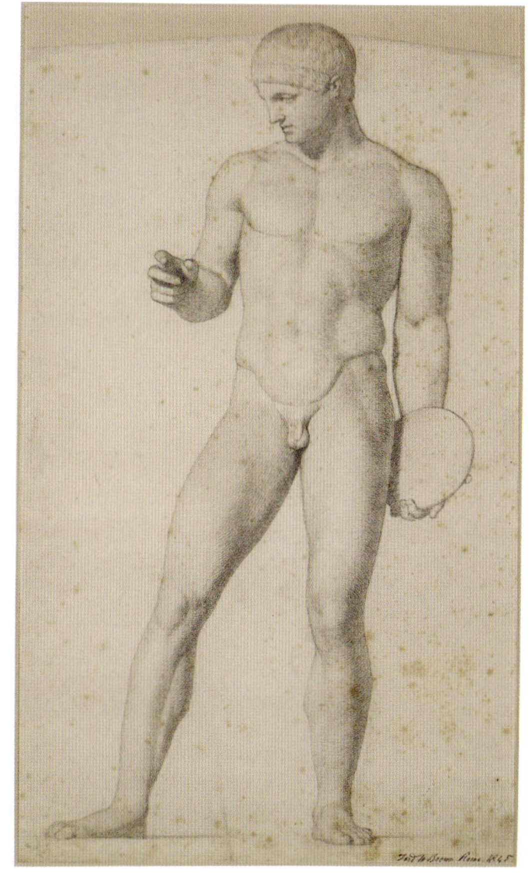

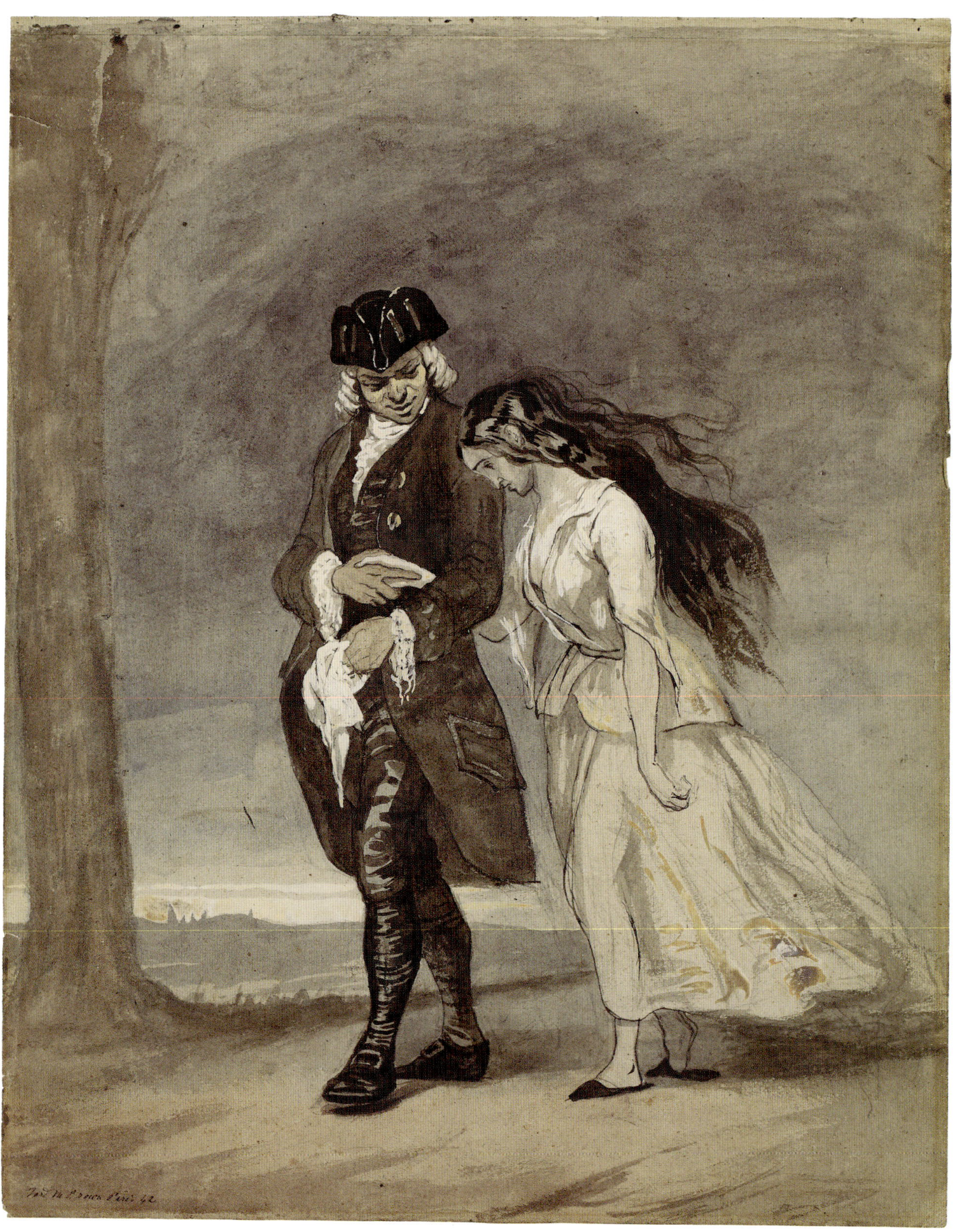

Sterne's ' Sentimental Journey': Yorick and Maria Walking, 1842 (cat. 1)

1. *Sterne's 'Sentimental Journey': Yorick and Maria Walking*, 1842

Pen and ink, watercolour and bodycolour over pencil; 561 × 439 mm
Insc. bl.: *Ford M Brown Paris 42*
Lit.: *Bennett*, C11
Exh.: *Grafton*, 1897 (175); *Huit Siècles de Vie Britannique à Paris*, Musée Gallieria, Paris, 1948 (585); *Ford Madox Brown*, 1964 (48)
1906P796

This watercolour is more familiarly known under the title *Sterne and Maria Walking*, referring to the author's own association with the character of Yorick. There is also the further physical resemblance to Sterne, though the watercolour actually depicts the characters of Yorick and Maria, reunited, walking together towards Moulines. It was one of the most popular scenes in the novel, and had previously been painted by Joseph Wright of Derby and Angelica Kaufmann. Brown's figure of Maria plays up the pathos of the scene; her expression is meek and sad, her body fragile and languid. She wears slippers, not mentioned in the text, which combined with her loose dishevelled hair add to Sterne's depiction of her as slightly unstable.

Brown has also caught the ambiguity of Sterne's portrayal of Yorick as 'sentimental' and good-hearted but also slightly 'sleazy' and bawdy. Here he kindly escorts the unfortunate Maria from her poplar, seen on the left, but her beauty and moving story have drawn him to her, and the reader. His expression appears concerned but there is the faintest glimmer of a grin as well.

Although he later became better known as a painter of British history and modern life, Brown continued to paint works with literary subjects, often based on compositions first produced as book illustrations.

2. *Sketch of Lear questioning Cordelia*, 1844

Sepia pen and ink over pencil; 201 × 277 mm (s.)
Insc. on verso: *Alfred the Great/ Compositional Sketches*
Lit.: *Hueffer*, p. 37; *Whitley*, p. 29; *Bennett*, C13
Exh.: *Shakespeare in Pictures*, Ulster Museum, Belfast, 1964 (4)
1906P754

In 1844, whilst living in Paris, Brown created a set of eighteen drawings to illustrate Shakespeare's tragic play *King Lear*. The majority of these drawings are now at the Whitworth Art Gallery, University of Manchester, but BMAG holds four related sheets of sketches. This sheet depicts the early scene in which Lear questions Cordelia's love for him. Already the vitality and zeal of the series is apparent in Lear's intense glare and the strong diagonal pose which cuts across the centre of the composition. Although the basic poses of the main characters remain the same, the position of the map, the extravagant design of the throne and the prominence of the intermediary figure, most likely representing Kent, are altered in the final version.

On the left is a pencil sketch of Goneril and Regan for the third drawing in the series *Cordelia parting from her Sisters*. The finished drawing for this scene is also in the Whitworth, and became the basis for Brown's first printed illustration published in *The Germ*, 1850 (cat. 24). In the top left corner is another pencil sketch of a female figure restrained by two figures either side of her, faintly drawn. This does not appear to have been used in the drawings but may have been an early idea for a group of figures depicting Cordelia being led away from her father.

On the reverse are sketches for *Alfred the Great*, perhaps inspired by the competition to redecorate the new Houses of Parliament, but never realised.

3. *Sketches of Lear imagining his unfaithful Daughters' Trial* and *Lear in the Storm*, 1844

Sepia pen and ink over pencil; 440 × 280 mm
Insc. on verso: *Alfred the Great/ FMB*
Lit.: *Hueffer*, p. 37; *Whitley*, p. 30; *Bennett*, C29
Exh.: *Shakespeare in Pictures*, Ulster Museum, Belfast, 1964 (4)
1906P755

This sheet of paper has been divided in half by Brown and contains sketches for two scenes from *King Lear*. The top sketch is for the scene in which Lear imagines himself at his unfaithful daughters' trial. It shows Lear standing by the farmhouse, symbolised by the two servants and the cooking pot, pointing with his right hand and holding onto his faithful courtier Kent. On the left are two seated figures in pencil representing Edgar and the Fool.

The lower half of the paper is a study for *Lear in the Storm*. Lear stands with his arms above his head and his clothes billowing out behind him. To the left is a faint pencil sketch of the Fool. Both of these figures are more fully developed in the final version at the Whitworth. On the back of this sheet of drawings are further sketches for *Alfred the Great*, and studies of two putti for the wings of *The Seeds and Fruits of English Poetry*, both in chalk.

4. *Sketch for Cordelia at the Bedside of Lear (Lear's Awakening)*, 1844

Sepia pen and ink over pencil; 152 × 232 mm
Insc. br.: *Ford M Brown Paris/ 44*
Lit.: *Whitley*, p. 30; *Bennett*, C31
Exh.: *Shakespeare in Pictures*, Ulster Museum, Belfast, 1964 (4)
1906P757

The drawing depicts the scene in which Cordelia returns from France to aid her ailing father. It was the first in the series to become a major painting, *Cordelia at the Bedside of Lear*, but it was not exhibited with the other drawings in Brown's solo exhibition in 1865. The composition for the realised painting, in the Tate collection (1849–54), is similar, but significantly Lear is now awake to register Cordelia at the foot of his bed. The scene is also set more definitely in a tent by the sea.

5. *List of historical Names and Dates over Sketches of King Alfred*, 1844–50

Pencil; sepia writing over pencil on verso; 175 × 112 mm
Lit.: *Bennett*, A32
Found unaccessioned (1978P513)

This page from one of Brown's notebooks reveals much about how he approached his paintings and his desire to be historically accurate in his work. It records a list of key historical figures from the medieval period and important dates relating to them. These notes were likely to have been made as Brown began working on *Chaucer at the Court of Edward III*. They may have been jotted down when undertaking research at the British Museum or, as his diary suggests, when he was in Rome and had access to the library of the English Academy. There he was able to procure 'the works and life of our first poet and fortunately … found that the facts known respecting him perfectly admitted of the idea … already conceived of the subject to wit, Chaucer reading his poëms to Edward the 3rd & his court bringing in other noted characters such as the black prince etc'.

6. *Costume Studies: French and Italian thirteenth- and fourteenth-century Costumes (Seven Drawings)*, 1845

Sepia pen and ink on tracing paper; 338 × 220 mm
Insc. bl.: *Rome/ 45*
Lit.: *Whitley*, p. 47; Roger Smith, 'Bonnard's "Costume Historique" – a
    Pre-Raphaelite Source Book', *Costume*, 1973, issue 7, pp. 28–37; Roy
    Strong, *And When Did You Last See Your Father?* (London, Thames and
    Hudson, 1978), p. 58; *Bennett*, A40.1
1906P737

These drawings also appear to relate to books from the library of the English Academy in Rome. Roger Smith has identified one of the sourcebooks for Brown's medieval pictures as Camille Bonnard's two-volume *Costume Historique* (1829–30), the origin of most of the figures in this drawing. Brown has copied the illustrations of Petrarch, Cimabue, a young Frenchman, and pages in thirteenth- and fourteenth-century costume. The hood from the figure of Cimabue was used for the seated man with his back towards the viewer in the foreground of *Chaucer at the Court of Edward III*. The head of the Count of Flanders in the top right hand corner of the same painting is a copy of an illustration in J. R. Planché's *British Costume: A Complete History of the Dress of the Inhabitants of the British Isles* (1834). Such sourcebooks were increasingly popular in the nineteenth century and were often written specifically to aid artists in their search for historical accuracy.

7. *Chaucer at the Court of Edward III: Early compositional Study*, 1845

Pencil with sepia ink frame outline; 330 × 240 mm
Insc. bl.: *[F] M Brown Rome/ 45*
Lit.: *Hueffer*, ill. p. 447ff.; *Whitley*, p. 31; Keith Andrews, *The Nazarenes: A
    Brotherhood of German Painters* (Oxford, Clarendon Press, 1964), pp.
    81, 130, pl. 72b; *Rabin*, p. 98, pl. 44; *Bennett*, A40.11
Exh.: *Grafton*, 1897 (190?); *Aberystwyth*, 1956 (40); *Visions* (7)
1906P681

In 1845 Ford Madox Brown began an enormous triptych, *The Seeds and Fruits of English Poetry*. The wings were a celebration of English poets and portrayed the figures of Milton, Spenser, Shakespeare, Byron, Pope and Burns, with medallions representing Goldsmith and Thomson. The central panel depicted an imagined scene from the life of Chaucer in which he reads 'The Legend of Custance' to Edward III and his household. The wings were later discarded and the central panel became *Chaucer at the Court of Edward III* (Art Gallery of New South Wales, Sydney).

This is one of two very early compositional studies at BMAG for the central panel (see also B15). It is interesting to see how soon Brown settled on the design, as many of the figures in this early drawing appear almost unchanged in the painting. It is difficult to tell which of the two BMAG drawings is the earlier. This study is the slightly more finished of the two, although the

Gothic arch is less visible, and more figures are depicted than in the earlier version. These include the cardinal and the man in medieval hood on the left, preparatory studies for which are also at BMAG (B27 and cat. 12).

8. *Chaucer at the Court of Edward III: Eight early Studies of Figures and Hands*, 1845

Pencil; 280 × 436 mm
Insc. br.: *Ford M Brown Rome/ 45*
Lit.: *Whitley*, p. 33; *Bennett*, A40.17
1906P766

This is an early sheet of studies for the central panel of *The Seeds and Fruits of English Poetry*. It shows Brown working out various characters and their poses using life models, and was executed in 1845 whilst he was living in Rome. Faint writing on the sheet may represent the names and addresses of models used during his stay in Italy. The main study on the left is for the figure of Edward III. Brown used the same elderly model for the figures of two courtiers that appear in the painting, and BMAG also holds drapery studies relating to these figures (B28–B29).

The hand studies, the figure of the page slumped over, and the head of a man wearing a crown of leaves do not appear to have been used in the final version.

9. *Chaucer at the Court of Edward III: Nude Studies for Figures of Byron, Burns and Shakespeare*, 1845

Black chalk; 294 × 328 mm
Insc. br.: *Ford M Brown Rome/ 45*
Lit.: *Whitley*, p. 32; *Bennett*, A40.18
1906P705

These life studies are for the full-length figures of Byron, Burns and Shakespeare from the wings of *The Seeds and Fruits of English Poetry*. The blockish simplicity of the nudes is unusual in Brown's oeuvre and suggests that he was inspired by the muscularity of the classical sculpture he saw in Rome.

10. *Study of a Statue of the 'Discobolus'*, 1845

Black chalk; 435 × 254 mm (s.)
Insc. br.: *Ford M Brown Rome 1845*
Lit.: *Whitley*, p. 46; *Bennett*, C32
1906P718

In 1845 Ford Madox Brown travelled to Italy for the health of his first wife, Elizabeth. Whilst in Rome he took advantage of the wealth of great art available to him. As this drawing shows he was extremely impressed by classical sculpture and made this drawing of a *Discobolus* (*Discophoros*). It is a Roman copy of a fifth-century BC Greek statue of which there are versions in the Louvre, the British Museum and the Vatican. In Rome, Brown met the artists Peter Cornelius and Friedrich Overbeck, who were members of the German art group known as the Nazarenes. He was influcnced by their imitation of early Italian Renaissance art and his encounters with them in Rome radically changed his approach to colouring and artistic style.

11. *Academic Study of a nude Male with Moustache and Arms folded*, 1846–49

Black chalk; 172 × 142 mm
Lit.: *Whitley*, p. 48, *Diary*, pp. 15, 24–27ff.; *Bennett*, C36
Exh.: *Exposed: The Victorian Nude*, Tate Britain, London, 2001–2 (25)
1906P708

In 1847 Ford Madox Brown began attending life classes run by his friend and fellow artist, Charles Lucy (1814–73) at Tudor Lodge in Mornington Crescent, Camden, and at the Dickinson Brothers Drawing Academy at 18½ Maddox Street, London. This drawing is one of four highly finished academic nudes by Brown in the BMAG collection (B96–B99). Together they show the range of poses set by the instructor to show off the muscular bodies of the models. Working-class men were sought for these models as their strenuous jobs provided them with toned bodies resembling classical sculptures.

A large number of artists attended these classes, which must have become a social meeting place. Despite his academic training in Belgium, Brown appears to have felt the need to attend such lessons, as suggested in a frustrated diary entry for 12 January 1848:

> …drew all day at the canvas. Lucy came to go to Dickinson's with me, found I was making my figures of Chaucer and Gower [for *Wycliffe reading his Translation of the Bible*] to short, quite took me aback. Went & began a pencil drawing at Dickinson's walked home with Lucy, came back and bought a bottle of wiskey to drown care with.

12. *Chaucer at the Court of Edward III: Study of a Man in medieval Hood*, 1847

Black chalk; 209 × 170 mm
Insc. br.: *Ford M Brown London/ 47*
Lit.: *Whitley*, p. 35; *Diary*, p. 7; *Bennett*, A40.24
1906P777

The hood is based on the illustration of the Count of Flanders in *British Costume: A Complete History of the Dress of the Inhabitants of the British Isles* by J. R. Planché, published in 1834 and reprinted in 1847 and 1874. Brown copied the hood and liripipe from Planché onto a sheet that is also in the BMAG collection (cat. 6). On 25 September 1847 he noted, 'got up Early – & got to work late, fumbled till 12 o'clock over the Hood of the left hand corner figure of the "knight" made a lirlipipe for it.' The next day he 'finished the drawing of the Hood & a drawing of the cloak for one of the Men next to him, "the chamberlain"'.

13. *Wycliffe reading his Translation of the Bible: Nude Study of Wycliffe*, 1847

Pencil; 253 × 104 mm
Lit.: *Whitley*, p. 41; *Bennett*, A48.13
Exh.: *Ford Madox Brown*, 1964 (56)
1906P730

At the end of November 1847 Brown realised that he would not complete his ambitious triptych *The Seeds and Fruits of English Poetry* in time for the following year's Free Exhibition. Whilst travelling home from his uncle's house in Foot's Cray, Kent, he devised a completely new composition, 'Wycliff reading his translation of the bible to John of Gaunt, Chaucer and Gower Present [and] arranged it in [his mind].' On reaching home he 'made a slight scetch of it'.

Although his diary is inconsistent, kept for two years then put aside and taken up for a few months and put away again, *Wycliffe* is one of the few paintings whose progress and completion is recorded in full. It gives insight into Brown's early research at the British Museum and the books consulted, as well as the models he used, and the hours worked. The drawings for *Wycliffe* held at BMAG are studies made at various times in the months November 1847 to April 1848, when Brown worked on the project, before drawing directly or tracing onto the canvas.

This is a nude study for the central figure of Wycliffe. It depicts a young man, whereas in the finished work Wycliffe is old and has a beard. This discrepancy reveals that Brown made use of professional nude models to help him find the correct pose of a figure before adding clothes. The model for the nude drawing might have been a man named 'Garret', recorded as having posed for 'sketches of Wycliff' on 20 December 1847.

14. *Wycliffe reading his Translation of the Bible: Drapery Study of Wycliffe*, 1847

Black chalk on pinkish paper; 358 × 203 mm (i. and p.)
Insc. br.: *Ford M Brown 1847*
Lit.: *Whitley*, p. 39; *Diary*, pp. 21–23; *Bennett*, A48.14
Exh.: *Ford Madox Brown*, 1964 (55)
1906P699

The face of this drapery study for Wycliffe has been drawn from the imagination and the figure has no hands. It is therefore likely that it was done from a lay figure in order to save money and keep the folds of cloth completely still. Brown's diary describes the long hours he spent arranging the cloth in exactly the right position, and hiring or buying lay models. On 28 December 1847, he 'tried to work did nothing all day but arrange the lay figure for Wicif [sic] & superintended the making of a gown for Chaucer, I am sadly idle'. The following day he worked again 'at arranging the dress of Wicliff' and 'muddled at a drawing of it till ½ past 2'. After a break for New Year he records that he finally 'drew at the draperies of Wicliff till ½ past 3, finished the study, went out for a walk'.

15. *Wycliffe reading his Translation of the Bible: Head of Wycliffe*, 1847

Pencil; 144 × 126 mm
Insc. bl.: *London*, br.: *Ford M Brown*
Lit.: *Hueffer*, ill. p. 447ff.; *Whitley*, p. 39; *Newman and Watkinson*, pl. 71; *Bennett*, A48.18
Exh.: *Ford Madox Brown*, 1964 (54)
1906P670

This detailed drawing of an old man is a study for Wycliffe, and was possibly drawn from a model called 'Old Coulton'.

16. *Wycliffe reading his Translation of the Bible: Study of John of Gaunt and Chaucer's left Hand*, 1847

Pencil and black chalk; 240 × 175 mm
Insc. br.: *(London)/ F.M Brown/ 47*
Lit.: *Whitley*, p. 40; *Bennett*, A48.11
Exh.: *Ford Madox Brown*, 1964 (58)
1906P725

This is one of two drawings of John of Gaunt which shows the figure first nude and then clothed. These studies reveal much about Brown's working process. He began, as taught in the art academies of Belgium, by making studies of nude models in order to get the correct anatomical details of the pose. He then drew the model clothed. This method was believed to make the figure more exact and was a process that had been practised since the Renaissance. The hand study is for the left hand of Chaucer who stands next to the poet Gower.

17. *Wycliffe reading his Translation of the Bible: Studies of Hands for John of Gaunt and Gower*, 1847

Black chalk; 151 × 215 mm
Insc. br.: *London/ F. M. Brown 1847*
Lit.: *Whitley*, p. 41; *Bennett*, A48.17
1906P746

Many of the drawings in the BMAG collection are carefully observed hand studies, including this sheet for John of Gaunt and Gower, two of the main characters in *Wycliffe*. It is a good example of Brown's economic use of paper, making all three drawings fit on one sheet, though the paper must be turned to find the correct position of the hands as they appear in the painting.

18. *Chaucer at the Court of Edward III: Drapery Study for Robert Burns*, 1848

Black chalk; 290 × 165 mm
Insc. br.: *Ford M Brown London/ 48*
Lit.: *Whitley*, p. 33; *Bennett*, A40.48
1906P745

This rather abstract-looking drapery study shows the intensity of Brown's preparations for a painting and his close observation of minute details such as the fall of the fabric. This is a study for the full-length figure of Robert Burns, one of the poets from the wings of *The Seeds and Fruits of English Poetry* which later became *Chaucer at the Court of Edward III*. At the top Brown has added lines to indicate Burn's tartan sash.

19. *Chaucer at the Court of Edward III: Drapery Study for the Black Prince*, 1848

Black chalk with touches of white; 206 × 165 mm
Insc. bl.: *Ford M Brown London/ 48*
Lit.: *Whitley*, p. 36; *Diary*, p. 41; *Bennett*, A40.43
1906P783

BMAG holds two drapery studies for the Black Prince which were done three years apart (see also B52). Brown put aside *Chaucer at the Court of Edward III* while working on several other pictures but took it up again in 1850. This chalk drawing is the earliest of the two studies and it is likely that Brown is referring to it when he notes in his diary that he used a model named 'Maitland & made a drawing of the surcoat of black Prince'.

20. *The Infant's Repast: Study of Mother and Child with separate Arm and Leg Studies of the Child*, 1848

Black chalk with grey wash; 253 × 175 mm
Insc. br.: *Ford Madox Brown London/ 48*
Lit.: *Work*, 1865, p. 5; *Twelve Pre-Raphaelite Drawings* (London, Methuen and Co., 1925), pl. 10; *Whitley*, p. 45; *Diary*, p. 27ff.; *Bennett*, A50.3
Exh.: *Grafton*, 1897 (189); *National Gallery British Art*, 1911–12 (4?); *Pre-Raphaelite Art*, Australian State Galleries, 1962 (5); *Artists of Victoria's England*, Cummer Gallery of Art, Jacksonville, Florida, 1965 (6); *Visions* (9)
1906P679

This study is for a small painting exhibited at the British Institution in 1851 under the title *The Young Mother* but also known as *The Infant's Repast* or *Mother and Child*. The surviving oil sketch now at Wightwick Manor, Wolverhampton, depicts a young mother in eighteenth-century costume nursing her child, watched by the family's spaniel. Brown summed up the subject in his 1865 solo exhibition catalogue by saying, '"doggy is jealous", this little picture, I think, needs no explanation. Never re-touched'.

A paid model, Mrs Ashley, and her own baby were used for this drawing. Brown records that she began to sit for *The Infant's Repast* on 13 October. A week later he had 'made a drawing of the head of Mrs Ashley', and on 26 and 30 October 'drew a study of childs head sucking' and 'worked 4 hours from Mrs Ashley & child, made drawing of the legs & arm etc.' The latter drawings may well be those on this sheet of studies with a close-up of the baby and separate studies of its legs and arms. Mrs Ashley continued to sit for him until February 1849.

The main inspiration appears to have been Charles West Cope's painting *The Young Mother*, exhibited at the Royal Academy in 1846 (oil on panel, V&A). The two versions of the subject are virtually the same size and share the full-length profile composition. In fact they are so similar that Brown must have seen it as an opportunity to both outdo an artistic rival and indulge his love of eighteenth-century subjects, clothing the mother in his favourite period costume rather than contemporary dress.

21. *Head Study of Daniel Casey (Full-Face)*, 1848

Black chalk; 250 × 175 mm
Insc. br.: *Ford M Brown/ 48*
Lit.: *Whitley*, p. 46; *Andrea Rose*, 1981, ill. p. 19; *Hong Kong*, 1984, p. 32; *Diary*, p. 44; *Newman and Watkinson*, p. 41; *Bennett*, B59. 2
1906P721

This is one of two studies at BMAG traditionally said to be of the Irish artist Daniel Casey, made during the 1848 Paris visit and finished in London for a now lost portrait of Casey (see also B122). This striking full-face pose is reminiscent of Dürer's *Self-Portrait* at twenty-eight. Made when Casey was the same age, Brown may have wanted to highlight his friend's artistic genius. In her forthcoming catalogue, however, Mary Bennett speculates that these portraits may not be of Casey. She suggests, in correspondence with the organisers of this exhibition, that the three-quarter head may be for the figure of Shakespeare in *The Seeds and Fruits of English Poetry*. However, as she points out, 'Fairfax Murray surely saw the Casey Self-Portrait in the artist's executive sale 1894' and made the initial identification. 'It's a puzzle.'

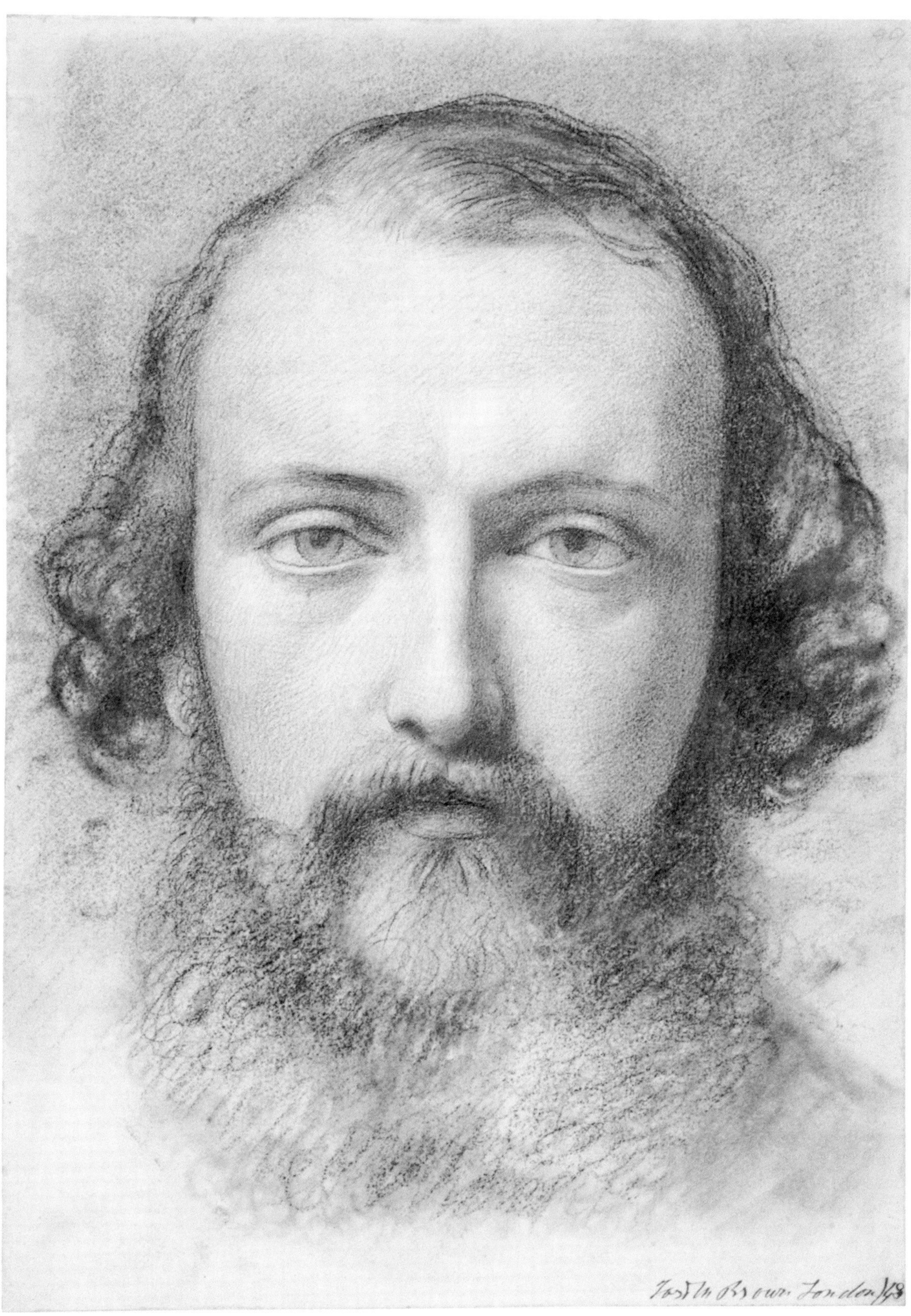

*Head Study of
Daniel Casey (Full-
Face)*, 1848 (cat. 21)

22. *Head Study of Emma Hill (later Mrs Madox Brown)*, 1848

Black chalk; 104 × 100 mm
Insc. br.: *F.M.B. / Xmas /48*
Lit.: *Whitley*, p. 48; *Rabin*, pp. 138–39, pl. 56; *The Pre-Raphaelites*, 1984, p. 256; Jan Marsh, *Pre-Raphaelite Sisterhood* (London, Quartet Books, 1985), pl. 1; *Newman and Watkinson*, p. 45; *Bennett*, A51.3
Exh.: *National Gallery British Art*, 1911–12 (33); *Ford Madox Brown*, 1964 (1); *Pre-Raphaelite Women*, BMAG, 1985–86 (2)
1906P789

This portrait of Emma Hill, who later became Madox Brown's second wife, was made around Christmas in 1848. It was drawn soon after Brown hired Emma as his model.

Brown's diary for 1848 is full of entries that record their early courtship. On 10 February he wrote, 'Began the veil of Cordelia, only laid in part of it when a girl as loves me came in & disturbed me'. On 23 February he was distracted again, 'arranged the Drapery of Lear, could not get it right, tried at it till three oclock, then Miss Stone came in & I did nothing more'. By 8 July Emma stops using her mother's maiden name of Stone and Madox Brown records, 'cleaned brushes – waited in vain for E to come back from the country'.

Although this is a portrait of Emma, it is also highly likely to have been a head study for Brown's painting *Cordelia at the Bedside of Lear* (Tate). Only the slightly open mouth is different but this appears to have recorded a particular facial feature of Emma's. Many of Brown's portraits show that her top lip naturally curled up to reveal her teeth (cat. 28, 29, 33).

23. *Young Woman in eighteenth-century Costume: Two Studies*, 1849

Pencil, laid down onto card; 375 × 232 mm
Insc. br.: *Ford M Brown London/ 49*
Lit.: *Twelve Pre-Raphaelite Drawings* (London, Methuen and Co., 1925), pl. 4; *Whitley*, p. 45; *Bennett*, A53
Exh.: *Grafton*, 1897 (173); *Pre-Raphaelite Drawings*, Arts Council Gallery, Cambridge, 1953 (4); *Artists of Victoria's England*, Cummer Gallery of Art, Jacksonville, Florida, 1965 (5)
1906P677

The eighteenth-century costume worn in these drawings of a young woman is almost certainly that worn by the young mother in Brown's painting *Infant's Repast* which he was finishing in January and February 1849. It is possible that Mrs Ashley, the model for *Infant's Repast*, also sat for these studies (see cat. 20 and B80). In these drawings the model sits awkwardly in an armchair, giving the impression of being restless and uncomfortable. If she was indeed Mrs Ashley, Brown's first description of her, in his diary, as someone who 'let the fire out 3 times & talked all day' seems rather apt for the fidgety woman depicted here.

24. *King Lear: Cordelia parting from her Sisters (The Germ: Art and Poetry)*, March 1850

Reprinted volume 1901
Etching; 178 × 222 (i.), 223 × 268 (p.)
Insc. etched under image: *Goneril: Regan: Lear: Fool: Cordelia: France:*
Lit: *Hueffer*, pp. 74, 98; *Diary*, pp. 71, 80; *Casteras*, 1991, p. 43ff.; *Engen*, p. 12ff.; *Goldman*, p. 9ff.; *Suriano*, pp. 63, 306; *Bennett*, D4
Inventoried in 1979 (1979P217.4)

This illustration accompanied William Michael Rossetti's poem *Cordelia* in the short-lived Pre-Raphaelite magazine *The Germ*. It was based on the earlier drawing *Cordelia parting from her Sisters* made in 1844. In this etching Brown includes the figure of the Fool writhing around Lear's deserted throne and has changed the background so that Lear and his retinue walk upstairs into the open rather than down a long corridor. His diary records the long hours spent on the work in the last week of March, when in just two days he worked twenty-one hours on the etching.

25. *Chaucer at the Court of Edward III: Two Studies of the Head of an old Woman*, 1851

Black chalk; 265 × 151 mm
Insc. br.: *Ford M Brown London / 51*
Lit.: *Whitley*, p. 36; *Bennett*, A40.52
Exh.: *National Gallery British Art*, 1911–12 (10); *Brussels*, 1929 (17); *English Eye I*, Midlands Federation Travelling Exhibition, 1958 (3)
1906P787

These two studies were actually used for the faces of two old men in Brown's painting *Chaucer at the Court of Edward III*. He used the face of an old woman looking down for the man sitting nearest the lectern on the left of the painting, and her face in profile for the old man with a beard on the far left. This study was completed in 1851: the same year that the painting was finished. Brown must have wanted to study an elderly person and found that the effect he wanted to copy was not dependent on the sex of the sitter.

26. *Chaucer at the Court of Edward III: Watercolour Version*, c. 1851

Watercolour with bodycolour; 365 × 386 mm
Lit.: *Rabin*, pp. 106–9, pl. 50; *Diary*, p. 74; *Bennett*, A40.2
Exh.: *Manchester*, 1911 (53, lent by J. R. Holliday); *Aberystwyth*, 1956 (41); *British Watercolours from Birmingham*, Arts Council of England Touring Exhibition, 1980–81 (57); *BMAG*, 1991 (92)
Bequeathed by J. R. Holliday, 1927 (1927P356)

Watercolour was a relatively unusual medium for Madox Brown, and here he intriguingly focuses on the top half of the *Chaucer at the Court of Edward III* composition. The drawing in fact only gives a suggestion of an arched frame rather than the completed arch of the realised painting. Instead of a vertical shape the measurements are nearly a square, with particularly regular paper edges by any standards. Mary Bennett discusses the problems relating to the two versions documented in Brown's diary, the first oil sketch given to Dr John Marshall and now in the Ashmolean Museum, Oxford, and the second sold to Brown's artist friend, Mark Anthony. The second sketch is referred to as measuring 20 × 13½ inches and is known to have been retouched by Brown, which implies that it is not the Birmingham version. The finished nature of this watercolour may even suggest that it is a contemporary version after Madox Brown. This debate should not however detract one from recognising the freshness and confidence that has been applied to a complex figurative composition. The profile that appears to be of Emma Hill in the right foreground dates the scene from at least 1848 when she first met Brown.

27. *The Pretty Baa-Lambs*, 1851–59

Oil on panel; 610 × 762 mm
Insc.: *F Madox Brown 1851–59*
Lit: *Work*, 1865, pp. 6–7; *Hueffer*, p. 74ff.; W. M. Rossetti, *Pre-Raphaelite Diaries and Letters* (London, 1900, reissued 1974), pp. 108–14; William Holman Hunt, *Pre-Raphaelitism*, 1905, I , p. 277; *Diary*, p. 74ff.; *Rabin*, pp. 206–14; Sara Cornell, *Art: A History of Changing Style* (Oxford, Phaidon, 1983), p. 342; *Newman and Watkinson*, pp. 58–61ff.; *Bendiner*, p. 135; Allen Staley, *The Pre-Raphaelite Landscape*, 2nd edn (New Haven, CT, and London, Yale University Press, 2001), p. 22ff.; Joyce H. Townsend, Jacqueline Ridge and Stephen Hackney, *Pre-Raphaelite Painting Techniques* (London, Tate Publishing, 2004), pp. 128–33; *Bennett*, A55
Exh: Royal Academy, 1852 (1291); *Works by Living Artists*, Academy of Arts, Newcastle upon Tyne, 1852 (55); *Works by Modern Artists*, St Enoch's Hall, Glasgow, 1854–55 (241); Liverpool Academy, 1859 (3); *Work*, 1865 (11); *A Pre-Raphaelite Collection*, Goupil Gallery, 1896 (11); *Ford Madox Brown*, 1964 (22); *Romantic Art in Britain: Paintings and Drawings 1760–1860*, Detroit Institute of Arts, 1968 (212); *Paintings in the Leathart Collection*, Laing Art Gallery, Newcastle upon Tyne, 1968 (17); Royal Academy Bicentenary, 1968–69 (378); *Pre-Raphaelites: Painters and Patrons in the North East*, Laing Art Gallery, Newcastle upon Tyne, 1989–90 (10); *Visions* (18); *Theodor Fontane and the Visual Arts*, Alte Nationalgalerie, Berlin, 1998 (31); *Love, Labour and Loss: 300 Years of British Livestock Farming in Art*, Tullie House Museum and Art Gallery, Carlisle, 2002 (95); *Pre-Raphaelite Vision: Truth to Nature*, Tate Britain, London, 2004 (27)
Prov.: Purchased from the artist by James Leathart 1859, sold 1896; H. Yates Thompson; Mrs E. M. Thompson (sold Sotheby's 27 June 1956, no. 81); bought Colnaghi
Purchased 1956 (1956P9)

Having successfully experimented with depicting women in eighteenth-century costume in previous compositions (see cat. 20 and 23), Brown chose to continue this theme for his first *plein-air* painting. In earlier works he had, like other Pre-Raphaelite artists, painted the landscape outdoors but the figures in the studio. In *The Pretty Baa-Lambs* he posed his models outdoors, wanting to depict on canvas the effect of bright sunlight exactly as he found it in nature. He described the painting process in his diary:

> The baa lamb picture was painted almost entirely in sunlight which twice gave me a fever while painting. I used to take the lay figure out every morning & bring it in at night or if it rained. Emma sat for the lady & Kate for the child. The lambs & sheep used to be brought every morning from Clappam [sic] common in a truck. One of them eat up all the flowers one morning in the garden where they used to behave very ill. The background was painted on the common. The medium I used was Robersons undrying copal (Flake White).

The meaning of the painting remains ambiguous. Brown insisted that 'this picture was painted out in the sunlight; the only intention being to render the effect as well as my powers in a first attempt of this kind would allow'. However, it also combined the theme of motherhood with an interest in the eighteenth century, both of which had preoccupied him in the previous two years.

28. *Portrait of Emma Hill (later Mrs Madox Brown)*, 1852

Pencil; 146 × 132 mm
Insc. br.: *FMB* [monogram] *1852*
Lit.: *Whitley*, p. 48; *Bennett*, B70
(1906P790)

By 1852 Emma had become Brown's favourite model. She had posed in all his main works including *Chaucer*, *The Pretty Baa-Lambs* and *Waiting*. This is a more intimate portrait of her, with the side profile and downward gaze recalling the portrait Brown made of her just after they had met in 1848 (cat. 22).

29. *The Last of England: Portrait of Emma Hill*, 1852

Chalks with scratching out on two sheets of paper; 164 × 177 mm
Insc. bl.: *FMB* [monogram] *Dec 52*
Lit.: *Hueffer*, ill. p. 447ff.; *Twelve English Pre-Raphaelite Drawings*, 1925, pl. 3; *Whitley*, p. 42; *Andrea Rose*, 1981, p. 21; *Newman and Watkinson*, p. 73; *Bennett*, A61.6
Exh.: *British Art*, Royal Academy of Arts, London, 1934 (1251); *English Drawings and Engravings*, Museum Toma Stelian, Bucharest, 1935–36 (37); *Pre-Raphaelite Drawings*, Arts Council Gallery, Cambridge, 1953 (6); *British Portraits*, Royal Academy of Arts, London, 1956–57 (738); *Pre-Raphaelite Art*, Australian State Galleries, 1962 (5); *Ford Madox Brown*, 1964 (72); *The Pre-Raphaelites*, 1984 (179); *Pre-Raphaelite Women*, BMAG, 1985–86 (4); *Visions* (21)
1906P791

This portrait study of Emma was made around Christmas 1852, with Emma continuing to model for *The Last of England* well into the New Year. Brown records Emma 'at the beginning of 53 … coming to sit … in the most inhuman weather from Highgate. This work representing an out door scene without sunlight I painted at it chiefly out of doors when snow was lieing on the ground.'

Whilst working on the painting in 1853 Brown spent four weeks on 'the madder ribbons of the bonnet' which are depicted being blown by the fierce wind. However, in this early head study of Emma, her ribbons are neatly tied and her hair lacks the windswept strands found in both the cartoon and the painting. This suggests that this study was done purely to capture Emma's likeness, which Brown was intent on portraying faithfully. However, capturing it in paint seems to have caused him a considerable amount of trouble, with references in his diary to alterations made because the work appeared 'very bad & made [me] miserable'.

30. *The Last of England: Cartoon*, 1852

Pencil, image edged with brown ink; 408 × 365 mm (oval), 431 × 390 mm (p.)
Insc. br.: *F. MADOX BROWN. 1852.*
Lit.: *Whitley*, p. 42; *Diary*, pp. 79–80ff.; Deborah Cherry, 'An Annotated Edition of the Diary and Selected Letters of Ford Madox Brown 1850–1870', unpublished PhD dissertation, University of London, 1977, p. 272; *Newman and Watkinson*, p. 92; *Barringer*, 2005, pp. 32–34ff.; *Bennett*, A61.5
Exh.: *Work*, 1865 (71); *Pre-Raphaelite Drawings*, Arts Council Gallery, Cambridge, 1953 (5); *English Eye I*, Midlands Federation Travelling Exhibition, 1958 (4); *Pre-Raphaelite Art*, Australian State Galleries, 1962 (4); *Ford Madox Brown*, 1964 (71); *The Pre-Raphaelites*, 1984 (178); *Theodor Fontane and the Visual Arts*, Alte Nationalgalerie, Berlin, 1998 (32); *Visions* (20)
1906P795

This finished preparatory drawing was produced in December 1852, and though close to the final composition it differs in a number of significant details. The painting was originally to be slightly more oval in shape with far fewer figures; only the reprobate, his mother, and the young woman with her arm round the straggly-haired boy from the final composition can be seen in this drawing. The name of the boat carrying the emigrants was altered from 'White Horse Lin[e] of Australi[a]' to the more symbolic 'Eldorado' in the painting (cat. 32). Emma's shawl also changed; she is seen here in a wide checked shawl. Unlike in the final painting, the man has no string attached to his hat, this having been added at the insistence of Brown's dealer D. T. White. In 1855 Brown took up the cartoon again, most likely with a view to selling it.

31. *An English Autumn Afternoon*, 1852–53, 1855

Oil on canvas; 717 × 1346 mm
Insc. bl.: *F. Madox Brown* (red paint)
Lit.: *Hueffer*, pp. 82–83ff.; W. M. Rossetti (ed.), *Pre-Raphaelite Diaries and Letters* (London, Hurst and Blackett Limited, 1900), pp. 111–14ff.; R. Ironside and J. Gere, *Pre-Raphaelite Painters* (Oxford, Phaidon, 1948), p. 23; *Newman and Watkinson*, p. 4ff.; Julius Bryant, 'Madox Brown's English Autumn Afternoon revisited', *Apollo*, July 1997, pp. 41–43; *Bendiner*, p. 21ff.; *Prettejohn*, 2000, p. 89; *Creative Quarters: The Art World in London 1700–2000*, Museum of London, 2001, pp. 78–79; *Bennett*, A60
Exh.: British Institute, 1855 (79); International Exhibition, 1862 (533); *Work*, 1865 (13); *Grafton*, 1897 (59); Wrexham, 1876 (523); Edinburgh, 1886 (899a), *Victorian Life*, Leicester Galleries, London, 1937 (92); *The Pre-Raphaelite Brotherhood*, BMAG, 1947 (7); *Pictures from Birmingham*, Agnew's, London, 1957 (54), Ford Madox Brown, 1964 (28); *Peintures et Aquarelles Anglaises 1700–1900*, Musée des Beaux Arts, Lyon, 1966 (15); *The Pre-Raphaelites*, 1984 (51); *Hong Kong*, 1984 (2); *Art Treasures of England: The Regional Collections*, Royal Academy of Arts, London, 1998 (129); *Pre-Raphaelite Vision: Truth to Nature*, Tate Britain, London, 2004 (29); *British Vision: Observation and Imagination in British Art 1750–1950*, Ghent Museum of Fine Arts, 2007–8 (196)
Prov.: Sent to auction at Phillips by the artist on completion in 1854; bought by R. Dickinson; C. Seddon; the artist; George Rae
Presented by the Public Picture Gallery Fund, 1916 (1916P25)

Many of the 'modern' subjects Brown chose to paint were inspired by places and events from his own life. This scene is a view of Hampstead from the window of Brown's lodgings and reveals his interest in capturing the light on an autumn afternoon. It was begun in October 1852 but took over two years to complete. There are few existing sketches and studies for Brown's landscapes and although there are several landscape paintings at BMAG, there is only one drawing relating to landscape in the collection (B153).

32. *The Last of England*, 1852–55

Oil on panel; 825 × 750 mm
Insc.: *F. Madox Brown 1855*
Lit: *Work*, 1865, pp. 8–9; *Hueffer*, p. 91ff.; Frances Winwar, *Poor Splendid Wings, The Rossettis and their Circle* (Boston, Little Brown and Co., 1933), p. 77ff.; H. C. Collins Baker, *British Painting* (London, Medici Society, 1933), p. 204; R. Ironside and J. Gere, *Pre-Raphaelite Painters* (Oxford, Phaidon, 1948), p. 24; Graham Reynolds, *Painters of the Victorian Scene* (London, B. T. Batsford, 1953), p. 18; *Rabin*, p. 139ff.; *Newman and Watkinson*, pp. 3–4ff.; Pamela Gerrish Nunn, *Problem Pictures: Women and Men in Victorian Painting* (Aldershot, Scolar

Press, 1995), p. 127ff.; *Bendiner*, p. 21ff.; *Prettejohn*, 2000, p.151; *Barringer*, 2005, pp. 32–34ff.; *Bennett*, A61
Exh: Liverpool Academy, 1856; International Exhibition, 1862 (110); *Work*, 1865 (14); Leeds, 1868 (1331); Bradford Art Treasures Exhibition, 1870 (225); Oldham, 1883 (152); Guildhall Art Gallery, London, 1897 (144); *Manchester*, 1911 (64); *National Gallery British Art*, 1911–12 (18); *British Empire Exhibition*, Wembley, 1925 (W6); *Brussels*, 1929 (13); *British Art*, Royal Academy, London, 1934 (557); *200 Years of English Art*, Rijksmuseum, Amsterdam, 1936 (10); *English Painting of the 18th and 19th Centuries*, Louvre, Paris, 1939 (9); *Aberystwyth*, 1956 (5); *Ford Madox Brown*, 1964 (29); *La Peinture Romantique et les Préraphaelites*, Musée du Petit Palais, Paris, 1972 (29); *The Pre-Raphaelites*, 1984 (62); *Exiles and Emigrants: Epic Journeys to Australia in the Victorian Era*, National Gallery of Victoria, Melbourne, 2005–6 (p. 26, ill. p. 27)
Prov.: Bought from the artist by D. T. White 1855; B. G. Windus (before 5 December 1855); sold Christie's 26 March 1859 (45); bought by Gambart; T. E. Plint; sold Christie's, 7 March 1862 (329); bought by Pilgrim; John Crossley, 1865; C. J. Pooley
Purchased in 1891 (1891P24)

Brown began this painting in 1852, inspired by the emigration of his friend, the sculptor Thomas Woolner, to Australia and his own thoughts of emigration to India due to severe financial hardship. The middle-class couple who dominate the oval are portraits of Brown and his future wife Emma Hill. Brown began painting the figures out of doors at the end of 1852, but after six weeks realised that the painting was too detailed to be finished for the 1853 Royal Academy exhibition. He stopped working on it until September 1854. It was finally finished a year later in September 1855, with Brown renting a room to exhibit the completed picture with a few other works including *The Pretty Baa-Lambs*. His dealer, D. T. White, bought it immediately for £150 and the pencil cartoon for £7 (cat. 30), before selling both on to the collector B. G. Windus. The financial boost given by the sale of the picture ended Brown's notions of emigrating to India.

33. *Sketch of Mrs Madox Brown (née Emma Hill)*, 9 May 1854

Pencil; 240 × 155 mm
Insc. br.: *F.M.B. May 9th/ 54*
Lit.: *Whitley*, p. 48; *Bennett*, B37
1906P792

This full-length portrait of Emma seated in her shawl is unusual in Brown's oeuvre. Most often the portraits of his family are quarter-length, creating a more emotionally intense view of the sitter. The Tate has a similar drawing on the back of a quarter-length portrait of Cathy. Again Emma is sitting on a high-backed chair. Brown may well have been making portraits to record his small family. This drawing is dated 9 May 1854, although there does not seem to be any particular relevance attached to this day. By this time, the couple had been married just over a year, and perhaps it was made to commemorate this fact.

34. *The Prisoner of Chillon: Study of a Corpse*, 1856

Pencil; 165 × 280 mm
Insc. br.: *FMB. University Hospital/ Study for prisoner of/ Chillon/ from Corpse FMB*
Lit.: Rev. Robert Avis Willmott, ed., *The Poets of the Nineteenth Century* (London, George Routledge and Co., 1857), p. 111; *Reid*, p. 49; *Whitley*, p. 42; *Diary*, p. 167; *Engen*, pp. 108–9; *Goldman*, p. 10; *Bennett*, C44.3
Exh.: *Ford Madox Brown*, 1964 (78); *Death, Heaven and the Victorians*, Brighton Museum and Art Gallery, 1970 (47); *Byron*, Victoria and Albert Museum, London, 1974 (S25); *Lord Byron*, Biblioteca Classense, Ravenna, 1988 (fig. 103, no cat.); *Visions* (37); *The Quick and the Dead: Artists and Anatomy*, Royal College of Art, London, 1997–98 (37); *Exposed: The Victorian Nude*, Tate Britain, London, 2001–2 (114)
Bequeathed by J. R. Holliday, 1927 (1927P352)

To make his illustration as realistic as possible Brown asked his friend John Marshall, an assistant surgeon at University College Hospital, London, to arrange access to a cadaver. Brown spent two days on this study of the dead body, arranging the corpse as he wanted it, even including a rope to stand in for the chain that ties the dead brother to the wall. On 13 April 1856 he described the sombre task in his diary:

> Out shopping, then to University hospital to ask John Marshall about a dead boddy. He got the one that will just do. It was in the vaults under the dissecting room. When I saw it first, what with the dim light, the brown & parchment like appearance of it & the shaven head, I took it for a wooden imulation of the thing. Often as I have seen horrors I really did not remember how hideous the shell of a poor creature may remain when the substance contained is fled. Yet we both in our joy at the obtainment of what we sought declared it to be lovely & a splendid corps. Marshall evidently loves a thing of the kind.

35. *The Prisoner of Chillon: Compositional Sketch*, 1856

Pencil; 133 × 99 mm (i.), 146 × 112 mm (p.)
Lit.: Rev. Robert Avis Willmott, *The Poets of the Nineteenth Century* (London, George Routledge and Co., 1857), p. 111; *Whitley*, p. 43; *Bennett*, C44.1
Exh.: *Ford Madox Brown*, 1964 (77)
Bequeathed by J. R. Holliday, 1927 (1927P353)

This loose early compositional sketch for Brown's illustration *The Prisoner of Chillon* depicts five figures in a dungeon. In the foreground, two figures lean over a third who is lying on the floor but chained to the wall. A shaft of light falls from a window on the right. In the background there is a shadow where Brown later adds a sixth person lurking in the doorway. Having made initial sketches, Brown produced detailed figure studies before incorporating these into a final compositional study very close to the engraved image.

36. *The Prisoner of Chillon*, pub. 1857

Wood-engraving; 127 × 95 mm (i.), 190 × 123 mm (p.)
Insc. engraved on image bl.: *DALZIEL Sc*, printed below image c.: *The Prisoner of Chillon*
Lit.: Rev. Robert Avis Willmott, ed., *The Poets of the Nineteenth Century* (London, George Routledge and Co., 1857), p. 111; *Hueffer*, p. 118ff.; *Gleeson White*, 1897, p. 106; *George and Edward Dalziel*, 1901, pp. 120, 122; *Reid*, pp. 48–49; *Whitley*, pp. 42–43; *Diary*, pp. 165–69ff.; *Casteras*, 1991, p. 14ff.; *Engen*, pp. 108–9; Paul Goldman, *Victorian Illustrated Books 1850–1870* (London, British Museum Publications, 1994), p. 82; *Goldman*, p. 10ff.; *Suriano*, p. 306; *Bennett*, D8

Presented by Charles Fairfax Murray, 1912 (1912P50)

In 1856 Brown was commissioned to illustrate Byron's poem *The Prisoner of Chillon* by the Dalziel brothers for the anthology *The Poets of the Nineteenth Century*. Early in his career he had depicted a scene from the poem in an oil painting, but for the new illustration he created a completely different composition. His diary entries over four consecutive days reveal how he used models, a cadaver and himself to make his figures as accurate as possible:

> 17th Drew in the dead body in the corrected sketch in Pen & Ink. It is rather dreary. Worked at sundries from self in the looking glass (8 hours).
> 18th worked all day from self in looking glass in shirts & draws. In the eveng had a model & so finished the figure of the jeering grave digger (8 hours).
> 19th accompts. Did not begin till 2 when a lean man sent by Rossetti came & so I used him & drew in the hands of the corps & the legs of the old grinning grave digger & one hand of his till 6.
> 20th 'Drawing the clothes of the old grave digger, made up a kind of sleeve & had it Pinned to my waistcoat.

37. *Stages of Cruelty: Study for the Child (Catherine Madox Brown)*, 1857

Black chalk on pale grey paper; 335 × 297 mm
Insc. bl.: *FMB 57*
Lit.: *Hueffer*, p. 131; *Whitley*, p. 43; *Diary*, p. 178ff.; *Newman and Watkinson*, p. 148; *Bennett*, A67.1
Exh.: *Brussels*, 1929 (16); *Pre-Raphaelites and their Followers*, Bournemouth Art Gallery, 1951 (104); *Some Pre-Raphaelite Paintings and Drawings*, Swansea Art Gallery, 1955 (8); *Ford Madox Brown*, 1964 (79); *Hong Kong*, 1984 (8)
Presented by A. E. Anderson, 1922 (1922P18)

Following the rejection of his design for *Cromwell on his Farm* by D. T. White, Brown thought up a new domestic subject in June 1856. At first it was called *Stolen Kisses are Sweet* but, inspired by Hogarth, it became the more moralistic *Stages of Cruelty*. The composition depicts a young woman spurning her lover, while a young girl in the foreground whips her dog with a bunch of Love-lies-bleeding. Brown used his second daughter Cathy as the model for the young girl, noting in his diary for 1857:

> as Hunt held out some prospect of Fairburns coming to buy the Lilac leaves, I set at it & painted the convolvulus out in the open air, composed & drew in the child, painted in the *Love-lies-Bleeding*, worked at the lovers head & at the girls, in all I suppose 3 weeks.

However, no commission came and the painting was worked on only intermittently during the 1860s. It was eventually finished in 1890 for Brown's Manchester patron Henry Boddington. By this time Cathy's own daughter Juliet had became the model for the girl in the completed canvas.

38. *Portrait: Thomas Carlyle*, c. 1859

Albumen photograph by 'Mr Thompson'; (top) 312 × 185 mm (bottom), 312 × 168 mm
Lit.: Jeremy Maas, *The Victorian Art World in Photographs* (London, Barrie & Jenkins, 1984), pp. 186–87
Exh.: *Thomas Carlyle 1795–1881*, National Portrait Gallery, London, 1981 (13)
Found unaccessioned (1975P329)

Although Brown met Carlyle, the essayist was too busy to sit for *Work* in person and instead posed for this photograph, possibly one of a number taken in the session at 'Mr Thompson's Photographic Establishment'. Brown was deeply impressed with the works of Thomas Carlyle (1795–1881) and several of them influenced his choice of subject matter. Carlyle's writings were known for their lively rhetoric which comes across in the letter he wrote to Brown agreeing to pose for the photograph:

> I think it a pity you had not put (or should not still put) some other man than me in your Great Picture. It is certain you could hardly have found among the sons of Adam, at present, any individual who is less in a condition to help you forward with it … I very well remember your amiable request, and the promise I made to you, to 'sit for some photographs'. That promise I will keep; and to that we must restrict ourselves, hand of Necessity compelling. Any afternoon I will attend here, at your studio, or where you appoint me, and give your man one hour to get what photographs he will or can of me. If *here*, the hour must be 3½ pm (my usual hour of quitting work, or to speak justly, the chamber of work); if at any other place, attainable by horseback, it will be altogether equally convenient to me; and the hour may such as enables me to arrive (at a rate of 5 miles *per* hour we will say!).

39. *Work*, commissioned 1852, finished 1863

Oil on canvas; 684 × 990 mm
Insc.: *F Madox Brown 1863*
Lit: *Work*, 1865, pp. 27–31; *Hueffer*, p. 162; Celina Fox, *Londoners* (London, Thames and Hudson/Museum of London, 1987), p. 180; Linda Burridge and John West, *Classroom Gallery* (Huntingdon, Elm Publications, 1992), pp. 290–94; *Newman and Watkinson*, p. 129; *Bennett*, A59.3
Exh: Liverpool Academy, 1866 (544); Mechanics' Institute, Newcastle upon Tyne, 1866 (30); *Coming of Age*, Cartwright Hall Art Gallery, Bradford, 1925 (56); *The Pre-Raphaelite Brotherhood*, BMAG, 1947 (11); *English Paintings from Birmingham*, Agnew's, 1957 (58); *Peintures et Aquarelles Anglaises 1700–1900*, Musée des Beaux Arts, Lyon, 1966 (89); *The British Royal Family*, Seibu Department Store, Tokyo, 1967 (89); *Paintings from the Leathart Collection*, Laing Art Gallery, Newcastle upon Tyne, 1968 (20); *Thomas Carlyle 1795–1881*, National Portrait Gallery, London, 1981–82 (11); *Hong Kong*, 1984 (3); *Pre-Raphaelites: Painters and Patrons in the North East*, Laing Art Gallery, Newcastle upon Tyne, 1989 (13); *Visions* (74); *Work and Leisure*, Bristol City Museum and Art Gallery and National Gallery, London 2007 (ill., no cat no.); *British Vision: Observation and Imagination in British Art 1750–1950*, Ghent Museum of Fine Arts, 2007–8 (22)
Prov.: Commissioned from the artist by James Leathart in November 1859; Harry Quilter; his sale Christie's 7 April 1906 (22); bought by Whitworth Wallis for J. R. Holliday
Bequeathed by J. R. Holliday, 1927 (1927P349)

This small version of *Work* was commissioned by James Leathart in 1852 for £315. It was completed in 1863, the same year as the original painting (now at Manchester Art Gallery). The two compositions are close though Brown notably replaced the portrait of his wife Emma, who sat for the lady holding a parasol on the left, with a portrait of Maria Leathart, wife of his patron.

The subject for *Work* was thought up in 1852 and the original painting commissioned in 1856 by T. E. Plint. The composition centres around navvies laying sewage pipes in Hampstead, London. These are the heroes of modern life who represent 'the

outward and visible type of work'. To the right are the 'brainworkers': F. D. Maurice, preacher and founder of the Working Men's College, and the essayist Thomas Carlyle. Behind them lie the Irish and itinerant workers who sleep because they can find no work. To the left is an impoverished flower seller let down by the fact that he has never 'been *taught to work*' and a lady carrying out religious work, distributing tracts. The scene also includes those who have no need to work, including a lady 'whose only business in life as yet is to dress and look beautiful for our benefit', and a rich man and his daughter at the back of the scene on horseback.

The ideas expressed in the painting show the influence of Carlyle's writings and the sociological concepts which Henry Mayhew published in *London Labour and the London Poor* (1851). In 1866 Leathart lent the painting to the Mechanics' Institute in Newcastle where it was unfavourably described as 'one of the extraordinary mistakes of the present day' in the *Newcastle Daily Journal*.

40. *Study for King René's Honeymoon: Architecture*, 1861

Brush and brown ink, with watercolour, over pencil on three sheets of paper; 445 × 318 mm
Insc. br.: *FMB* [monogram] _ *61*
Lit.: *Whitley*, p. 44; *Hueffer*, pp. 199–200; *Bendiner*, pp. 73–75ff.; *Bennett*, C58
Exh.: *Aberystwyth*, 1956 (42); *Ford Madox Brown*, 1964 (82); *William Morris and the Middle Ages*, Whitworth Art Gallery, Manchester, 1984 (65); *Visions* (57)
Bequeathed by J. R. Holliday, 1927 (1927P351)

In 1861 John Pollard Seddon (1827–1906) commissioned Morris, Marshall, Faulkner & Co. to produce ten decorative panels depicting the Fine and Applied Arts for an architect's desk of his own design (now at the V&A). On Brown's suggestion the door panels were decorated with scenes from the honeymoon of the medieval King René of Anjou, a patron of the arts whose life had been popularised by Sir Walter Scott in his novel *Anne of Geierstein* (1829). This is a study for *Architecture* showing King René sitting with his new wife, surrounded by architectural plans and instruments. Edward Burne-Jones (1833–1898) designed *Painting* and *Sculpture* and Dante Gabriel Rossetti (1828–1882) painted *Music*. The cabinet was made by the furniture firm of Seddon's father, and was exhibited at the 1862 International Exhibition in London. This study is considered the earliest of several versions, and is thought to relate to the original Seddon commission rather than the later stained glass design.

41. *Elijah and the Widow's Son*, 1863–64

Engraved woodblock; 227 × 150 mm
Insc. on reverse in ink: *Elijah & the Widow's Son/ 88/…*
Exh.: *Book Illustration of the 'Sixties' (Loans from J. N. Hart)*, BMAG, 1924 (515)
Acquired through the executors of J. N. Hart, c. 1965 (2006.1040.88)

This engraved woodblock was produced for *Dalziels' Bible Gallery*. The design is seen in reverse from the final printed version, with the paper remaining uninked where the wood has been gouged out.

42. *Elijah and the Widow's Son*, 1864

Oil on canvas; 525 × 343 mm
Insc. cr.: *FMB* [monogram] / *64*
Lit.: *Work*, 1865, p. 15; *Hueffer*, p. 440; *Newman and Watkinson*, p. 138;
    Bendiner, p. 26ff.; *Bennett*, A82.1
Exh.: *Work*, 1865 (33); *Grafton*, 1897 (15?); *Aberystwyth*, 1956 (39); *Pre-
    Raphaelite Art*, Australian State Galleries, 1962 (8); *The Bible in Art*,
    Russell-Cotes Art Gallery, Bournemouth, 1963 (38); *The Pre-
    Raphaelites*, 1984 (127); *Visions* (75)
Prov.: J. H. Trist, 1982; J. Bibby, 1899; L.W. Hodson (sold Christie's 25
    June 1906) (142); Sir J. T. Middlemore, Bt
Presented by Sir J. T. Middlemore, Bt, 1912 (1912P23)

Elijah and the Widow's Son was the most popular of Brown's three
compositions for *Dalziels' Bible Gallery*. The dealer Gambart
bought a small watercolour version, which he later sold to
Frederick Leyland (present owner unknown), and Frederick
Craven of Manchester, a collector of watercolours, commissioned
a larger version in 1868 (V&A). The painting in the BMAG
collection is the only oil variant and was commissioned by a
Brighton wine merchant, James Trist, for 100 guineas. Trist was so
pleased with it that he later sent Brown a case of wine.

43. *Dalziels' Bible Gallery: Joseph's Coat: Compositional Sketch and Four Studies for Jacob's Granddaughter*, 1863–65

Pencil; 391 × 291mm
Insc. bl.: *FMB 1865* [altered from 1855, possibly postdated]
Lit.: *Whitley*, p. 43; Jane Butler, 'A Pre-Raphaelite Shibboleth: Joseph', *The
    Journal of Pre-Raphaelite Studies*, Nov. 1982, vol. III, no. 1, pp. 78–90;
    The Pre-Raphaelites, 1984, p. 206; *Bennett*, C96.1
Exh.: *Ford Madox Brown*, 1964 (87)
1906P788

These drawings have in the past been identified as studies for the
painting *The Coat of Many Colours* (Walker Art Gallery,
Liverpool), but are in fact for the illustration *Joseph's Coat* from
Dalziels' Bible Gallery. The sheet gives an insight into how Brown
worked. On the right is an early compositional sketch drawn with
loose lines and little detail. It already contains the major elements
of the composition such as Jacob sitting on a raised platform with
his granddaughter, the dog in the centre, and four of Joseph's
brothers standing around his blood-stained coat of many colours.
Brown has boxed in the sketch and uses the spare paper to focus
on the figure of Jacob's granddaughter whose pose appears to
have troubled him. The sheet contains three nude sketches of this
child in various positions and one of the model in costume, in the
pose of the middle nude. This is the pose taken up in the finished
illustration. At the top right of the paper there is a small sketch of
the front wheel of a tricycle-like object which does not appear to
be related to the composition. Although it appears to be dated
1865, this might be a case of Brown mistakenly backdating his
work as the design was certainly begun by 1864 if not before. Jane
Butler suggests it may be a study for an illustration to Charles
Well's drama *Joseph and his Brethren* (1824), which D. G. Rossetti
was keen to have republished in the 1850s.

44. *Dalziels' Bible Gallery: Joseph's Coat*, 1863–65

Engraved woodblock; 177 × 173 mm
Insc. on verso: *Joseph's Coat/ Dalziel/ 2…*
Exh.: *Book Illustration of the 'Sixties' (Loans from J. N. Hart)*, BMAG,
1924 (521)
Acquired through the executors of J. N. Hart, c. 1965 (2006.1040.22)

As can be seen from the woodblock in the final design, Brown
added a man on a ladder in the background as a reference to
Jacob's ladder.

45. *The Entombment: Finished Design*, 1867

Black pen and ink; 263 × 234 mm (i. to border), 264 × 240 mm (p.)
Insc. br.: *FMB* [monogram]
Lit.: *Hueffer*, p. 221ff.; *Whitley*, p. 44; *Sewter*, I, p. 78 and II, pl. 252; *The
    Pre-Raphaelites*, 1984, pp. 215–16; *Pre-Raphaelites: Painters and Patrons
    in the North East*, Laing Art Gallery, Newcastle upon Tyne, 1989, p. 61;
    Bendiner, pp. 72, 106; *Bennett*, C123
Presented by the Trustees of the Public Picture Gallery Fund, 1916
(1916P27)

This is the finished drawing from which the engraved illustration
for Catherine Winkworth's *Lyra Germanica – The Christian Life*
was made by Thomas Bolton. The scene depicts Christ's shrouded
body being carried into the tomb by St John the Evangelist and
Nicodemus. St Joseph of Arimathea, St Mary Altera and the Virgin
Mary stand behind them whilst Mary Magdalene kneels in the
bottom left corner. The original design for *The Entombment* was a
cartoon for Morris, Marshall, Faulkner & Co. for one of the lights
in the chancel window of Gatcombe Church on the Isle of Wight.

46. *The Entombment*, pub. 1868

Wood-engraving; 107 × 95 mm (i.), 238 × 170 mm (p.)
Insc. engraved on image br.: *FMB* [monogram], and under image bl.:
    T Bolton Sc
Lit.: Catherine Winkworth, *Lyra Germanica – The Christian Life*
    (London, Longman & Co., 1868), p. 38; *Whitley*, p. 44; Eric de Maré,
    The Victorian Woodblock Illustrators (London, Gordon Fraser, 1980),
    p. 113; *The Pre-Raphaelites*, 1984, p. 215; *Casteras*, 1991, ill. pp. 15, 104;
    Goldman, pp. 10, 365; *Suriano*, pp. 64, 306, ill. p. 66
Presented by Charles Fairfax Murray, 1912 (1912P51)

In notes made for his Manchester friend, Charles Rowley, in 1883,
Brown explained his inclusion of the archaic nimbuses in the
composition, 'The golden Aurioles or Nimbuses are not intended
to represent facts but rather that traditional glory which for all
good Christians attaches to certain of the great personalities in
the divine drama or legend.' He also revealed his dedication to
historical accuracy noting that, 'the tomb itself is formed
according to the most recently received archaeological views'.

47. *Down Stream (Last Year's First of May)*, pub. 1871

Wood-engraving; 102 × 143 mm (i.), 135 × 225 mm (p. irregular)
Insc. engraved on image bl.: *Jenkin Sc*, br.: *FMB* [monogram], printed
    below image: *DRAWN BY F. MADOX BROWN./ DOW[NS]TREAM*
    [worn letters] *ENGRAVED BY C. M. JENKIN.*
Lit.: Dante Gabriel Rossetti, 'Down Stream', *Dark Blue*, October 1871, vol.
    II, pp. 211–12; William Michael Rossetti, ed., *Dante Gabriel Rossetti: His
    Family-Letters* (London, Ellis & Elvey, 1895), II, p. 246; *Hueffer*, pp.
    263–64; *Gleeson White*, 1897, p. 81; *Reid*, p. 50; Eric de Maré, *The
    Victorian Woodblock Illustrators* (London, Gordon Fraser, 1980), p. 113;
    Casteras, 1991, pp. 15, 104; *Newman and Watkinson*, pl. 127; *Engen*, p.
    109; *Goldman*, p. 10ff.; *Bendiner*, p. 95; Lisa J. Nicoletti, 'Resuscitating
    Ophelia: Images of Suicide and Suicidal Insanity in Nineteenth-
    Century England', PhD dissertation, University of Wisconsin, 1999, pp.
    169–70; *Suriano*, pp. 65, 306; *Bennett*, D23
Presented by Charles Fairfax Murray, 1912 (1912P49)

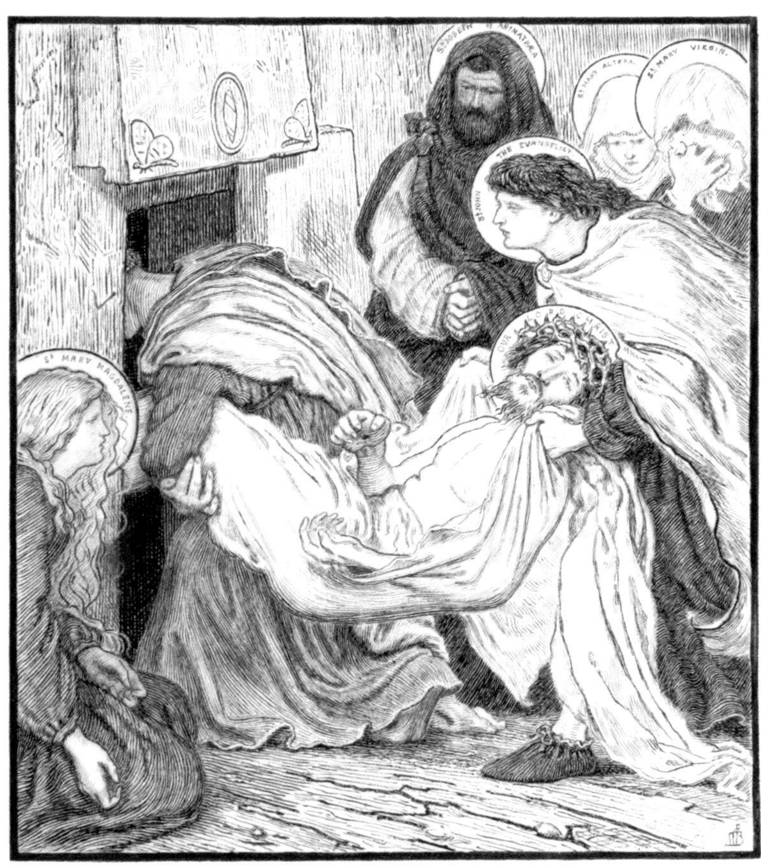

LEFT: *The Entombment: Finished Design*, 1867 (cat. 45)

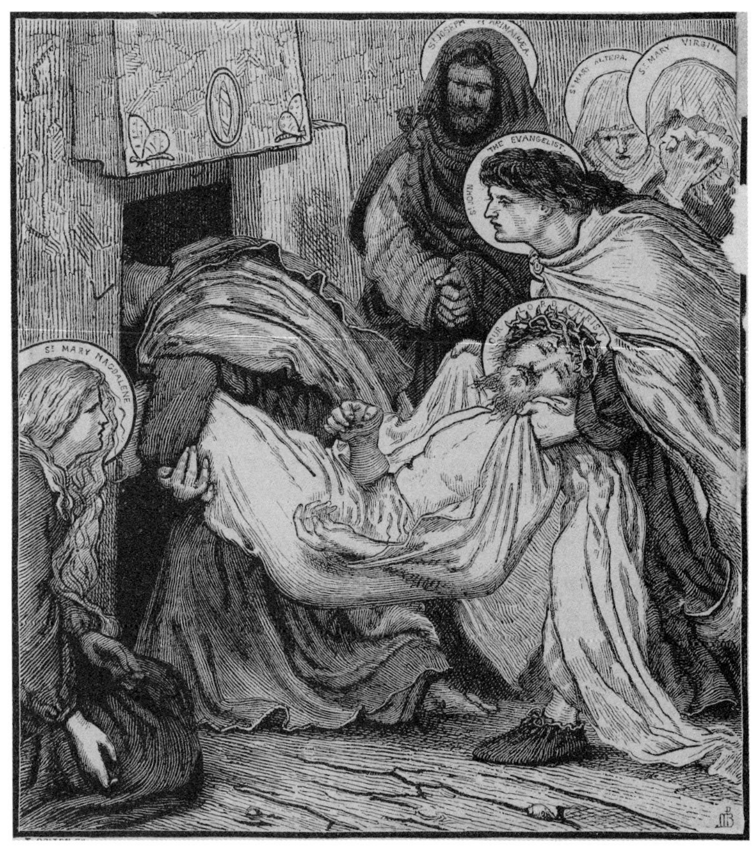

BELOW: *The Entombment*, pub. 1868 (cat. 46)

In the early 1870s Rossetti helped to set up *Dark Blue*, a short-lived magazine containing articles and poems. The foreword to the second volume sets out its liberal aspirations to show 'both sides of every question' and encourage debate. Brown made two illustrations for 'Down Stream', a poem by Rossetti published in the magazine in 1871. Rossetti was evidently very pleased with the illustrations and told his brother William: 'I'm Dark Blued at last, owing to Brown, who was asked to illustrate something of mine for them if I would contribute.' In a congratulatory letter to Brown he wrote, 'I expect to see you in a few days, but must meanwhile write to say how very excellent I think your drawing in "Dark Blue". It is like a tenderer kind of Hogarth and seems to me the most successful of your book illustrations.'

48. *Down Stream: (This Year's First of June)*, pub. 1871

Wood-engraving; 45 × 110mm (i.), 225 × 141 mm (p.)
Insc. engraved bl.: *FMB* [monogram]
Lit.: Dante Gabriel Rossetti, 'Down Stream', *Dark Blue*, October 1871, vol. II, pp. 211–12; *Hueffer*, p. 264; *Gleeson White*, 1897, p. 81; Eric de Maré, *The Victorian Woodblock Illustrators* (London, Gordon Fraser, 1980), p. 113; *Casteras*, 1991, ill. pp. 15, 104; *Goldman*, pp. 10, 274, 370; Lisa J. Nicoletti, 'Resuscitating Ophelia: Images of Suicide and Suicidal Insanity in Nineteenth-Century England', PhD dissertation, University of Wisconsin, 1999, pp. 169–70; *Suriano*, pp. 65, 306; *Bennett*, D24
Presented by Charles Fairfax Murray, 1912 (1912P45)

This is the more sedate tailpiece which depicts the poem's tragic ending. Although it lacks the vitality of the main illustration, Rossetti was pleased with it and told Brown, 'the little one is pretty too'.

49. *Stained Glass Design: Cartoon for Zachariah, The High Priest*, 1872

Black chalk; 934 × 476 mm (s.)
Insc. bl.: *The property of the/ artist F Madox Brown*, br.: *FMB* [monogram] *–72*, around halo: *Powells bleu* [?] *St light*, on cloak, *24 green*
Lit.: *Sale Catalogue*, 1894, p. 16; Harold Rathbone, *The Cartoons of F. M. Brown* (London, Autotype Company, 1895), pl. 5; *Hueffer*, p. 446; *Whitley*, p. 49; *Sewter*, I, p. 107ff. and II, pls. 450, 451; *Bennett*, C178
Exh.: *Centenary of William Morris*, Victoria and Albert Museum, London, 1934 (34)
Transferred from Birmingham Municipal School of Art, 1912 (1912P149)

In 1873 Morris, Marshall, Faulkner & Co. completed their commission to produce two large stained-glass windows in the church of St John the Baptist, Knaresborough. Brown provided designs for both windows including this cartoon for Zachariah, the Old Testament priest and father of St John the Baptist. In the final window, Zachariah is depicted carrying out his duties as a priest, swinging his censer and wearing a gold cape lined with green. The angel on his cape may well represent the archangel Gabriel who appeared to Zachariah to tell him that Elizabeth, his wife, would fall pregnant. A year later the company completed the nave window for All Saints' Church in Leigh, Staffordshire, reusing this cartoon for the figure of Zachariah.

After the reorganisation of the Morris firm in 1875, Brown was replaced as the chief supplier of cartoons by Edward Burne-Jones. This created a rift between Brown and Morris that lasted until 1885. As the inscription suggests, Brown was conscious of the value of such cartoons as independent works of art, and insisted on their return.

50. *Convalescent: Portrait of Emma Madox Brown*, 1872

Pastel on paper; 475 × 435 mm
Insc. bl.: *FMB* [monogram] *Octr _72*
Lit.: *Sale Catalogue*, 1894, p. 10; *Hueffer*, p. 271ff.; *Andrea Rose*, 1981, p. 24; *Newman and Watkinson*, p. 165; *Bennett*, B44
Exh.: *Pre-Raphaelite Women*, BMAG, 1985–86 (5); *Visions* (97) (1906P793)

Brown's portrait of Emma recovering from a serious illness depicts her looking pale, but with an abundance of red hair. She clutches a posy of pansies, which in the language of flowers signify, 'You occupy my thoughts' or victory: both appropriate sentiments after her alarming malady.

Despite the personal nature of the portrait, Brown and his family saw it as a notable work. Hueffer lists it among 'Brown's more important works', also recording that Brown contributed it to a raffle in aid of the widow of a Manchester artist named Holding. This necessitated the making of a duplicate portrait in February 1873. As late as 1891 the composition became the basis for the title page illustration to Mathilde Blind's *Dramas in Miniature*. This scene, entitled *The Perfume of the Breath of May*, illustrates the final scene in Blind's short story 'The Message' where an impoverished woman, on her deathbed in a charity hospital, receives a glimmer of happiness from a small posy of flowers. Emma herself had died in 1890 after another long illness.

51. *Portrait of Miss Iza Duffus Hardy*, 1872

Pastel and coloured chalks on brown paper; 771 × 556 mm
Insc. tl.: *IZA HARDY/ FMB* [monogram] *72*
Lit.: *Sale Catalogue*, 1894, p. 10, *W. M. Rossetti*, II, p. 491; *Bendiner*, p. 68; *Bennett*, B19
Exh.: *Grafton*, 1897 (83); *Manchester*, 1911 (19); *National Gallery British Art*, 1911–12 (28)
Presented by Charles Fairfax Murray, 1903 (1904P498)

This was the first drawing by Ford Madox Brown to enter the Birmingham collection in 1904. It was one of several gifts from Charles Fairfax Murray received whilst the Museum and Art Gallery was gathering subscriptions to buy the first instalment of what is now Birmingham's celebrated drawing collection. It is likely that Fairfax Murray bought the drawing from the sale of Brown's household effects following his death in 1893.

Iza Duffus Hardy (1850–1922) was the daughter of Sir Thomas Duffus Hardy (1804–1878), Deputy Keeper of the Public Record Office, and his second wife Lady May Anne Hardy, novelist and travel writer (1824–1891). Iza also became an author, publishing over thirty books and numerous short stories in the 1870s and 1880s. The Browns and the Hardys were, according to William Michael Rossetti, close friends, and he notes that both Mrs Hardy and Iza were 'warmly attached to my wife', Brown's first daughter Lucy.

52. *Stained Glass Design: Cartoon for The Young Milton*, 1874

Black chalk; 572 × 300 mm
Insc. tr.: *2 gown/ 3 shirt/ 4 slashe[d]*, bl.: *FMB* [monogram] *c74*, br.: *The Young Milton / [ ]f the A…* [remaining piece of inscription rubbed out]
Lit.: *Sale Catalogue*, 1894, p. 15; Harold Rathbone, *The Cartoons of F. M.*

Brown (London, Autotype Company, 1895), pl. 20; *Hueffer*, p. 446;
Sewter, I, pp. 45, 241, 307 and II, pl. 325; *Bennett*, C167
Exh.: *English Eye I*, Midlands Federation Travelling Exhibition, 1958 (2);
  Morris & Company in Cambridge, Fitzwilliam Museum, Cambridge,
  1980, ex cat.
Presented by the Reverend John Richard Dorman, 1957 (1957P34)

This cartoon of *The Young Milton* was produced for a set of
windows in the Combination Room of Peterhouse College,
Cambridge, executed by Morris, Marshall, Faulkner & Co.
According to Hueffer, this cartoon was entered into Brown's
account book in late 1872 although work on the windows was not
completed until 1874. This must account for Brown's loose dating
of the cartoon: 'c. 74.' In the completed stained-glass window,
Milton is depicted with long hair and a brown cloak lined in blue.
He holds a hat and the edge of his robes in his left hand and an
open book in his right. In 1873 Brown also produced a cartoon of
the blind and old Milton for Cragside, Rothbury.

53. *Dalziels' Bible Gallery: Elijah and the Widow's Son*, pub. 1881

Wood-engraving; 230 × 150 mm (i.), 285 × 221 mm (p.)
Insc. engraved on image bl.: *DALZIEL Sc*
Lit.: George and Edward Dalziel, *Dalziels' Bible Gallery* (London, George
  Routledge & Sons, 1881), ill. no. 60; *Art Pictures* (London and New York,
  Society for Promoting Christian Knowledge, 1894), p. 156; *Gleeson
  White*, 1897, p. 146; *George and Edward Dalziel*, 1901, p. 252; *Reid*, pp.
  49–50; *Goldman*, pp. 10, 43, 370; *Suriano*, pp. 65, 306; *Bennett*, D11
Presented by Charles Fairfax Murray, 1912 (1912P48)

The strong diagonal and compressed space of this design adds to
the feeling of oppressive summer heat in which Brown sets the
miracle of Elijah bringing a child back to life. He depicts the
moment when Elijah emerges with the revived child, who 'is
represented as in his grave-clothes, which have a far-off
resemblance to Egyptian funeral trappings; having been laid out
with flowers in the palms of his hands, as is done by women in
such cases'. To Brown such details were vital to the viewer's
understanding of the illustration and he explained in his solo
exhibition catalogue that, 'without this, the subject (the coming
to life) could not be expressed by the painter's art, and till this
view of the subject presented itself to me I could not see my way
to make a picture of it'.

   Such attention to detail and historical accuracy reveals that he
approached religious illustrations in the same fastidious way as
his history paintings. The costumes were based on his 'study of
Egyptian combined with Assyrian, and other nearly contemporary
remains' which he was able to look at in the British Museum. He
used the symbol of a bird's shadow to signify 'the return of the
body to the soul', an idea which was prompted by his research
into Middle Eastern customs.

54. *Dalziels' Bible Gallery: Joseph's Coat*, pub. 1881

Wood-engraving; 180 × 175 mm (i.), 570 × 400 mm (p.)
Insc. engraved on image bl.: *DALZIEL Sc*, on image br.: *FMB*
Lit.: *Work*, 1865, p. 21; George and Edward Dalziel, *Dalziels' Bible Gallery*
  (London, George Routledge & Sons, 1881) (22); *Art Pictures* (London
  and New York, Society for Promoting Christian Knowledge, 1894), p. 38;
  Gleeson White, 1897, p. 146; *George and Edward Dalziel*, 1901, p. 252;
  Reid, p. 50; *Goldman*, pp. 10, 370; *Suriano*, pp. 65, 306; *Bennett*, D10
Presented by Charles Fairfax Murray, 1912 (1912P47)

Although *Dalziels' Bible Gallery* was published in 1881, most of
the illustrated designs, including Brown's, were made in the early
1860s. Like all three of Brown's illustrations for the *Bible Gallery*,
Joseph's Coat shows figures claustrophobically compressed within
a small space with minute details. In order to remain as realistic
as possible, Brown used a landscape from the Holy Land for the
background. Although he had not travelled to the Middle East
himself, he copied a watercolour study painted in the summer of
1851 by his friend Thomas Seddon of the hills above Jerusalem,
entitled *The Well of Enrogel* (Harris Museum and Art Gallery,
Preston).

   In December 1863 Brown sent his patron George Rae a list of
potential subjects. From this, in March 1864, Rae commissioned
an oil version of *Joseph's Coat* retitled *The Coat of Many Colours*
(Walker Art Gallery, Liverpool). However, work on the painting
was only begun after Brown had finished the pen-and-ink
drawing for the illustration in October that year (British
Museum). An oil replica (1871, Museo de Arte, Ponce, Puerto
Rico) and a watercolour sketch (1866–67, Tate) were also
produced from the illustration design.

55. *Stained Glass Design: The Marriage of Editha with Sigtrygg, King of Northumbria* (St Editha's, Tamworth, Staffordshire)

Copy by Thomas Matthews Rooke, 1909
Watercolour; 932 × 765 mm (s.)
Lit.: *Hueffer*, p. 447; *Sewter*, I, pp. 184, 241; John Bryson and J. C. Troxell,
  Dante Gabriel Rossetti and Jane Morris: Their Correspondence (Oxford,
  Clarendon Press, 1976), pp. 86–87 (letter 50); *Bendiner*, p. 42; Charles
  Nugent, *British Watercolours in the Whitworth Art Gallery, University of
  Manchester* (London, Philip Wilson Publishers, 2002), p. 64
Exh: *Rooke*, BMAG, 1992 (36); *Rooke*, Sheffield, 1993 (92)
Presented by the Library of the University of Birmingham from the J. R.
  Holliday Bequest (1959P40)

This watercolour is one of three copies of clerestory windows in
St Editha's, Tamworth, designed by Ford Madox Brown for
Morris, Marshall, Faulkner & Co. in 1873. The windows depict
the Legend of St Editha and the Occupation of Tamworth Castle
by Marmion. This first window illustrates the marriage of St
Editha and shows Athelstan, King of the West Saxons, giving away
his sister, Editha, to Sigtrygg, King of Northumbria, as Aella,
Bishop of Lichfield, looks on.

   The designs appear to have caused some controversy as a
letter from Dante Gabriel Rossetti to Jane Morris suggests:

   Some of cartoons of Old Brown's (made for Top's firm)
   are being published in an architectural paper. Really I must
   say they are inconceivable. Every figure (it is a long series) is
   passing one hand through the stone mullion of the window
   into the next panel of glass!! – each panel containing one
   figure. It is called the Story of St Edith [sic]. I must say if this
   series was what reduced Top to desperation, I think every one
   would have sympathised with him [replacing Brown as
   designer] if he had only shown the cartoons.

James Richardson Holliday, an avid collector of Morris & Co.
stained glass cartoons, commissioned the watercolour copies
from Thomas Matthews Rooke (1842–1942). Rooke was a
talented painter who produced watercolours and oils of religious,
imaginative and architectural subjects.

Catalogue

Ford Madox Brown: Catalogue of Drawings, Prints, Designs, Watercolours and Archive Material at Birmingham Museums and Art Gallery

Introductory Note

The following catalogue of 174 items is a complete listing of works on paper by Ford Madox Brown at Birmingham Museums and Art Gallery. Each work is identified by the capital B sequence number and accompanying accession number. The collection was purchased from the artist and collector Charles Fairfax Murray in July 1906 as part of the second phase of acquiring a collection of Pre-Raphaelite drawings through public subscription from local patronage. For an account of this outstanding acquisition see recent publications on the Birmingham collection: *John Everett Millais: Illustrator and Narrator*, Lund Humphries, 2004; and *Hidden Burne-Jones*, D Giles Ltd, 2007.

The following works on paper have been arranged alphabetically by title, with strength and depth in sketches and studies for historical compositions, notably *Chaucer at the Court of Edward III* as well as *Wycliffe reading his Translation of the Bible, The Spirit of Justice*, 1844 drawings for *The Ascension* and *Oure Ladye of Saturday Night*. Working drawings and finished designs for illustration, ranging from Laurence Sterne's *Sentimental Journey* and early sketches for *Lear and Cordelia* and for *Dalziels' Bible Gallery* are also well represented. Other groupings to emerge include portraits of known and unidentified models spanning much of the artist's career, and a small selection of late designs for stained glass.

Measurements are given in millimetres, height before width. The addition of an asterisk indicates the inclusion of the work in the accompanying exhibition. The drawings are frequently but not exclusively on cream wove Whatman paper. The 1906 accession number refers to the Charles Fairfax Murray provenance, the 1927 accession number to the Bequest of J. R. Holliday.

The result aims to be very much a reference listing, and should be seen alongside A. E. Whitley's seminal *City of Birmingham Art Gallery & Museum: Catalogue of Drawings* catalogue (1939) and the much anticipated catalogue of Ford Madox Brown's work by Mary Bennett to be published by Yale University Press. Building on the precedent of an online Burne Jones Resource Site launched in 2007, a Pre-Raphaelite Resource Site, including Madox Brown and extended catalogue entries of the Birmingham collection, is scheduled to be completed in 2009.

LAURA MacCULLOCH AND TESSA SIDEY

B1 *Alfred the Great: Sketch of Alfred drawing in the Sand*, 1843–45 *
Verso: *List of historical Names and Dates, over Sketches of King Alfred*, 1843–50
Pencil; sepia writing over pencil on verso; 175 × 112 mm
Insc. verso: *Edward III Born in 1312 / Chaucer born in 1328 / Black Prince in 1330 / English Language becomes legal in 1362 / Wicliffe Translated the Bible in 1377 / Order of the Garter 1349 / Wicliffe* <u>Preaches reform</u> *1362 / Black Prince Died in 1376 / Edward the IIIrd died in 1377 / King John Prisoner/ in London from 1357 till – 1360 / Came back & died 1364 / Black Prince Married 1365 / Richard born to him in 1367 / Queen Phillipa died in 1359 / Black Prince returned in / [John] of Gaunt also 1372–*
Found unaccessioned, 1978 (1978P513)
(*Bennett*, A32)

***

B2 *Angels watching the Crown of Thorns: Study of clasped Hands*, 1846
Black chalk; 166 × 280 mm
Insc. br.: *Southend / F. M Brown/46*
1906P727 (*Bennett*, A43.2)

***

B3 *Architecture: Study of Gothic Arches and fourteenth-century Vaulting*, 1850
Black pen and ink over pencil on grey paper; 188 × 409 mm
Insc. br.: *Ford M Brown London/50*
1906P714 (*Bennett*, A48.28)

Mary Bennett relates the archway in this study to the oil sketch of *Wycliffe reading his Translation of the Bible* in Cartwright Hall Art Gallery, Bradford.

B4 *The Ascension* (formerly Forbes Magazine Collection), 1844–1900
Toned photographic print; 175 × 80 mm
Found unaccessioned, 1978 (1978P512)
(*Bennett*, A37)

B5 *The Ascension: Study of Angels and Hands*, 1844
Sepia pen and ink over pencil; 360 × 178 mm
Insc. b.: *Different sketches for a design of the Ascension Paris/ Ford Brown/44*
1906P668 (*Bennett*, A37.4)

In 1844, while living in Paris, Ford Madox Brown entered a competition to paint a large altarpiece of *The Ascension of Christ* for the church of St James, Bermondsey. He was unsuccessful and the commission was given to the relatively unknown British artist John Wood (1801–1877).

B6 *The Ascension: Study of a Group of Angels*, 1844
Sepia pen and ink over pencil; 280 × 150 mm
Insc. br.: *(Paris) / F. M Brown/44*
1906P669 (*Bennett*, A37.5)

B7 *The Ascension: Study of a Group of six flying Angels*, 1844
Verso: *Two nude Angels holding onto each other*
Sepia pen and ink over pencil; sepia brush over pencil on verso; 173 × 228 mm
Insc. bl.: *(Paris)*, br.: *Ford M Brown/44*

1906P698 (*Bennett*, A37.6)

B8 *The Ascension: Study for kneeling Apostle*, 1844
Verso: *Head of a Child*
Black chalk touched with white on brown-toned laid paper; 283 × 220 mm
Insc. br.: *Ford M Brown/44 / (Paris)*
1906P695 (*Bennett*, A37.7)

B9 *The Ascension: Drapery Study of a praying Apostle*, 1844
Verso: *The Spirit of Justice: Seated Figure in ecclesiastical Robes, gripping Staff with left Hand raised in a Blessing*
Black chalk; 233 × 185 mm
1906P752 (*Bennett*, A37.8)

B10 *The Ascension: Study for an Apostle*, 1844
Verso: *The Spirit of Justice: Body of seated Figure in ecclesiastical Robes holding a Staff and Book*
Black chalk; 316 × 137 mm
Insc. bl.: *Ford M Brown/44 (Paris)*
1906P697 (*Bennett*, A37.9)

B11 *The Ascension: Study for an Apostle*, 1844
Verso: *The Spirit of Justice: Sketch of a standing, naked Child*
Black chalk; 319 × 137 mm
Insc. bl.: *Ford M Brown 44 (Paris)*
1906P696 (*Bennett*, A37.10)

B12 *The Ascension: Study for the Figure of Christ*, 1844
Sepia pen and ink over pencil; 212 × 155 mm (s.)
1906P694 (*Bennett*, A37.3)

***

B13 *Caricature: Composite Drawing: A Stunner*, 1861–63
Verso: *A Victorian woman in her Underwear* (considered to be by Burne-Jones)
Pencil on paper; 212 × 90 mm
1980P37

B14 *Caricature: Composite Drawing: Bewigged Head*, 1861–63
Pencil on paper; 136 × 79 mm
1980P38

The reference to Madox Brown in B13 and B14 remains largely conjectural; see Stephen Wildman in *Re-framing the Pre-Raphaelites*, ed. Ellen Harding (Aldershot, Scolar Press, 1996), p. 256.

***

Chaucer at the Court of Edward III (*The Seeds and Fruits of English Poetry*)

Ford Madox Brown began the triptych, *The Seeds and Fruits of English Poetry*, in 1845, but later abandoned the wings to concentrate on the central panel as a single composition, which was exhibited as *Geoffrey Chaucer reading the 'Legend of Custance' to Edward and his Court, at the Palace of Sheen, on the Anniversary of the Black Prince's forty-fifth Birthday*, Art Gallery of New South Wales, Sydney (hereafter *Chaucer at the Court of Edward III*). Several of the drawings that follow relate to both the central and side wings, and for clarity are catalogued here under one title: *Chaucer at the Court of Edward III*.

B15 *Chaucer at the Court of Edward III: Early compositional Study*, 1845
Verso: *The Seeds and Fruits of English Poetry: Study for the Figure of Milton and two Designs for Tombstones*, 1845–46
Pencil with sepia; 254 × 185 mm
Insc. br.: *Ford M Brown Rome/4* [5 cut]
1906P680 (*Bennett*, A40.10)

This early compositional sketch is slightly less finished than the drawing below, although the Gothic arch is more defined.

B16 *Chaucer at the Court of Edward III: Early compositional Study*, 1845 *
Pencil with sepia frame outline; 330 × 240 mm
Insc. bl.: *[F] M Brown Rome/45*
1906P681 (*Bennett*, A40.11)

B17 *Chaucer at the Court of Edward III: Nude Studies of two Boys*, 1845
Pencil; 243 × 232 mm
Insc. br.: *Ford M Brown Rome/45*
1906P767 (*Bennett*, A40. 15)

B18 *Chaucer at the Court of Edward III: Nude Studies of four Figures*, 1845
Pencil; 287 × 385 mm
Insc. br.: *Ford M Brown London* [crossed out] *Rome/45*
1906P671 (*Bennett*, A40.16)

B19 *Chaucer at the Court of Edward III: Eight early Studies of Figures and Hands*, 1845 *
Pencil; 280 × 436 mm
Insc. br.: *Ford M Brown Rome/ 45*
1906P766 (*Bennett*, A40.17)

B20 *Chaucer at the Court of Edward III: Nude Studies for Figures of Byron, Burns and Shakespeare*, 1845 *
Black chalk; 294 × 328 mm
Insc. br.: *Ford M Brown Rome/45*
1906P705 (*Bennett*, A40.18)

B21 *Chaucer at the Court of Edward III: Drapery Study for Robert Burns*, 1847
Black chalk; 355 × 212 mm
Insc. bl.: *Ford M Brown London/ 47*
1906P744 (*Bennett*, A40.19)

B22 *Chaucer at the Court of Edward III: Study of right Leg and left Foot for one of the Poets*, 1847
Black chalk; 294 × 125 mm (s.)
Insc. br.: *Ford M Brown London 47*
1906P711 (*Bennett*, A40.20)

This study is most likely to be for the legs of Milton.

B23 *Chaucer at the Court of Edward III: Study of left Leg for Figure of Shakespeare*, 1847
Black chalk; 313 × 122 mm (s.)
Insc. br.: *Ford M Brown London 47*
1906P706 (*Bennett*, A40.21)

B24 *Chaucer at the Court of Edward III: Drapery Study for Milton*, 1847
Black chalk; 355 × 200 mm
Insc. bl.: *[F] M Brown London/47*
1906P743 (*Bennett*, A40.22)

B25 *Chaucer at the Court of Edward III: Drapery Study for Shakespeare*, 1847
Black chalk; 350 × 170 mm

Insc. br.: *Ford M Brown London/47*
1906P707 (*Bennett*, A40.23)

B26 *Chaucer at the Court of Edward III: Study of a Man in medieval Hood*, 1847 *
Black chalk; 209 × 170 mm
Insc. br.: *Ford M Brown London/47*
1906P777 (*Bennett*, A40.24)

B27 *Chaucer at the Court of Edward III: Study for the Cardinal*, 1847
Black chalk; 297 × 178 mm
Insc. bl.: *Ford M Brown London 47*
1906P780 (*Bennett*, A40.25)

B28 *Chaucer at the Court of Edward III: Drapery Study in profile for Courtier*, 1847
Black chalk; 238 × 170 mm
Insc. br.: *Ford M Brown London/47*
1906P735 (*Bennett*, A40.26)
See B19

B29 *Chaucer at the Court of Edward III: Drapery Study,* 1847
Black chalk; 158 × 128 mm
Insc. br.: *Ford M Brown London/47*
1906P734 (*Bennett*, A40.27)
See B19

B30 *Chaucer at the Court of Edward III: Female nude Study of a Muse holding onto a Rail,* 1847
Pencil; 290 × 147 mm
Insc. br.: *Ford M Brown London/47*
1906P776 (*Bennett*, A40.28)

B31 *Chaucer at the Court of Edward III: Female nude Study of a Muse,* 1847
Pencil; 267 × 146 mm
Insc. br.: *F. M B. London/47*
1906P775 (*Bennett*, A40.29)

The above two drawings have been identified as almost certainly the two figures Brown drew on 14 October 1847, recording in his diary that 'Miss Chamberlayne came. Worked well till 4 in spite of her talking propensities. Made outlines of the nude of the two figures of "Muses of impassioned & satirical poetry".'

B32 *Chaucer at the Court of Edward III: Nude Study for seated Lady,* 1847
Pencil; 233 × 182 mm
Insc. br.: *Ford M Brown London/47*
1906P768 (*Bennett*, A40.30)

B33 *Chaucer at the Court of Edward III: Nude Study of a Woman with right Arm raised,* 1847
Pencil; 132 × 192 mm
Insc. br.: *Ford M Brown London/47*
1906P772 (*Bennett*, A40.31)

B34 *Chaucer at the Court of Edward III: Two Studies of Back of seated Woman's Head,* 1847
Pencil; 128 × 201 mm
Insc. br.: *Ford M Brown London/47*
1906P769 (*Bennett*, A40.32)

These studies of the same model are for two of the women with the back of their heads facing the viewer in *Chaucer.*

B35 *Chaucer at the Court of Edward III: Two Studies of a seated Woman in three-quarter length pose and from the Back,* 1847
Pencil; 155 × 230 mm

Insc. br.: *Ford M Brown London/47*
1906P770 (*Bennett*, A40.33)

B36 *Chaucer at the Court of Edward III: Nude Study of a Woman,* 1847
Pencil; 289 × 135 mm
Insc. br.: *Ford M Brown London/47*
1906P773 (*Bennett*, A40.34)

This nude study is for the figure of a girl seated with an older woman in *Chaucer.*

B37 *Chaucer at the Court of Edward III: Sketch of Woman supporting another Figure (Lay Figure),* 1847
Pencil; 175 × 161mm
Insc. bl.: *Ford M Brown 47*
1906P774 (*Bennett*, A40.35)

B38 *Chaucer at the Court of Edward III: Study of the Heads and Shoulders of two Women,* 1847
Pencil; 164 × 254 mm
Insc. br.: *Ford M Brown London /47*
1906P771 (*Bennett*, A40.36)

The left study may well be for the figure of Edward III's mistress, Alice Perrers. The right one is thought to be Joanna, the Fair Maid of Kent, the wife of Edward the Black Prince.

B39 *Chaucer at the Court of Edward III: Drapery Study for Edward III with Outline of a Child,* 1847
Black chalk; 270 × 175 mm
Insc. br.: *Ford M Brown London/ 47*
1906P779 (*Bennett*, A40.37)

B40 *Chaucer at the Court of Edward III: Study for Head of Jester,* 1847
Pencil; 237 × 176 mm
Insc. br.: *Ford M Brown London/47*
1906P778 (*Bennett*, A40.38)

B41 *Chaucer at the Court of Edward III: Head of Alexander Pope,* 1847
Black chalk; 327 × 258 mm
Insc.: *Pope after Roubilliac Ford M Brown London/47*
1906P713 (*Bennett*, A40.39)

B42 *Chaucer at the Court of Edward III: Study of two Hands,* 1847
Black chalk; 170 × 238 mm
Insc. br.: *Ford M Brown London/47* (sepia ink over pencil inscription: *'Chaucer at the ...'*)
1906P749 (*Bennett*, A40.40)

B43 *Chaucer at the Court of Edward III: Study of Head of Milton copied from Sculpture,* 1848
Black chalk; 163 × 176 mm
Insc. br.: *Ford M Brown London/48*
1906P719 (*Bennett*, A40.41)

This study for Milton is likely to have been copied from Michael Rysbrack's bust of 1737 on the monument to the poet in Westminster Abbey.

B44 *Chaucer at the Court of Edward III: Nude Studies for Squire and Courtier talking to Gower,* 1848
Pencil; 160 × 269 mm
Insc. br.: *Ford M Brown London 48*
1906P782 (*Bennett*, A40.42)

B45 *Chaucer at the Court of Edward III: Drapery Study for the Black Prince,* 1848 *
Black chalk with touches of white; 206 × 165 mm
Insc. bl.: *Ford M Brown London/48*
1906P783 (*Bennett*, A40.43)

B46 *Chaucer at the Court of Edward III: Three Studies of Hands,* 1848
Black chalk; 281 × 201 mm
Insc. br.: *Ford M Brown London/48*
1906P751 (*Bennett*, A40.44)

The hand on the bottom left is a study for the blind figure of Milton. Above, the right hand of Byron holds a scroll, while on the right there is a drawing for Burns's right hand.

B47 *Chaucer at the Court of Edward III: Four Studies of Hands,* 1848
Black chalk touched with white; 305 × 312 mm
Insc. br.: *Ford M Brown London 48*
1906P750 (*Bennett*, A40.45)

B48 *Chaucer at the Court of Edward III: Study of clasped right Hand for Figure of Shakespeare,* 1848
Black chalk; 214 × 103 mm
Insc. br.: *Ford M Brown London 48*
1906P748 (*Bennett*, A40.46)

This hand study is for the figure of Shakespeare in the abandoned wings of *The Seeds and Fruits of English Poetry.*

B49 *Chaucer at the Court of Edward III: Study of left Hand for Figure of Robert Burns,* 1848
Black chalk heightened with touches of white chalk; 119 × 200 mm
Insc. br.: *Ford M Brown London/48*
1906P747 (*Bennett*, A40.47)

B50 *Chaucer at the Court of Edward III: Drapery Study for Robert Burns,* 1848 *
Black chalk; 289 × 165 mm
Insc. br.: *Ford M Brown London/48*
1906P745 (*Bennett*, A40.48)

B51 *Chaucer at the Court of Edward III: Drapery Study,* 1848
Black chalk; 105 × 116 mm
Insc. br.: *London / Ford M Brown/48*
1906P781 (*Bennett*, A40.49)

B52 *Chaucer at the Court of Edward III: Drapery Study for the Black Prince,* 1851
Black and white chalks on brown-toned paper; 211 × 185 mm (image and paper, irregular shape)
Insc. bc.: *Ford M Brown London 51*
1906P785 (*Bennett*, A40.50)

B53 *Chaucer at the Court of Edward III: Study for Squire's Legs,* 1851
Black chalk heightened with white; 230 × 232 mm
Insc. br.: *Ford M Brown London/51*
1906P786 (*Bennett*, A40.51)

B54 *Chaucer at the Court of Edward III: Head of old Woman,* 1851 *
Black chalk; 265 × 151 mm
Insc. br.: *Ford M Brown London/51*
1906P787 (*Bennett*, A40.52)

B55 *Chaucer at the Court of Edward III: Watercolour Version*, c. 1851 *
Watercolour with bodycolour; 365 × 386 mm
1927P356
See *Bennett* (A40.2) for a full discussion of this watercolour.

B56 *Convalescent: Portrait of Emma Madox Brown*, 1872 *
Pastel; 475 × 435 mm (s)
Insc. bl.: *FMB* [monogram] *Octr _ 72*
1906P793 (*Bennett*, B44)

B57 *Costume Sketches: Armour and Costume*, 1844
Sepia pen and ink over pencil; 363 × 225 mm
Insc.: *Edward 1st & IInd/ Richard IInd / Henry 6th & Edward 4th / Henry 4 Ford M Brown Paris/ 44*
1906P740 (*Bennett*, A31.5)
Mary Bennett catalogues this sketch under *The Spirit of Justice*.

B58 *Costume Study: Archbishop's Dress*, 1845
Sepia pen and ink on tracing paper; 173 × 95 mm
Insc. in reverse tl.: *Archévéque MCCCC*, br. *Rome/45*
1906P739 (*Bennett*, A40.9 (3))

B59 *Costume Studies: French and Italian thirteenth- and fourteenth-century Costumes (Seven Drawings)*, 1845 *
Sepia pen and ink on tracing paper; 338 × 220 mm
Insc. bl.: *Rome/45*
1906P737 (*Bennett*, A40.9 (1))

B60 *Costume Study: Seigneur de Rimini*, 1845
Sepia pen and ink on tracing paper; 167 × 94 mm
Insc. b. *Seigneur de Rimini/MCCCC Rome/45*
1906P738 (*Bennett*, A40.9(2))
The above three drawings (1906P737–739) were made after illustrations in Camille Bonnard's *Costumes Historiques*, a sourcebook of medieval costumes printed between 1829 and 1830.

B61 *Dalziels' Bible Gallery: The Death of Eglon*, 1863–64
Engraved woodblock; 150 × 185 mm
Insc. in ink on reverse: *Death of Eglon / Judges Chap 3 v 21/ 72/ Dalziel/ No 520* [label] */ BAM loan J N Hart Esq/ No 57* [label]
Acquired through the executors of J. N. Hart, c. 1965 (2006.1040.53)
The text is taken from Judges III, 15–31 and tells the story of the murder of Eglon by Ehud and the ultimate victory of the Israelites over the Moabites.

B62 *Dalziels' Bible Gallery: The Death of Eglon*, pub. 1881
Wood-engraving; 150 × 184 mm (i.), 213 × 253 mm (p.)
Insc. engraved on image bl.: *FMB* [monogram], on image bc.: *DALZIEL Sc*
Presented by Charles Fairfax Murray, 1912 (1912P46) (*Bennett*, D12)

B63 *Dalziels' Bible Gallery: The Death of Eglon*, pub. 1881
Wood-engraving on India paper, in bound volume; 152 × 188 mm (i.)
Insc. engraved on image bl.: *FMB* [monogram], on image bc.: *DALZIEL Sc*
Presented by Wilfred Phillips, 1920 (1920P713.1.) (*Bennett*, D12)

B64 *Dalziels' Bible Gallery: The Death of Eglon*, pub. 1881
Wood-engraving on India paper, in bound volume; 152 × 188 mm (i.)
Insc. engraved on image bl.: *FMB* [monogram], on image bc.: *DALZIEL Sc*
Presented by Wilfred Phillips, 1920 (1920P713.2.) (*Bennett*, D12)

B65 *Dalziels' Bible Gallery: Elijah and the Widow's Son*, 1863–64 *
Engraved woodblock; 227 × 150 mm
Insc. on reverse in ink: *Elijah & the Widow's Son/ 88/ Dalziel/ 515/ BAM loan J N Hart Esq No 35*
Acquired through the executors of J. N. Hart, c. 1965 (2006.1040.88)

B66 *Dalziels' Bible Gallery: Elijah and the Widow's Son*, pub. 1881 *
Wood-engraving; 230 × 150 mm (i.), 285 × 221 mm (p.)
Insc. engraved on image bl.: *DALZIEL Sc*
Presented by Charles Fairfax Murray, 1912 (1912P48) (*Bennett*, D11)
The text for the design is I Kings XVII, 17–24.

B67 *Dalziels' Bible Gallery: Elijah and the Widow's Son*, pub. 1881
Wood-engraving on India paper, in bound volume; 231 × 149 mm (i.)
Insc. engraved on image bl.: *DALZIEL Sc*
Presented by Wilfred Phillips, 1920 (1920P713.1.60) (*Bennett*, D11)

B68 *Dalziels' Bible Gallery: Elijah and the Widow's Son*, pub. 1881
Wood-engraving on India paper, in bound volume; 231 × 149 mm
Insc. engraved on image bl.: *DALZIEL Sc*
Presented by Wilfred Philips, 1920 (1920P713.2.60) (*Bennett*, D11)

B69 *Dalziels' Bible Gallery: Joseph's Coat (Compositional Sketch and four Studies for Jacob's Granddaughter)*, 1863–65 *
Pencil on paper; 391 × 291 mm
Insc. bl.: *FMB 1865* [altered from 1855, possibly postdated]
1906P788 (*Bennett*, C96.1)

B70 *Dalziels' Bible Gallery: Joseph's Coat*, 1863–65 *
Engraved woodblock; 177 × 173 mm
Insc. in ink on verso: *Joseph's Coat/ Dalziel/ No 52 (label)/ BAM Loan J N Hart Esq No 34*
Acquired through the executors of J. N. Hart, c. 1965 (2006.1040.22)

B71 *Dalziels' Bible Gallery: Joseph's Coat*, pub. 1881 *
Wood-engraving; 180 × 175 mm (i.), 570 × 400 mm (p.)

Insc. engraved on image bl.: *DALZIEL Sc*, on image br.: *FMB*
Presented by Charles Fairfax Murray, 1912 (1912P47) (*Bennett*, D10)
The source for this design is Genesis XXXVII, 31–34.

B72 *Dalziels' Bible Gallery: Joseph's Coat*, pub. 1881
Wood-engraving on India paper, in bound volume; 178 × 174 mm (i.)
Insc. engraved on image bl.: *DALZIEL Sc*, on image br.: *FMB*
Presented by Wilfred Phillips, 1920 (1920P713.1.22) (*Bennett*, D10)

B73 *Dalziels' Bible Gallery: Joseph's Coat*, pub. 1881
Wood-engraving on India paper, in bound volume; 178 × 74 mm (i.)
Insc. engraved on image bl.: *DALZIEL Sc*, on image br.: *FMB*
Presented by Wilfred Phillips, 1920 (1920P713.2.22) (*Bennett*, D10)

B74 *Decorative Sketch: Venus reclining on a Shell in the midst of the Sea*, 1848–49
Sepia pen and ink over pencil; 231 × 220 mm
Insc. cr.: *Ford M Brown London/48(9)*
1906P741 (*Bennett*, C39)

B75 *Decorative Design: Ornamental Pattern*, 1850
Watercolour and bodycolour over pen and ink and pencil on two sheets of paper; 250 × 197 mm
Insc. bl.: *Ford M Brown London / 1850*
1927P358 (*Bennett*, C41)
In correspondence Kathryn Ferry suggests Owen Jones as a possible source and specifically his *Elevations, Sections and Details of the Alhambra* of 1845, which 'includes pages of pattern including the borders of mosaic dados as illustrated later in the *Grammar of Ornament*'. The central orange portion, however, reminds her 'more of borders in medieval manuscript illuminations'.

B76 *Down Stream (Last Year's First of May)*, pub. 1871 *
Wood-engraving by C. M. Jenkin; 102 × 143 mm (i.), 135 × 225 mm (p.)
Insc. engraved on image bl.: *Jenkin Sc*, on image br.: *FMB*, printed below image: *DRAWN BY F. MADOX* BROWN./ *'DOW[NS]TREAM'* [worn letters]/ *ENGRAVED BY C. M. JENKIN.*
Presented by Charles Fairfax Murray, 1912 (1912P49) (*Bennett*, D23)
This is the first of two illustrations for 'Down Stream', a poem by Rossetti published in the magazine *Dark Blue*.

B77 *Down Stream (This Year's First of June)*, pub. 1871 *
Wood-engraving by C. M. Jenkin; 45 × 110 mm (i.), 225 × 141 mm (p.)
Insc. engraved: *FMB* [monogram]
Presented by Charles Fairfax Murray, 1912 (1912P45) (*Bennett*, D24)

B78 *The Establishment of Flemish Weavers in Manchester A.D. 1363: Four Studies of Parts of a Horse*, 1879–82
Black, white and red chalk on rough brown paper; 570 × 650 mm
Insc. verso: *F.M.B*
Presented by Harold Hartley, 1905 (1905P14) (*Bennett*, A109.2)
   Angela Thirlwell and Mary Bennett have related this drawing of different parts of a horse to *The Establishment of Flemish Weavers in Manchester A.D. 1363*, one of a series of twelve murals painted to decorate Manchester Town Hall and completed in 1882.

B79 *Female: Two Studies of young Woman in eighteenth-century Costume*, 1849 *
Pencil; 375 × 232 mm
Insc. bl.: *Ford M Brown London/49*
1906P677 (*Bennett*, A53)

The Germ: see *King Lear*

B80 *The Infant's Repast: Study of a Mother and Child*, 1848
Black and white chalk; 298 × 98 mm
Insc. br.: *Ford M Brown London/48*
1906P678 (*Bennett*, A50.2)

B81 *The Infant's Repast: Study of Mother and Child with separate Arm and Leg Studies of the Child*, 1848 *
Black chalk with grey wash; 253 × 175 mm
Insc. br.: *Ford Madox Brown London/48*
1906P679 (*Bennett*, A50.3)

B82 *King Lear: Sketch of Lear questioning Cordelia*, 1844 *
Verso: *Alfred the Great: Compositional Sketches*, 1843–1845
Sepia pen and ink over pencil; 201 × 277 mm (s.)
1906P754 (*Bennett*, C13)
   This is from Act I, sc. i of the play.

B83 *King Lear: Sketches of Lear imagining his unfaithful Daughters' Trial* and *Lear in the Storm*, 1844 *
Verso: *Alfred the Great: Compositional Studies and Sketches* and *The Seeds and Fruits of English Poetry: Studies of a Cherub*, 1843–49
Sepia pen and ink over pencil; pencil on verso; 440 × 280 mm
Insc. on verso cl.: *Alfred the Great / FMB*
1906P755 (*Bennett*, C29)
   The top sketch refers to the scene where Lear imagines himself at his unfaithful daughters' trial (Act 3, sc. vi, lines 33–39.); the lower half of the paper is a study for *Lear in the Storm* (Act III, sc. ii, 1–24).

B84 *King Lear: Kent accuses Oswald*, 1844
Verso: *Study for Lear recounts his Wrongs to Regan*
Sepia pen and ink with pencil underneath; 151 × 235 mm (s.)
Insc. bl.: *Ford M Brown Paris/44*
1906P756 (*Bennett*, C24)
   This sheet shows Kent accusing Oswald of

---

disloyalty to King Lear (Act II, sc. iv, 50–125), while the reverse sketch depicts Lear complaining to Regan about Goneril's unkindness (Act II, sc. iv, 122–32).

B85 *King Lear: Sketch for Cordelia at the Bedside of Lear (Lear's Awakening)*, 1844 *
Sepia pen and ink over pencil; 152 × 232 mm
Insc. br.: *Ford M Brown Paris/44*
1906P757 (*Bennett*, C31)
   This drawing depicts Act IV, sc. vii, 30–58, in which Cordelia comes to the aid of her father, finally realised as *Cordelia at the Bedside of Lear*, 1848–49, oil on canvas, Tate.

B86 *King Lear: Cordelia parting from her Sisters (The Germ: Art and Poetry)*, March 1850 *
Reprinted volume, 1901
Etching; 178 × 222 mm (i.), 223 × 268 mm (p.)
Insc. etched under image: *Goneril: Regan: Lear: Fool: Cordelia: France:*
Inventoried in 1979 (1979P217.4) (*Bennett*, D4)

B87 *King Lear: Cordelia parting from her Sisters (The Germ: Art and Poetry)*, March 1850 *
Reprinted volume, 1901
Etching; 178 × 222 mm (i.), 223 × 268 mm (p.)
Insc. etched under image: *Goneril, Regan, Lear: Fool: Cordelia: France:*
Presented by Elisa Korb, 2005 (2007.1800) (*Bennett*, D4)
   See also *Lear and Cordelia*

B88 *King René's Honeymoon: Study for Architecture*, 1861 *
Brush and brown ink, with watercolour, over pencil on brown paper; 445 × 318 mm
Insc. br.: *FMB* [monogram] _ *61*
1927P351 (*Bennett*, C58)

B89 *The Last of England: Cartoon*, 1852 *
Pencil, image edged with brown ink; 408 × 365 mm (oval), 431 × 390 mm (p.)
Insc. br.: *F. MADOX BROWN 1852*
1906P795 (*Bennett*, A61.5)

B90 *The Last of England: Portrait of Emma Hill*, December 1852 *
Chalks with scratching out on two sheets of paper; 164 × 177 mm
Insc. bl.: *FMB* [monogram] *Dec 52*
1906P791 (*Bennett*, A61.6)

B91 *Lear and Cordelia: Four Studies of Hands*, 1849
Black chalk; 250 × 173 mm (top right corner of paper cut out)
Insc. br.: *Ford M Brown London/49*
1906P758 (*Bennett*, A51.4)
   This study of outstretched hands may have been made from Ford Madox Brown's model, and later wife, Emma Hill.

B92 *Lyra Germanica – The Christian Life: Abraham and Isaac*, pub. 1868
Wood-engraving by Joseph Swain; 125 × 54 mm (i.), 235 × 170 mm (p.)
Insc. printed bl.: *F. M. Brown*, br.: *Swain Sc*
Presented by Charles Fairfax Murray, 1912 (1912P42) (*Bennett*, D15)

This is one of three illustrations by Brown for *Lyra Germanica – The Christian Life*, the second series of an anthology of hymns translated from German by Catherine Winkworth and published in 1868.

B93 *Lyra Germanica – The Christian Life: Finished Design for The Entombment*, 1867 *
Black pen and ink; 263 × 234 mm (i.), 264 × 240 mm (p.)
Insc. br.: *FMB* [monogram]
Presented by the Trustees of the Public Picture Gallery Fund, 1916 (1916P27) (*Bennett*, C123)

B94 *Lyra Germanica – The Christian Life: The Entombment*, pub. 1868 *
Wood-engraving by Thomas Bolton; 107 × 95 mm (i.), 238 × 170 mm (p.)
Insc. engraved on image br.: *FMB* [monogram], under image bl.: *T. Bolton Sc*
Presented by Charles Fairfax Murray, 1912 (1912P51) (*Bennett*, D13)
   This illustration is printed above a verse by Viktor Strauss.

B95 *Male: Sketch of Man reclining on Steps with Hands together*, 1844
Sepia pen and ink over pencil; 242 × 225 mm
Insc. br.: *(Paris)/F. M. Brown/44*
1906P724 (*Bennett*, A31.6)
   Mary Bennett considers this sketch to be related to the figure of Wisdom in *The Spirit of Justice*.

B96 *Male: Academic nude Study, half-length with Moustache and Arms folded*, 1846–49 *
Black chalk; 172 × 142 mm
1906P708 (*Bennett*, C36)

B97 *Male: Academic Study of Nude holding a Staff*, 1847
Pencil; 252 × 134 mm
Insc.: *Ford M Brown/47 London*
1906P672 (*Bennett*, C35)

B98 *Male: Academic Study of Nude posed as a Sculptor*, 1847
Chalk with grey wash; 387 × 175 mm
Insc. br.: *Ford M Brown /47 London*
1906P709 (*Bennett*, C37)

B99 *Male: Academic Study, three-quarter length Nude, with Moustache and clenched Fists*, 1847
Black chalk; 302 × 174 mm
Insc. br.: *Ford M Brown/47*
1906P710 (*Bennett*, C38)

B100 *Morris & Company Revised Index: Catalogue of Stained Glass Cartoons by Edward Burne Jones, Ford Madox Brown, William Morris, Philip Webb, Simeon Solomon, Arthur Hughes etc*, 1900–40
Pen and ink with pencil annotations, and small photo inserts and pen-and-ink drawings; 325 × 215 mm
Insc. handwritten: (front cover) *Revised/ Glass Cartoon Index* (inside front cover) *Morris and Company / 449 Oxford Street London W*
Presented anonymously, 1940 (1940P604.4)

B101 *Morris & Company Windows Book: Photographic Album of Stained Glass Designs by Dante Gabriel Rossetti, Ford Madox Brown, William Morris, Edward Burne-Jones, Simeon Solomon and Philip Webb*, 1900–5
Photographs laid into bound volume; 381 × 323 mm
Insc. impressed on front: *Morris & Company,/ 449 Oxford Street,/ London, W / This book Must Not Be Taken From The Showroom*
Presented anonymously, 1940 (1940P604.5)

Oure Ladye of Good Children: see *Oure Ladye of Saturday Night*

B102 *Oure Ladye of Saturday Night: Seven Sketches*, 1846
Pencil; 180 × 220 mm
Insc. b.: *Sketches & Studies for a cartoon of "Oure Layde of Saturday Night/ Black Heath / F.MB./ 46*
1906P682 (*Bennett*, A44.2)
   The cartoon *Oure Ladye of Saturday Night* (Tate) was retitled *Our Ladye of Good Children* in an American exhibition of 1857–58. The scene depicts a Madonna-like mother washing her child, aided by an angel. According to Brown, this represented the English ritual of bathing children before going to bed.

B103 *Oure Ladye of Saturday Night: Four Studies for Angel holding Child*, 1846–47
Pencil; 250 × 220 mm
1906P673 (*Bennett*, A44.3)

B104 *Our Ladye of Saturday Night: Study of Angel holding Child*, 1847
Black chalk; 250 × 147 mm
Insc. br.: *Kensington F.M. Brown/47*
1906P674 (*Bennett*, A44.4)

B105 *Oure Ladye of Saturday Night: Study of Arm and Hands of Angel holding Bowl of Water*, 1847
Black chalk; 103 × 231 mm
Insc. br.: *Kensington/ Ford M Brown/47*
1906P685 (*Bennett*, A44.10)

B106 *Oure Ladye of Saturday Night: Drapery Study for Angel holding Bowl of Water*, 1847
Black chalk; 422 × 265 mm
Insc. br.: *FM Brown 1847 Kens[ington]*
1906P684 (*Bennett*, A44.11)

B107 *Oure Ladye of Saturday Night: Study of Head of Angel holding Bowl of Water*, 1847
Black chalk with rubbing and grey wash; 258 × 215 mm
Insc. br.: *Ford M Brown/47* Kensingto[n]
1906P675 (*Bennett*, A44.12)

B108 *Oure Ladye of Saturday Night: Study of Child seated on Knees of the Virgin and two separate Studies of Child's Legs*, 1847
Verso: *Frieze design for the tent border in Cordelia at the Bedside of Lear* (Tate, identified by Mary Bennett)
Pencil; pen and ink with pencil on verso; 146 × 119 mm
Insc. br.: *F.MB./47*
1906P687 (*Bennett*, A44.6)

B109 *Oure Ladye of Saturday Night: Three Studies of Arms and Legs of Child*, 1847
Pencil, 219 × 127 mm
1906P688 (*Bennett*, A44.7)

B110 *Oure Ladye of Saturday Night: Three Studies of Child's Legs on Virgin's Knees*, 1847
Pencil on buff paper; 212 × 104 mm
Insc. bl.: [cut]*B./47 Kensington*
1906P689 (*Bennett*, A44.8)

B111 *Our Ladye of Saturday Night: Studies of right Foot and left Hand of Child*, 1847
Pencil on light brown paper; 67 × 107 mm
Insc. bl.: *FMB./47 Kensington*
1906P690 (*Bennett*, A44.9)

B112 *Oure Ladye of Saturday Night: Drapery Study of Virgin*, 1847
Black chalk; 288 × 255 mm
Insc. bl.: *F M Brown 1847 Kensington*
1906P686 (*Bennett*, A44.5)

B113 *Oure Ladye of Saturday Night: Study of Head of Virgin*, 1847
Black chalk with wash; 244 × 222 mm (s.)
Insc. br.: *FMB/47*
1906P676 (*Bennett*, A44.13)

B114 *Parisina's Sleep: Study for Prince Azo and Parisina*, 1842
Black chalk with pencil side drawing; 415 × 418 mm
Insc. bl.: *FMB/42* (in pencil)
1927P355 (*Bennett*, A27.1)

B115 *Parisina's Sleep: Study for Head of Prince Azo*, 1842
Black chalk with grey wash; 432 × 310 mm
Insc. bl.: *FMB/42 Paris*
1906P716 (*Bennett*, A27.2)

B116 *Parisina's Sleep: Study for Head of Parisina*, 1842
Black and white chalk with grey wash; 320 × 299 mm
Insc. br.: *Ford M Brown 1842 (Paris)*
1906P717 (*Bennett*, A27.3)
   These three studies for the now untraced painting are based on a poem of the same name by Byron. The poem tells how Prince Azo killed his wife, Parisina, after discovering her adulterous affair with his illegitimate son, Hugo. Brown chooses to depict the scene where Prince Azo first hears Parisina talk of Hugo in her sleep, and in his rage contemplates murdering her.

B117 *The Poets of the Nineteenth Century: The Prisoner of Chillon (Compositional Sketch)*, 1856 *
Verso: *Profile of a Man's left Eye and Nose*
Pencil; 133 × 99 mm (i.), 146 × 112 mm (p.)
1927P353 (*Bennett*, C44.1)

B118 *The Poets of the Nineteenth Century: The Prisoner of Chillon: Study of Corpse*, 1856 *
Verso: Designs for Decoration
Pencil; 165 × 280 mm
Insc. br.: *FMB. University Hospital / Study for prisoner of / Chillon / from Corpse FMB*
1927P352 (*Bennett*, C44.3)

B119 *The Poets of the Nineteenth Century: The Prisoner of Chillon*, pub. 1857 *
Wood-engraving; 127 × 95 mm (i.), 190 × 123 mm (p.)
Insc. engraved on image bl.: *DALZIEL Sc*, printed below image c.: *The Prisoner of Chillon*
Presented by Charles Fairfax Murray, 1912 (1912P50) (*Bennett*, D8)
   This is an illustration to Byron's poem *The Prisoner of Chillon* commissioned by the Dalziel brothers for the anthology *The Poets of the Nineteenth Century*.

B120 *Portrait: Ford Madox Brown*, c. 1865
After Elliott & Fry (albumen carte de visite)
Modern photographic print, 138 × 111 mm (i.), 145 × 118 mm (p.)
Found unaccessioned, 2007 (2007.2600)

B121 *Portrait: Thomas Carlyle*, c. 1859 *
Albumen photograph by 'Mr Thompson'; (top) 312 × 185 mm, (bottom) 312 × 168 mm
Found unaccessioned, 1975 (1975P329)

B122 *Portrait: Head Study of Daniel Casey (Three-quarter View)*, 1848
Black chalk; 253 × 177 mm
Insc. br.: *Ford M Brown London /48*
1906P720 (*Bennett*, B59.1)

B123 *Portrait: Head Study of Daniel Casey (Full-Face)*, 1848 *
Black chalk; 250 × 175 mm
Insc. br.: *Ford M Brown London/48*
1906P721 (*Bennett*, B59.2)
   Mary Bennett has doubts as to whether these two drawings are of Daniel Casey.

B124 *Portrait: Miss Iza Duffus Hardy*, 1872 *
Pastel and coloured chalks on brown paper; 771 × 556 mm
Insc. tl.: *IZA HARDY. / FMB* [monogram] *72*
Presented by Charles Fairfax Murray, 1903 (1904P498) (*Bennett*, B69)

B125 *Portrait: Emma Hill (later Mrs Madox Brown)*, 1848 *
Black chalk; 104 × 100 mm
Insc. bl.: *F.M.B. / Xmas/48*
1906P789 (*Bennett*, A51.3)

B126 *Portrait: Emma Hill (later Mrs Madox Brown)*, 1852 *
Pencil; 146 × 132 mm
Insc. br.: *FMB* [monogram] *1852*
1906P790 (*Bennett*, B70)
   See also *The Last of England*

B127 *Portrait: Sketch of Mrs Madox Brown (née Emma Hill)*, 9 May 1854
Pencil; 240 × 155mm
Insc. br.: *F.M.B. May 9th/54*
1906P792 (*Bennett*, B37)
   See also *Convalesent: Portrait of Emma Hill*

B128 *The Repose in Egypt: Compositional Sketch*, 1847
Pencil; 160 × 190 mm
Insc. below image c.: *il Rinfresco in Egytta. / Dedicated to ye fellowes of Christ his college OXFOR[D]/* bl.: *London*, br.: *Ford M Brown*

1847
1906P683 (*Bennett*, A45)

B129 *Sculpture: Study of a Statue of the 'Discobolus'*, 1845 *
Black chalk; 435 × 254 mm (s.)
Insc. br.: *Ford M Brown Rome 1845*
1906P718 (*Bennett*, C32)

The Seeds and Fruits of English Poetry: see *Chaucer at the Court of Edward III*

B130 *William Shakespeare: Study for Invitation Card*, 1849–50
Pencil; 146 × 95 mm (s.)
Insc. bc.: *GULIELMUS SHAKSPEAR*
1906P798 (*Bennett*, A54.2)

B131 *William Shakespeare: Invitation Card*, 1850
Wood-engraving; 147 × 111 mm (s.)
Insc.: *AD MLC/ To View / the Picture/ By/ Ford Madox Brown Esq/ On view at the/ Galleries of Art,/ Messrs Dickinson & Co/ 114,/ New Bond Street*
1906P798.1 (*Bennett*, D5)
   These two objects relate to the portrait of William Shakespeare that Brown was commissioned to paint by the Dickinson Brothers in 1849 (Manchester Art Gallery).

B132 *The Spirit of Justice: Study for Baron and his Advisor, with Sketches of Erudition and Wisdom*, 1844–45
Sepia pen and ink over pencil; 361 × 230 mm
Presented by Harold Hartley, 1905 (1905P18) (*Bennett*, A31.4)
   Madox Brown submitted *The Spirit of Justice* for the third competition to decorate six arched compartments in the newly rebuilt House of Lords.
   See also *Costume Studies: Armour and Costume* and *Male: Sketch of Man reclining on Steps with Hands together*

B133 *The Spirit of Justice: Drapery Study of Erudition*, 1844–45
Verso: *Drapery Study and outline Sketch of two Legs*
Black chalk on laid paper; 200 × 199 mm
Insc. on reverse tr.: *sketch for figure in right of Justice*
1906P753 (*Bennett*, A31.7)

B134 *The Spirit of Justice: Study for Wisdom*, 1844–45
Black chalk with grey wash; 315 × 238 mm
1906P712 (*Bennett*, A31.8)
   This drawing has been identified by Mary Bennett in her forthcoming catalogue.

B135 *The Spirit of Justice: Study for Head of Baron*, 1844–45
Black chalk; 283 × 175 mm
1906P715 (*Bennett*, A31.9)

B136 *The Spirit of Justice: Study for Head of Bishop*, 1844–45
Black chalk; 317 × 255 mm
1906P723 (*Bennett*, A31.10)

B137 *The Spirit of Justice: Study for Head of Bishop*, 1844–45
Black chalk with grey wash; 440 × 357 mm
1906P722 (*Bennett*, A31.11)

B138 *The Spirit of Justice: Study of the uplifted left Arm of Justice*, 1844–45
Black chalk on laid paper; 448 × 320 mm
Presented by Harold Hartley, 1905 (1905P17) (*Bennett*, A31.12)

B139 *The Spirit of Justice: Study for Head of Counsellor in a Coronet*, 1844–45
Black chalk with touches of blue chalk; 455 × 315 mm
Presented by Harold Hartley, 1905 (1905P21) (*Bennett*, A31.13)

B140 *The Spirit of Justice: Study of Head of Counsellor*, 1844–45
Black chalk on grained paper; 424 × 306 mm
Presented by Harold Hartley, 1905 (1905P20) (*Bennett*, A31.14)

B141 *The Spirit of Justice: Drapery Study of central Figure*, 1844–45
Verso: *Part of a Drapery Study*
Pencil on laid paper; 263 × 229 mm
Insc. in pencil br.: *FMB 1843* (misdated?)
Presented by Harold Hartley, 1905 (1905P16) (*Bennett*, A31.15)

B142 *The Spirit of Justice: Study for Head of Widow*, 1844–45
Black chalk; 434 × 371 mm
Presented by Harold Hartley, 1905 (1905P19) (*Bennett*, A31.16)

B143 *Stages of Cruelty: Study for the Child (Catherine Madox Brown)*, 1857 *
Black chalk on pale grey paper; 335 × 297 mm
Insc. br.: *FMB 57*
Presented by A. E. Anderson, 1922 (1922P18) (*Bennett*, A67.1)

B144 *Stained Glass Design: Christ blessing little Children*, 1862
After Ford Madox Brown
Brush, ink and wash over pencil, squared up for transfer; 656 × 516 mm
Insc. tr.: *SP 307* [or 1] / *Christ blessing little / Children*
1927P350 (*Bennett*, C81.1)
   This is a working copy, made in 1862, by Morris, Marshall, Faulkner & Co. after one of Brown's earliest designs for stained glass. It was produced for the stained-glass windows of St Peter's Church in Cranbourne, Berkshire.

B145 *Stained Glass Design: Cartoon for Zachariah, The High Priest*, 1872 *
Black chalk; 934 × 476 mm (s.)
Insc. bl.: *The property of the/ artist F Madox Brown*, br.: *FMB* [monogram] *–72*, around halo: *Powells bleu*[?] *St light*, on cloak, *24 green*
Transferred from Birmingham Municipal School of Art, 1912 (1912P149) (*Bennett*, C176)

B146 *Stained Glass Design: Cartoon for The Young Milton*, 1874 *
Black chalk; 572 × 300 mm

Insc. tr.: *2 gown / 3 shirt / 4 slashe*[d], bl.: *FMB* [monogram] *c74*, br.: *The Young/ Milton/* [o]*f the A …*[rubbed out]
Presented by Reverend John Richard Dorman, 1957 (1957P34) (*Bennett*, C167)

B147 *Stained Glass Design: Cartoon for St Simon*, 1874
Black chalk; 1385 × 514 mm (s.)
Insc. in halo: *Aup R/ top of* [illegible word], tr.: *2 cloak 3 lining* [and corresponding numbers on the figure's clothes], bl.: *FMB* [monogram]*–74*, bc.: *Bottom of feet* [and illegible writing]
Transferred from Birmingham Municipal School of Art, 1912 (1912P150) (*Bennett*, C214)
   The cartoon is for the figure of St Simon, recognisable by the fish he is holding, in a three-light window in the north aisle of Llandaff Cathedral.

B148 *Stained Glass Design: The Marriage of Editha with Sigtrygg, King of Northumbria* (St Editha's, Tamworth, Staffordshire)
Copy by Thomas Matthews Rooke (1842–1942), 1909 *
Watercolour; 932 × 765 mm (s.)
Presented by the Library of the University of Birmingham from the J. R. Holliday Bequest (1959P40)
   The Whitworth Art Gallery, University of Manchester, holds copies of the original 1873 cartoons, produced by Morris, Marshall, Faulkner & Co. and in the collection of Manchester Art School but now lost (see *Bennett*). This is the first of the three clerestory windows by the altar on the south side of St Editha's, Tamworth.

B149 *Stained Glass Design: St Editha and the Nuns of St Mary* (St Editha's, Tamworth, Staffordshire)
Copy by Thomas Matthews Rooke, 1909
Watercolour; 930 × 760 mm (s.)
Label on reverse: *Messrs Charles Roberson & Co., Longacre, London*
Presented by the Library of the University of Birmingham from the J. R. Holliday Bequest (1959P41)
   This is the second of the clerestory windows at St Editha's, Tamworth. It shows Editha, deserted by Sigtrygg, as the superior of a nunnery she has founded in Tamworth. Surrounded by the nuns of her convent, she sees a vision of the Virgin and Child, Patroness of the Benedictine Order, to whom the nunnery belonged. At the top there is a depiction of Editha's convent.

B150 *Stained Glass Design: William the Conqueror, Lord Marmion and St Editha* (St Editha's, Tamworth, Staffordshire)
Copy by Thomas Matthews Rooke, 1909
Watercolour; 922 × 765 mm (s.)
Presented by the Library of the University of Birmingham from the J. R. Holliday Bequest (1959P42)
   William the Conqueror rests upon his sword while he presents the deeds of Tamworth Castle to his champion Marmion. In the next two windows Marmion, having dispossessed Editha's nunnery, is struck by the offended saint. The

wound will only heal when Marmion repents and allows a new nunnery to be built. The top window shows Marmion's castle at Tamworth.

Madox Brown's designs for St Editha's are catalogued by Mary Bennett as C186–200.

B151 *Sterne's 'Sentimental Journey': Study of Yorick and La Fleur talking to Maria's Mother*, 1842
Verso: *The Body of Harold brought before William the Conqueror: Eight Sketches of Figure Groups*, c. 1844
Sepia pen and ink over pencil; pencil on verso; 570 × 435 mm
Insc. br.: *Ford M Brown Paris/ 42*
1906P797 (*Bennett*, C10)

B152 *Sterne's 'Sentimental Journey': Yorick and Maria Walking*, 1842 *
Pen and ink, watercolour and bodycolour over pencil; 561 × 439 mm
Insc. bl.: *Ford M Brown Paris 42*
1906P796 (*Bennett*, C11)

These two drawings come from the eighteenth-century novel *A Sentimental Journey through France and Italy by Mr Yorick* by Laurence Sterne.

B153 *Tree Trunk Study with Roots*, c. 1847?
Verso: *Two Studies of Tree Trunk*
Black chalk, heightened with white chalk on buff paper; 245 × 385 mm
Insc. on verso: *Studies by FMB*
1927P357 (*Bennett*, A47)

B154 *Unknown Subject: Compositional Sketch*, 1843–50
Pencil; 206 × 260 mm (s.)
1906P742 (*Bennett*, A46)

Wycliffe reading his Translation of the Bible: see also *Architecture*

B155 *Wycliffe reading his Translation of the Bible: Nude Study of Chaucer*, 1847
Pencil on J Whatman paper; 252 × 175 mm
Insc. br.: *London / Ford M. Brown/ 47*
1906P736 (*Bennett*, A48.6)

B156 *Wycliffe reading his Translation of the Bible: Study of Chaucer*, 1847
Pencil; 251 × 175 mm
Insc. br.: *London / F. M Brown/47*
1906P729 (*Bennett*, A48.7)

B157 *Wycliffe reading his Translation of the Bible: Nude Study of Gower*, 1847
Pencil; 251 × 175 mm
Insc. br.: *London / F. M Brown/47*
1906P733 (*Bennett*, A48.8)

B158 *Wycliffe reading his Translation of the Bible: Study of Gower*, 1847
Pencil on J Whatman paper; 251 × 145 mm
Insc. br.: *London / F.M.Brown/47*
1906P732 (*Bennett*, A48.9)

B159 *Wycliffe reading his Translation of the Bible: Nude Study of John of Gaunt and Chaucer's right Hand*, 1847
Pencil and black chalk; 253 × 177 mm

Insc. br.: *London / F M Brown/47*
1906P726 (*Bennett*, A48.10)

B160 *Wycliffe reading his Translation of the Bible: Study of John of Gaunt and Chaucer's left Hand*, 1847 *
Pencil and black chalk; 240 × 175 mm
Insc. br.: *(London)/ F.M Brown / 47*
1906P725 (*Bennett*, A48.11)

B161 *Wycliffe reading his Translation of the Bible: Study of Wycliffe*, 1847
Black chalk; 174 × 80 mm
Insc. br.: *London / F.M.Brown/47*
1906P700 (*Bennett*, A48.12)

B162 *Wycliffe reading his Translation of the Bible: Nude Study of Wycliffe*, 1847 *
Pencil; 253 × 104 mm
1906P730 (*Bennett*, A48.13)

B163 *Wycliffe reading his Translation of the Bible: Drapery Study of Wycliffe*, 1847 *
Black chalk; 358 × 203 mm (i. and p.)
Insc. br.: *Ford M. Brown 1847*
1906P699 (*Bennett*, A48.14)

B164 *Wycliffe reading his Translation of the Bible: Study of Drapery for Chaucer*, 1847
Black chalk; 350 × 217 mm
Insc. bl.: *Ford M Brown 1847 London*
1906P731 (*Bennett*, A48.15)

B165 *Wycliffe reading his Translation of the Bible: Study of Legs of John of Gaunt and two Studies of Feet for Wycliffe*, 1847
Black chalk; 285 × 340 mm
Insc. bc.: *F M Brown/47*
1906P728 (*Bennett*, A48.16)

B166 *Wycliffe reading his Translation of the Bible: Studies of Hands for John of Gaunt and Gower*, 1847 *
Black chalk; 151 × 215 mm
Insc. br.: *London / F. M. Brown 1847*
1906P746 (*Bennett*, A48.17)

B167 *Wycliffe reading his Translation of the Bible: Head of Wycliffe*, 1847 *
Pencil; 144 × 126 mm
Insc. bl.: *London*, br.: *Ford M Brown [1847]* (a photograph published in 1896 shows it was originally inscribed with the date 1847 which was later cut off)
1906P670 (*Bennett*, A48.18)

B168 *Wycliffe reading his Translation of the Bible: Study for Constance and Child*, 1847
Pencil; 134 × 143 mm
Insc. bl.: *London*, br.: *F.M.Brown 1847*
1906P692 (*Bennett*, A48.19)

B169 *Wycliffe reading his Translation of the Bible: Unfinished Study for Head of Constance*, 1847
Pencil; 105 × 117 mm
1906P701 (*Bennett*, A48.20)

B170 *Wycliffe reading his Translation of the Bible: Portrait of Elizabeth Bamford modelling for Figure of Constance*, 1848
Pencil; 97 × 125 mm
Insc. bl.: *Miss Elizabeth Bamford*, br.: *London / Ford M.Brown 1848*

1906P693 (*Bennett*, A48.21)

B171 *Wycliffe reading his Translation of the Bible: Study for Head of Constance*, 1848
Chalk over pencil, 135 × 155 mm
Insc. bl.: *London*, br.: *Ford M Brown 1848*
1906P691 (*Bennett*, A48.22)

B172 *Wycliffe reading his Translation of the Bible: Study for Head of Chaucer*, 1848
Pencil, 176 × 148 mm
Insc.: *London/ F.M.Brown/ 48*
1906P702 (Bennett, A48.23)

B173 *Wycliffe reading his Translation of the Bible: Study of Monk representing the Catholic Faith*, 1848
Black chalk with sepia pen and ink, squared up; 247 × 245 mm (i.), 278 × 275 mm (p.)
Insc.: *Ford M.Brown 1848 London*
1906P703 (*Bennett*, A48.24)

B174 *Wycliffe reading his Translation of the Bible: Study of young Woman representing the Protestant Faith*, 1848
Black chalk; 245 × 247 mm (i. roundel), 277 × 278 mm (p. roundel)
Insc.: *Ford M Brown 1848 London*
1906P704 (*Bennett*, A48.25)

The above two drawings are for the corner spandrels of *Wycliffe*. The drawing for the Catholic Faith has been squared up for transfer onto canvas.

The following works are presently missing from the BMAG collection:

Cordelia's Portion, wood engraving (1912P41), *Lyra Germanica –The Christian Life: He that soweth*, wood engraving (1912P43), *The Traveller*, wood engraving (1912 P44), *Study for Work: Thomas Carlyle* pen and Indian ink, with a note on old catalogue card, 'at the house of J R Holliday but not traced by his art executor (Sydney Cockerell) at the time of the former's death in 1927, (1905P15).

The following works were given an accession number but were never actually received by BMAG, being transferred to the Fitzwilliam Museum, Cambridge, by Charles Fairfax Murray (776 (1–7)):

A Man proposing to a Girl in a Garden, sepia pen and ink (1906P759), *The Leave-Taking before the War*, sepia pen and ink (1906P760), *Storming a Breach*, sepia pen and ink (1906P761), *Soldier carried from the Field by his Comrades*, sepia pen and ink (1906P762), *Soldier invalided home with Loss of a Leg*, sepia pen and ink (1906P763), *The Soldier telling the Story of his Battles to his Grandchildren at the Seaside*, sepia pen and ink (1906P764), *Wife reading Gazette during the War*, sepia pen and ink (1906P765).

A drawing by Thomas Seddon of Ford Madox Brown's *Work* made in preparation for the engraving after Brown's painting was formerly listed as 794'06 but was never actually acquired by BMAG. It was presented instead by Charles Fairfax Murray to the Fitzwilliam Museum, Cambridge, in 1908 (668).

Index

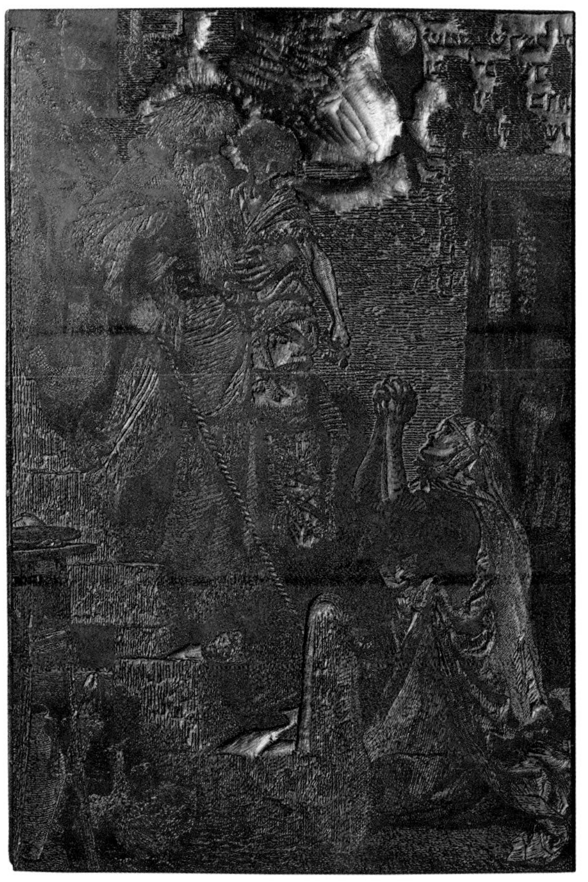

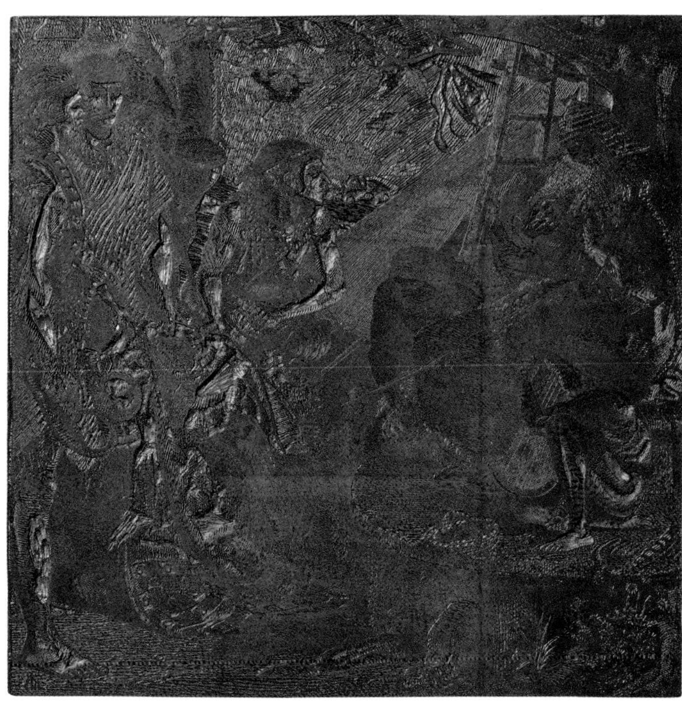

LEFT: *Dalziels' Bible Gallery: Elijah and the Widow's Son*, 1863–64 (cat. 41)

ABOVE: *Dalziels' Bible Gallery: Joseph's Coat*, 1863–65 (cat. 44)